The Flowering of Modern Chinese Poetry

The Flowering of Modern Chinese Poetry

An Anthology of Verse from the Republican Period

Translated by Herbert Batt and Sheldon Zitner
with introductions by Michel Hockx

McGill-Queen's University Press
Montreal & Kingston • London • Chicago

ISBN 978-0-7735-4765-0 (cloth)
ISBN 978-0-7735-4766-7 (paper)
ISBN 978-0-7735-9944-4 (ePDF)
ISBN 978-0-7735-9945-1 (ePUB)

Legal deposit third quarter 2016
Bibliothèque nationale du Québec

Printed in Canada on acid-free paper that is 100% ancient forest free (100% post-consumer recycled), processed chlorine free

This book has been published with the help of a grant from the Canadian Federation for the Humanities and Social Sciences, through the Awards to Scholarly Publications Program, using funds provided by the Social Sciences and Humanities Research Council of Canada.

McGill-Queen's University Press acknowledges the support of the Canada Council for the Arts for our publishing program. We also acknowledge the financial support of the Government of Canada through the Canada Book Fund for our publishing activities.

Library and Archives Canada Cataloguing in Publication

The flowering of modern Chinese poetry : an anthology of verse from the Republican period / translated by Herbert Batt and Sheldon Zitner ; with introductions by Michel Hockx.

Includes bibliographical references.
Issued in print and electronic formats.
ISBN 978-0-7735-4765-0 (cloth). – ISBN 978-0-7735-4766-7 (paper). – ISBN 978-0-7735-9944-4 (pdf). – ISBN 978-0-7735-9945-1 (epub)

1. Chinese poetry – 20th century – Translations into English. I. Batt, Herbert J., 1945–, translator II. Zitner, Sheldon P., translator III. Hockx, Michel, writer of introduction

PL2658.E3F56 2016 895.11'508 C2016-901891-1
C2016-901892-X

Contents

For Chinese texts of poems in this anthology please visit www.modernchineseverse.com

Translators' Preface

HERBERT BATT AND SHELDON ZITNER

The years from 1918 to 1949 witnessed an outpouring of poetry written in a form and style new to Chinese literature. Our anthology seeks to present the best of the vernacular verse that came to be called "New Poetry," translated into English.[1] This collection contains over two hundred and fifty poems by fifty poets, with a short biography introducing each author. Chinese originals of our poems can be found on our website, which also contains a list of critical readings for further study: www.modernchineseverse.com.

The rise of vernacular verse in China in the early twentieth century coincided with a period of intense social dislocation. While this is not a history book, the momentous social and political transformation in early twentieth-century China is the backdrop – in a sense, the engine – of the rise of New Poetry. Many of these poems were written in response to this upheaval, which involved imprisonment and execution of Communist revolutionaries, famine and oppression suffered by the peasants, and Japanese troops' burning of villages. Other poems speak of the authors' experiences of the joys and sorrows of love, friendship, and family life, often set against the backdrop of war.

Our aim is to give a nuanced picture of the astonishingly rapid development of vernacular verse in China from its first appearance just before the May Fourth Movement of 1919 through 1949, the year of Mao Zedong's Communist takeover.[2] Our collection presents a catholic perspective and readers will meet the works of master poets still virtually unknown to Western audiences. We include poetry by Liu Dabai, Chiang Kai-shek's[3]

1 Our translations render the stanza structure of the original poems, but we do not attempt to replicate rhyme in the relatively few poems that employ it.

2 When one of our authors continued writing after 1949, we include selections from this later work, twenty-one poems in all.

3 We use the pinyin system to spell Chinese words with the exception of "Chiang Kai-shek," the conventional spelling of the name as pronounced in a southern Chinese dialect. (See glossary under "Chiang Kai-shek.")

minister of education; by Lu Xun, the leftist leader of the anti-Chiang Kai-shek intellectuals; by Tian Jian, the innovator of Mao's revolutionary folk poetry; and by Ji Xian, who fled Mao to the island of Taiwan.

We have striven to include significant figures who have not always received the attention they deserve. The collection is distinguished by a rich selection of women poets. The poetry of previously untranslated female author Fang Lingru appears here, as well as the first English translation of verse by the novelist Ding Ling.

The introduction to our volume is provided by Michel Hockx, professor of Chinese and director of the Liu Institute for Asia and Asian Studies at the University of Notre Dame. Vernacular poetry appeared as part of a radical transformation of Chinese culture. Innovative writers produced a new poetry written in the common people's language, known as *baihua*.[4] In his introduction, Hockx traces the linguistic origins of *baihua* verse from its roots in the nineteenth century. He explains the New Poetry's challenge to justify itself in the face of the millennia-old tradition of classical Chinese poetry, and describes the different schools or styles of vernacular poetry that developed within the new literary movement. We identify five such schools and have organized the volume accordingly, with sections devoted to each of them: Pioneers, Formalists, Symbolists, "Peasants and Soldiers" Poetry, and the Nine Leaves poets. Hockx contributes introductions to each of these sections to explain the distinctive characteristics of each school and where they fit in the overall development of the New Poetry. Within these sections each author's poetry is preceded by a short critical biography. The biographies provide an overview of the poets' lives and literary careers, their political involvement (where relevant), discussion of their style and influences as well as the themes and content of their poetry, and – in some cases, for writers who have been unjustly neglected – an argument for the importance of their work. A glossary at the end of the book explains historical terms and persons mentioned in the introductions and the short biographies.

4 Besides ours, there is no volume in print exclusively devoted to vernacular poetry from the Republican period. Michelle Yeh's *Anthology of Modern Chinese Poetry* features vernacular poets who published on the island of Taiwan and in Hong Kong after 1949, in the People's Republic of China after 1980, together with selections of poetry from Republican China written before 1949.

In the latter part of the introduction Hockx explains how the New Poetry movement has given birth to the modern vernacular poetry of the post-Mao era. Since 1979 "obscure" poets like Yang Lian, Bei Dao, and Shu Ting have regenerated mainland Chinese poetry. Hong Kong has produced major poets such as Leung Ping-kwan and Taiwan has produced masters of the New Poetry like Yang Mu, who continued his prolific career as a professor in the United States.[5] The verse of these authors is exemplary of the quality which Chinese vernacular poetry has achieved after 1949 both on the mainland and in Taiwan, in Hong Kong, and in the Chinese diaspora. Our anthology presents to English-language readers the beginnings of this modern, innovative poetry. Its rise reflects the rise of modern China.

5 For translations of these recent poets see the following: *Non-Person Singular: Collected Shorter Poems of Yang Lian*, translated by Brian Holton and edited by Tony Barnstone; *Shu Ting: Selected Poems*, edited by Eva Hung; *City at the End of Time: Poems by Leung Ping-kwan*, co-translated with Gordon Osing; and *No Trace of the Gardener: Poems of Yang Mu*, co-translated with Lawrence Smith.

The Flowering of Modern Chinese Poetry

Introduction: The Making of Modern Chinese Poetry in the Twentieth Century

MICHEL HOCKX

Scholars of modern Chinese literature often presume that fiction is the preeminent literary genre of the twentieth century and should be considered as representing the "mainstream." It is true that novels and short stories have been laden with many moral and political imperatives. As early as 1902, the influential writer and political reformer Liang Qichao claimed that fiction, especially novels, was the best tool for reforming and strengthening the nation. The reason he gave was that fiction, more than any other genre, was capable of spreading new ideas and new values among a wide readership. For many people involved in what became known as the "New Culture Movement" in China in the 1910s and 1920s, the need to overhaul China's traditional Confucian culture arose from a political imperative. Art and literature needed to change because the country needed to change, and they needed to become more like Western art and literature because Western countries were strong and powerful. As a result of this emphasis on fiction, and on a utilitarian approach to literature, modern Chinese poetry has not been given its due. It deserves much more attention than scholars have given it so far.[1]

Although poetry is not the kind of writing that draws huge audiences, poetry sections have appeared in Chinese literary magazines throughout the twentieth century, many poetry magazines have long publication histories, and leading fiction writers like Lu Xun, Fei Ming, Shen Congwen, and Ding Ling have also written poetry. In historical terms, studying the development of modern Chinese poetry is crucial because of all the genres it

1 The most comprehensive English-language study is Michelle Yeh's *Modern Chinese Poetry: Theory and Practice since 1917*. Yeh emphasizes the marginality of the New Poetry in its own historical and cultural context, but argues that it is exactly because of its marginal position that modern Chinese poetry was relatively free from moral and political expectations, and therefore more at liberty to experiment.

has always had the most to prove, struggling to justify itself against not only the utilitarian spirit of the time but also the intimidating cultural value of classical Chinese poetry, which continues to be widely read, taught, and enjoyed by Chinese readers all over the world. Throughout the twentieth century and up to the present, modern Chinese poetry has had to defend itself against accusations of not being "Chinese" enough. Whereas reforms in other literary genres were widely accepted (very few Chinese readers nowadays would expect a modern novel or a modern play to resemble novels and plays from the classical tradition), the specific experiments engaged in by modern poets, including the use of vernacular language, free verse, and obscure imagery, have often been frowned upon. One consequence of this is that modern poetry, even nowadays, is often referred to as "New Poetry" to distinguish it from that written in the classical style, which continues to be practiced and appreciated by many.

At no time were these anxieties about tradition and modernity, Chineseness and foreignness, more acute than during the Republican period, to which this anthology is devoted. By the late nineteenth century the once-powerful Chinese empire was collapsing, its authority weakened from within, its borders encroached upon by foreign powers from without. Following a revolution led by Sun Yat-sen (1866–1925), China ceased to be an empire; it became a republic in 1911. A period of social and intellectual turmoil ensued. Political conflict, repudiation of tradition, and growing nationalism fragmented the country, creating tensions in all levels of society. Chinese literature was caught up in this upheaval. For many it had become a symbol of the nation's stagnation. Classical poetry had long been considered integral to Confucian values, so the call for a new kind of verse carried with it an implicit rejection of the old system and its Confucian morals and world-view. The elitism of classical poetry, which was comprehensible only to the most highly educated, became a target of the reformers' invective. Literature became a battleground. Conservatives and progressives struggled over basic literary principles. Reformers saw literature as a new frontier in which visions of a new China could take shape.

The struggle in politics and the arts went on until 1949, when the Republic was overthrown by the Communist revolution led by Mao Zedong (1893–1976). His victory resulted in the founding of the People's Republic of China on the Chinese mainland. His new Communist regime imposed its strictures upon artistic expression. The Republican government moved to the island of Taiwan, where it continues to use the name "Republic of China," but in literary history the term "Republican period" is widely used to refer to the period from 1911 to 1949. Almost all the poems in this volume were written in this period; all of the poets included were active during it.

In my introductory comments to the various sections of this anthology I shall have more to say specifically about this period, but in this general introduction I aim for the *longue durée*, placing the Republican period in the context of broader developments in twentieth and twenty-first century Chinese literature. I will begin with a brief sketch of the chief characteristics of classical Chinese poetry in order to explain the tradition that the modern poets confronted.

WHAT CAME BEFORE

Classical poetry is written in literary Chinese (*wenyan)*, a traditional form of the Chinese language modelled on the written language used two thousand years ago. Until the twentieth century this was the standard form of written Chinese. It is very different from any modern spoken dialect of the language. The *wenyan* vocabulary, the immense vocabulary of classical verse, is made up of tens of thousands of Chinese characters, some extremely intricate in their orthography. Many of these would have been – and continue to be – illegible to all but those with an advanced knowledge of written Chinese. A vast number of *wenyan* characters are unused in spoken Chinese. The syntax of classical poetry is highly compressed, often elliptical. Personal pronouns and articles are excluded. This is a language far removed from the common speech of the people and comprehensible only to the literati.

From a Western perspective, perhaps the most perplexing thing about seeing a classical Chinese poem printed in a book or magazine is that it does not look like poetry. The traditional way of printing Chinese poetry was to print the text in continuous lines, without the line-breaks and generous white margins common to Western poetic tradition. Classical Chinese poetry, in other words, is not typographically distinct from prose. Yet a trained reader can recognize a classical poem as such upon reading a few lines because it contains many formal characteristics, especially on the level of prosody and language, that make it immediately recognisable. These characteristics have changed over time, with new genres emerging in different periods, the most famous ones being the verse (*shi*) of the Tang dynasty

(618–907 CE) and the lyrics (*ci*) of the Song dynasty (960–1279 CE). What ties all the classical genres of poetry together is the idea that poetry is meant to be read or sung out loud, and therefore should possess clear rhythmic and musical qualities regulated through some form of prosody. Part of what is appreciated in the art of classical Chinese poetry is the poet's ability to be creative within the context of prosodic rules.

Most classical Chinese poems, when read out loud, fall into short lines, usually of five or seven syllables. In most cases the same line-length is maintained throughout a poem, depending on the genre. It is common that every pair of these poetic lines should end on syllables that fall into a particular rhyme category. This does not mean that the pairs of lines actually rhyme when read aloud in modern pronunciation. In fact, long before the modern period classical poems had already ceased to "rhyme" in that sense, as the tables used to determine the rhyme-sounds date from the Han dynasty (206 BCE–220 CE). However, in pre-Republican times, poets and critics knew and accepted these artificial rhyme tables and appreciated their skilful use in poetry. Another way in which lines are paired on the basis of language is by means of tone. Chinese is a tonal language. In classical verse pairs of lines are arranged in corresponding syllables of either "level" tones or "oblique" tones. Again, this tonal structure is based on obsolete pronunciations of the characters and was no longer orally detectable long before the modern period.

Classical Chinese poems often break into line-pairs that are linked to each other in content. This is achieved by means of parallelism and antithesis, meaning that one line is followed by a second line in which the words belong to the same "meaning category" (e.g. emotions, nature images, etc.), while at the same time contrasting each other (e.g. spring vs. autumn, joy vs. sorrow, etc.). Again, many of these so-called "categorical correspondences" were well established within the culture and had been observed for more than two millennia by the time modern poetry arrived on the scene.

Classical Chinese poetry is divided into a number of genres, such as *fu*, *shi*, *ci*, and *qu*, all of which have their own prosodies and which would never be mistaken for one another. A *fu* is a long "rhapsody" in lines of equal length in which a single topic or scene is described in great detail and with the greatest possible display of vocabulary. *Shi* poems are more lyrical and are usually written in lines of five or seven characters in length, with strict rules for rhyme, parallelism, and tone contrast. The genres of *ci* and *qu* were originally linked to sets of tunes from older songs or opera arias, which determined the prosody of the poem. Poetry in general was usually described with the term *yunwen*, rhymed writing.

Classical poetry is distinct not only in its form but also in its content. Poets do not express their emotional experiences directly; instead, they project their feelings into the objects they describe. The typical classical poem juxtaposes a natural scene with a personal or social situation. Discerning the connection between the natural setting and the human condition constitutes the ultimate experience of the poem. An example may illustrate this point. A well-known poem by the Tang poet Li Shangyin (c. 813–58 CE) describes a view of the capital city Chang'an at sundown. The poem expresses sorrow over the decline of the empire, but its decline and the poet's dejection are not stated explicitly; rather they are expressed by his description of the sunset over the seat of government. This implicit assumption of the interplay between nature and human experience rests on the Confucian doctrine of the continuity between the natural world and the human psyche.

In short, the artistry of classical poetry derives not only from its substance but also from its style, and its demonstrations of verbal skill and technical ingenuity. Since the stylistic demands of the classical form are ultimately inseparable from it, the challenge for the emerging generation of writers in the early twentieth century was how to conceive of a new poetry without any strict form or prosody at all. They faced a blank page.

BEGINNINGS

The beginnings of modern Chinese poetry are usually traced to the so-called "Literary Revolution" of 1917. This movement started when Hu Shi, a professor at Beijing University who had just returned from a long period of study in the United States, published an article entitled "Some Modest Proposals for Literary Reform." In it he called for the abolition of classical Chinese as the written language, claiming it was a dead language that could not express modern ideas. He urged writers to use language similar to the spoken vernacular instead. Vernacular writing had a long tradition in popular literature but was not normally used for formal literary expression. Hu Shi referred to the replacement of Latin by vernacular languages in Europe during the Renaissance, and called for a "Chinese Renaissance" to take place. Many young intellectuals (mostly professors who were Hu's colleagues, together with their students) enthusiastically responded to the call. They founded journals devoted to experiments in this new kind of literature, and to theoretical articles about what it should be. By 1922 their campaign had been so successful that the vernacular was officially introduced as the language of primary and secondary education throughout China. The language that developed in the process was a mixture of vernacular Chinese grammar and Japanese vocabulary, usually referred to somewhat deceptively as *baihua*, or "plain language." This was the common spoken language with a liberal addition of Japanese coinages for terms new to Chinese culture.

Why was so much of the vocabulary borrowed from Japan? Chinese characters are used to write Japanese. Late nineteenth-century Japanese language-reformers had preceded the Chinese in selecting appropriate combinations of Chinese characters to translate modern Western concepts, ranging from words like "democracy" to a new word for "literature" in the Western sense of the combination of poetry, drama, and fiction. Chinese language-reformers borrowed these character-combinations from the Japanese, and introduced the new words into the Chinese vernacular. Some Europeanized grammatical structures were borrowed as well, as will be discussed later.

As far as poetry is concerned, two basic changes took place during the early days of the Literary Revolution (1917–22) which had a lasting effect on the development of Chinese poetry. First, on the conceptual level, Hu Shi and others, under the influence of Japanese, began to use the word *shi*, originally the name of one particular genre of poetry (as mentioned above), to refer to poetry in general. This may have indicated their wish to move away from a definition of poetry in terms of rhyme and prosody to a freer and more fluid form. A second major change was the introduction of the Western way of printing poetry on the page, line by line, rather than continuously like prose as had been the tradition. This was practised first in the magazine *New Youth*, the highly influential Beijing University–based monthly where Hu Shi had published his 1917 manifesto, but was quickly taken up by editors and publishers throughout the country. This has clearly been the most successful innovation, as nowadays even classical poetry is printed this way. Some avant-garde poets of the early 1920s, like Guo Moruo (see the "Pioneers" section), went so far as to print their poems (and other writing) horizontally rather than vertically, as had been the tradition in Chinese writing. Yet the change to printing horizontally as a rule, rather than as an exception or as an avant-garde gesture, was not made state policy until after 1949.

For many poets, and for those who proposed new literary theories in those early days, the introduction of *baihua* ("plain language") into poetry was not a simple matter. It was often pointed out that since *baihua* is a bi-syllabic language (i.e. most words consist of two syllables, whereas in classical Chinese most words are one syllable), it would be difficult to write in lines of five or seven syllables. Likewise, if there were no standard pronunciation for *baihua,* people would not know how to rhyme, or would do so on the basis of their own dissimilar dialects, which would create confusion.[2] For many of the "New Poets," as Hu Shi and his fellow reformers were soon called, no matter how reformist they were, poetry distinguished itself from prose by formal means such as rhyme and regular line-length. During the late 1910s, literary theorists such as Liu Bannong and others began to search for poetic forms that would "fit" the *baihua* language, being of the opinion that form and language cannot be separated.

Eventually a solution to the problem was put forward by one of the leading reformers, Zhou Zuoren, who also taught at Beijing University as professor of Chinese literature. He argued that in *baihua* one simply cannot write in a fixed form, and therefore must write free verse. As a model of this new way of writing, he presented his own translations of poetry from languages as diverse as Ancient Greek and Modern Japanese. Western examples were of huge importance to the New Literature movement, and most of those experimenting with new ways of writing in Chinese were also avid translators. Zhou Zuoren's translations were all free verse renderings of the poems' meaning only, with no attempt made to capture any of the prosodic qualities of the original works. Zhou explained that when one translated a poem into Chinese, one should do so as literally as possible and not be afraid of producing a translation whose syntax and diction appeared unnatural and awkward, reflecting the syntax and diction of the foreign original. For the first generation of poets, whose works are represented in the first section of this anthology, these characteristics (free verse form, foreign-looking language) applied equally to the writing of original poetry in Chinese. Indeed, when read in Chinese, some of the poems collected here may sound "foreign" in their diction and syntax and might be

2 In the different regions of China dozens of dialects of widely differing pronunciation are spoken.

mistaken for translations from a Western language. Some poets even went as far as to use foreign terms in their Chinese poems, partly as an act of exoticism and partly because in some cases they were genuinely unsure about how to render a foreign concept into Chinese. The anglophile poet Bian Zhilin, for instance, uses the word "serenade," printed in English, in the title of his poem "A Demon's Serenade" (pub. 1931). The free use of foreign words in New Poetry suggests that this was verse produced for an in-crowd of young intellectuals who had been educated in foreign languages.

Modern poetry written in free verse with unfamiliar diction caused anxiety among those poets and critics who preferred the classical style. This was not just because it was experimental or appeared to be incompetently written but because it seemed "un-Chinese." Even nowadays it is not uncommon to encounter Chinese intellectuals who prefer not to read any modern poetry (even if they do read modern fiction and watch modern drama) because they simply do not feel it can be considered "poetry" in the traditional sense. This is especially interesting by comparison with developments in European and American poetry. In the West, modernist poetry has tended toward complex expressions of individual perspectives and experiences, with little interest in expressing collectivist perspectives or national identity. The Western modernist canon, consisting of poetry written in a variety of European languages, is by and large shared by literary elites across most Western countries. In contrast, modern Chinese poetry – after the initial revolutionary efforts by Hu Shi and others – experienced a kind of backlash, with certain poets searching for ways of writing vernacular verse (i.e. using the modern language) in a variety of newly designed bound forms. The forms that emerged during the 1920s and that were used, for instance, by the poets of the Crescent Moon Society, have often been referred to as "national" forms, possessing more "Chineseness" by virtue of the fact that they are more regulated and more musical compared to the pioneers' free verse. The idea that national cultural identity in poetry could only be obtained by writing in bound forms or by trying to emulate the classical tradition has been so pervasive in China throughout the twentieth century that we will consider a couple of different expressions of this anxiety.

As has been mentioned, the pioneers we have been discussing belong to the first section of this anthology. I shall now discuss in turn the poets whose works appear in the book's remaining sections: the formalists, the symbolists, the "peasants and soldiers" poets, and the Nine Leaves poets.

FORMALISM

One of the first critics of free verse was the poet Wen Yiduo, a founding member of the Crescent Moon Society. He was mainly active in the 1920s, and is known as the inventor of what is sometimes derogatively called the *doufugan ti* or "dried bean curd form." (When printed on the page, his highly regular poems resemble symmetrical blocks of bean curd.) Wen Yiduo wrote his poetry in *baihua*. Although he was decidedly a New Poet and rejected classical conventions, he was also an ardent nationalist and unable to abandon the idea of a formal structure for the new verse. He endeavoured to capture some of the rhythmic qualities of classical poetry by dividing his lines into groups of "feet" consisting of two or three syllables, one of which was stressed. He based this prosody on European, especially English, models. He also advocated the use of rhyme, based either on modern Mandarin pronunciation of the characters or on a popular system of Beijing-opera rhyme tables known as the "Thirteen Tracks."[3] The most famous example of this metre is the poem "Stagnant Water" (1925), the first lines of which read as follows in the English translation included in this volume:

This ditch is rank with the water of despair.
A brisk wind cannot stir it to ripple.
Why not toss in more scrap copper and iron?
Might as well add soup and rotten vegetables.

The original Chinese lines, marked to show the metre, read as follows. The end rhyme in lines two and four (*lun* rhyming with *geng*) comes from the "Thirteen Tracks" system:

zhe shi / yi gou / juewang de / sishui
qing feng / chuibuqi / bandian / yilun
bu ru / duo reng xie / potong / lantie
shuaixing / po ni de / shengcai / cangeng

Wen's rigid forms of equal numbers of feet per line, together with patterned rhyme, did not find a wide following, but his technique of dividing the lines into feet or segments of two or three characters with one stressed remained

3 Cf. Lloyd Haft, *The Chinese Sonnet: Meanings of a Form.*

popular throughout later periods. It can perhaps be seen as one that fits the *baihua* language.

Wen's formal structure was employed by his contemporary Xu Zhimo, the leader of the Crescent Moon Society, today the most widely enjoyed of the early twentieth-century poets. A later poet who made extensive use of structured prosody in combination with the *baihua* language was Wu Xinghua, who was mainly active in Beijing during the War of Resistance against Japan (1937–45). Wu Xinghua did not believe that it was possible to write poetry without having a fixed form; he regarded form as a bridge between poet and reader. Wu was nostalgic for the classical period, when readers and poets knew what to expect of each other and readers could anticipate, after reading one line of a poem, what was to follow in the next. He went so far as to claim that poetic lines that were not regular in form should be considered "ungrammatical," because they would be confusing to readers looking for regularity and parallelism. In other words, Wu suggested that a defect in poetic form was a defect in language. This was starkly different from modernist poetry in the West, which deliberately sought to abandon and disrupt established patterns of form and meaning. Wu Xinghua wrote that it was the duty of modern poets to study classical poetry and to develop new and suitable forms, to make sure that modern Chinese poetry would not "get off the right track." Precisely what the right track was he did not say, but we see his strong identification with a shared cultural identity of which poetry is an important expression.

When Wu's views were discussed by poets and critics in Taiwan in the 1950s, almost forty years after the Literary Revolution of 1917, the critic Xia Ji'an (T.A. Hsia) still agreed that poetry in *baihua* had yet to prove its value and was far from established. Xia also made explicit an assumption that was likely shared by many poets and critics in the first half of the century, namely that writing in the vernacular involved making literature accessible for the "common people" or, as Xia put it, "when you write in *baihua* you have to draw some inspiration from peasants and soldiers." The underlying assumption was that if poetry were only to be appreciated by a literate elite then there was no need for it to adopt vernacular language. For critics like Xia, the whole point of Hu Shi's 1917 revolution had been an attempt to broaden the readership of poetry, making it more accessible to the common people. Although he believed that this was laudable, Xia and other critics were not convinced that writing poetry in the vernacular could ever make for better poetry.

SYMBOLISM

At the same time as Xu and Wen were endeavouring to formulate a new structure based on English meter for vernacular verse, poets like Bian Zhilin and Dai Wangshu, who studied in France, were imitating the symbolist style originated by Baudelaire and developed by Rimbaud and Verlaine. Following their European models, these New Poets used images to express the depths of the psyche. Their metaphors and allusions often had a deliberately abstract and ambiguous quality, being without any concrete referent. The symbolist Ji Xian wrote, "Modern poetry holds as true the internal world of the imagination and regards as illusory the external world of the senses." Much negative criticism of New Poetry was aimed at the perceived rootlessness and surrealism of its symbolism. The first and most radical of the symbolists, Li Jinfa, imitated the style of French surrealists like Louis Aragon and André Breton. The result was something no Chinese reader had encountered before. Irate critics went so far as to deny that such confabulations of bizarre, disconnected images could be poetry at all.

The symbolists have come to be considered more successful in terms of poetic form. In contrast to the rigorous prosodies of the formalists, their verse was characterized by a subtle, irregular musicality that comes out especially when read aloud, as in the case of Dai Wangshu's famous poem "Rainy Lane." Later literary historians have generally hailed the symbolists for their ability to present an aesthetically successful fusion of the experimentalism of the pioneers and the intricate regularity of the formalists.

Symbolist poetry arose in an age of political and social chaos in China. As Japanese troops advanced, poets became increasingly uneasy about verse written simply for artistic enjoyment. Symbolists like He Qifang turned their backs on aestheticism to support Mao's Communist rebels, employing their skill at symbolic detail to write realistic poems about the sufferings of ordinary people at the hands of both the Japanese invaders and Chiang Kai-shek's Republican government. The exception was Ji Xian, who persisted in depicting an imaginary symbolic world. He fled Mao's victorious forces to Chiang Kai-shek's island republic on Taiwan, where he would be recognized among Taiwanese poets as "the high priest of modernism."

PEASANTS AND SOLDIERS

As early as 1942, when Mao gave his famous talks on literature and art at the forum in Yan'an, he criticized the literature of the preceding decades, including the New Poetry, for being too difficult and too narrow in content for ordinary people to understand. These talks soon became guidelines for a new style of revolutionary art, addressing "the masses" as its audience. Mao called upon writers to descend to the level of peasants and soldiers (i.e. the working classes, who were the focus of Mao's Marxist movement), and particularly encouraged the collection of local folksongs as a means of inspiration for poets. Mao's standards reflect the kind of verse that the Communist poet Tian Jian had been writing since the mid-1930s, propagandist poetry in simple language for the common people that tended to culminate in revolutionary slogans:

When cotton is picked in this hill country,
We carry it home. Someone takes it away
And we swallow our bitterness –
How many times have we played pack-beasts for nothing!

Have no fear!
Let the wind blow
And the rain pour.
When the storm is over,
Everything under heaven will be ours!
(from "Song of the Hill Country," 1935)

The storm was the Communist revolution led by Mao, which had begun in the 1920s and ultimately overthrew Chiang Kai-shek's government in 1949.

Mao's critique of modern Chinese poetry is different from others we have discussed, in that he does not hark back to classical poetry as a model, but rather appeals to popular culture and the basic appetites of the common people. At the same time, it must be recalled that Mao himself was a poet, and that all the poems he ever wrote and published were written in classical forms and genuinely accessible only to those with ample grounding in the classical tradition.[4]

4 Mao never wrote any "peasants and soldiers" poems, or any works that could be recognized as New Poetry at all. For that reason his verse is not included in this anthology.

THE NINE LEAVES POETS

The rigidity with which Mao enforced his guidelines, pressing literature into political service, strangled the artistic quality of vernacular verse written in regions under his control. In the late 1940s a group of nine poets published in two journals in Shanghai, which still lay outside Mao's domain. This group would come to be known as the "Nine Leaves" poets. Four of them studied before 1945 at Southwest United University, where they encountered the modernist verse of W.H. Auden and T.S. Eliot. They did not hesitate to write about politics, but they also treated apolitical themes like love and poetic creation, and they did so from rigorously individual perspectives. Their penchant for Western models and their intellectual independence put them out of favour with Mao's publishing establishment after 1949. For the following thirty years, until the beginning of the more liberal Deng Xiaoping era, they could not publish their own verse. Even "writing for the drawer" became dangerous during the Cultural Revolution (1966–76), when writers were subject to unannounced searches, beatings, and public denunciation. When Deng took power, the surviving members of the Nine Leaves were among the first poets to emerge from deep freeze. Their individualistic use of imagery represents a bridge from the pre-1949 vernacular poetry to the "obscure" poets of the 1980s and 90s. In fact, the term "obscure" first appeared in 1979 as a criticism of a group of poems that included "Autumn" by Du Yunxie, one of the Nine Leaves poets. Two of the Nine Leaves poets (Chen Jingrong and Zheng Min) are female, which is a high proportion when compared to the overall presence of female poets in the modern Chinese poetic canon.

THE POST-MAO ERA

Partly as a result of the discrepancy between Mao's literary theories and his poetic practice, during the 1950s and 1960s aspiring mainland Chinese poets were caught in a double bind. On the one hand, classical poetry was still being taught in schools, was practised by Mao and other members of the elite, and was presented as one of the great heritages of the Chinese people. On the other hand, poets who wrote in the vernacular were expected to do no more than produce simple folksongs on politically approved topics. More ambitious forms of modern poetry, which would have challenged the classical tradition, were discouraged by the government, were not permitted to be taught in schools, and ceased to appear in print, as all publishing was controlled by the regime.[5] This was the situation for twenty years, during the 1950s and 1960s.

The decades that followed Mao's death in 1976 witnessed a change. In the early 1970s, after the schools were closed, many young Chinese intellectuals were living in the countryside, sent there by the government to learn socialism among the peasants during the Cultural Revolution. They were starting to feel alienated both from the peasants amid whom they lived and from the government that sent them there. A favourite pastime was reading the so-called "Brown Cover Books" (*huangpi shu*). These were translations of Western literature, including modernist literature, which were printed and circulated in small quantities in the 1950s and early 1960s. They also included some volumes of vernacular Chinese poetry written in the 1930s and 1940s. Originally intended to be read only by higher Communist Party cadres, these books gradually found their way into the hands of the youth sent to the countryside, who read and copied them avidly. Through the reading of these books, some were encouraged to try their hand at writing themselves. Many of the poets who would later become known as the "Obscure Poets" or *menglong shiren* started their careers as underground writers during the early 1970s.

As the contemporary poet Bei Dao later explained, what attracted them most about the *huangpi shu* was the language of the translations, which was so unlike both the political language of the "Mao style" and the language of classical literature that they had studied in school. Bei Dao called this language the translation style (*fanyi ti*) and described it as something neither foreign nor Chinese, and completely new. Of course it was not really new, as most of the translators of the *huangpi shu* had themselves been writers and poets during the 1930s. The original poetry of several *huangpi shu* translators appears in our anthology, including that of Bian Zhilin, who translated Baudelaire, Mallarmé, Verlaine, and Valéry. In this way the second major "revolution" in modern Chinese poetry was brought about under the influence of a style that emerged from the practice of translation. Once again the result was a poetry predominantly written in free verse.

When Bei Dao's work moved above ground and into open publication after 1978, it was neither his language nor his form that first attracted the

5 Some poets, like the symbolist Bian Zhilin and the Nine Leaves poet Yuan Kejia, turned to the politically safer task of translation of foreign literature, which – curiously – continued to be published under Mao, even as the regime rejected Chinese poetry based on foreign models.

attention of readers but his highly emotional defence of individualism in the famous poem "The Answer," which recalls poetry from the 1920s by Guo Moruo in its presentation of the figure of the poet as "hero." Old guard "Peasants and Soldiers" poets Ai Qing and Zang Kejia attacked the individualism and scepticism of Bei Dao as Western cultural decadence. The Communist regime had identified the state socialism it had built with Chinese nationalism. Because Communist China had experienced no spiritual crisis like the capitalist West, Ai and Zang claimed, Bei Dao's expression of alienation had no place in China.

Before long, however, debate about this new post-Mao poetry did move onto the familiar ground of form and language. While Bei Dao and others' innovative verse was allowed to be published, it was labelled by the authorities as obscure (*menglong*), implying that it was unintelligible for the "masses." The young poets gladly accepted this description of their style and many of them (Bei Dao, Duoduo, Gu Cheng, Yang Lian, etc.) enjoyed writing a kind of poetry in which the language called attention to itself. The "obscure images" presented by these poets are not meant to be understood transparently but to be enjoyed first of all on the level of language, often offering the possibility of multiple interpretation. A good example is Bei Dao's 1970s poem cycle "Notes from the City of the Sun" (English translation, 1983), and especially the last poem:[6]

LIVING
A net

In the Chinese the visual quality of the character that stands for "net" – 网 – adds to the aesthetic quality of the language. For Communist critics at the time, this was difficult to understand. One of them even criticized Bei Dao saying that it was absurd to have a poem in which the title was longer than the text itself! Many Chinese readers have problems with these so-called "obscure poems" because they do not understand them, not just on the level of meaning, but often on the level of language. Like Wu Xinghua, whose comments on form and grammar are mentioned above, many contemporary readers of "obscure" poetry state that its language is simply

6 The translation is from Bei Dao, *The August Sleepwalker*, trans. Bonnie S. McDougall.

"wrong" and "ungrammatical," rather than merely difficult or unconventional. Moreover, Bei Dao and other contemporary poets are nowadays again being criticized by postcolonial critics concerned about Western influence on Chinese poetry and wary of the loss of the classical tradition.

We must ask ourselves if such anxieties stem from literary or from political concerns. Certainly politics plays a role. But there are other issues as well. Poets have refused to consider the possibility of mixing the "national forms" and the "translation style," for instance by writing free verse in classical *wenyan* or classical parallel verse in *baihua*. One reason for this refusal is the identification of the two genres with conflicting worldviews: traditional poetry with Confucianism and the New Poetry with a progressive outlook. It seems that in classical verse and New Poetry, we are dealing with two rival constellations of form, language, and probably also content. It has proven very difficult for the two to co-exist. Two examples may suffice to clarify this point. Many modern Chinese poets like Feng Zhi, working in the Europeanized tradition, have experimented with traditional Western forms such as the sonnet. Others have worked with newly developed forms such as Wen Yiduo's "Stagnant Water" metre. But no one has attempted to write modern poetry in a classical Chinese form (which is entirely possible, despite the bi-syllabic nature of modern Chinese). Such poetry would have the very same form as classical poetry – the same conventional number of syllables per line, the same rhyme scheme, the same parallel line structure, the same tone patterns – but its syntax would be that of common speech and its vocabulary would be *baihua*, not the elaborate vocabulary of the classical tradition. But this idea has been anathema. Secondly, until very recently it was almost impossible to come across modern-style and classical-style poems alongside each other in the same anthology or magazine. Only since the development of the internet, which has given rise to novel ways of interaction between poetry-lovers throughout China, have we seen the emergence of websites simultaneously devoted to both styles of poetry.

We should take into account the role of education. No twentieth-century Chinese person could appreciate classical poetry if it were not taught and explained to them. The language, images, and references to other classical works are simply too difficult to understand at first sight. As long as classical poetry continues to be given so much emphasis in education, it will always be difficult for modern poetry to establish itself. To illustrate this: when I studied literature in school in the Netherlands, classical European poetry was dealt with briefly in the earlier stages of the curriculum. In later years we read modernist poetry, which was considered to be more difficult and challenging and therefore more suitable for reading at a higher academic level. In China the order is reversed: middle-school students read modern poetry in the early years of the curriculum because it is considered simple and straightforward, before they are encouraged to study the "difficult" texts of the classical tradition. Against this background, it is almost inevitable that most pupils come away with a life-long conviction that classical poetry is more significant culturally than its modern counterpart.

However, none of this matters if we take into account the fact that modernist poets, as a rule, do not write in order to serve as a bridge between poet and reader who share a single culture. If classical poetry did (and still does) perform this function in China, then perhaps we should simply say that in modern poetry we are dealing with a completely different kind of writing that cannot be expected to rise to the same level of cultural prominence in China as its classical counterpart. But that does not make it less valuable. In the end, the value of modern Chinese poetry, especially the poetry in the Westernized style that is collected in this anthology, lies in its ability to bring about a creative fusion of "Chinese" and "foreign" language, subject matter, and imagery.

PART ONE

Pioneers

Introduction

MICHEL HOCKX

The poets represented in the first section of this anthology are traditionally referred to as "pioneers" to emphasize the newness of their way of writing and thinking about poetry. Naturally, the fact that they attracted so much attention and were subsequently canonized indicates that there must have been even more "pioneering" pioneers before them, as well as others contemporary to them who were less successful in their own experiments. So in order to understand better how these canonized pioneers were different from others, we should look at the choices they made in the modernization of poetry.

THE USE OF *BAIHUA*

Surely the most revolutionary aspect of the New Poetry advocated by Hu Shi and others from 1917 onwards was the use of the vernacular (*baihua*). Although this might not always show in translation, the reader of the following pages will most likely find that the diction of these poems is more straightforward and less ornate than that of much classical Chinese poetry. For example, compare two descriptions of cowardice in the face of invasion, the first by a great classical poet, the second by a pioneer of the New Poetry:

> Still the dogs of Chieh bark at Yao,
> And the Tartar crew mock the imperial command.
> In the middle of the night I sigh four and five times,
> Worrying ever over the great empire's affairs.
> Still the war-banners cover the sides of the two mountains
> Between which flows the Yellow River.
> Our generals like frightened fowls dare not advance,
> But linger on, watering their idle horses.
> (from Li Bai, "To His Friend, Wei, the Good Governor"[1])

1 From *The Works of Li Po*, tr. Shigeyoshi Obata, 179.

In my home town
Amid gunsmoke and splashing blood,
Bodies strewn all over the ground,
  Soldiers,
  Bandits,
  The mayor's gunmen,
Who can tell who's on whose side?
If I weren't such a coward
I'd take a gun
And annihilate them all.
  (from Xu Yunuo, "If I Weren't Such a Coward")

The particular type of *baihua* used by the New Poets was heavily influenced by vocabulary and grammatical structures borrowed from European languages, especially English. The European flavour of this language reveals the origins of early New Poetry in the "translation style," as I have argued in the general introduction. Contemporaries of Hu Shi, such as the Nanjing-based group of Harvard graduates publishing the journal *Xueheng* (*The Critical Review*), insisted that poetry must be written in classical Chinese and they continued to do so. Many of the New Poets themselves, including Lu Xun, continued to write classical poetry as well, but chose not to publish it then (although some of it was published posthumously). As Zhu Ziqing, represented here with his long masterpiece "Annihilation," once said: "I wrote classical poetry throughout this time but I chose not to publish it so as not to harm 'the movement.'"

FREE VERSE

Hu Shi was not the first person to introduce Europeanized diction into Chinese poetry. Two decades earlier a similar attempt had been made by Huang Zunxian, who proclaimed a "Poetry Revolution" in 1895. Huang's choices, however, were different from Hu's. Huang was unable to conceive of poetry written in irregular forms. He experimented with folk-song prosodies, but he is most remembered for the introduction of foreign words and concepts into poetry written in the standard classical five-syllable line. One of his most famous lines, *wo shou xie wo kou* ("my hand writes my mouth"), is ironically often quoted as evidence of Huang's advocacy of the vernacular – ironically, because Huang condenses the vernacular sentence

"My hand writes what my mouth says" into a five-syllable line in the compressed syntax of classical poetry while retaining *baihua* vocabulary. In fact, this five-syllable line appears in a long poem consisting of nothing but five-syllable lines strictly arranged according to classical prosody.

Free verse, then, was the most significant innovation carried out by Hu Shi and his colleagues. Writing in free verse was a matter of principle for these early New Poets: rejecting the strict prosodies of classical poetry was a symbol of rebellion against the prescriptions of Confucian morality. Writing free verse was thus a crucial aspect of the movement for a "New Culture." Nevertheless various elements of classical prosody, including rhyme, parallelism, and repetition, continue to appear throughout the writing of poets like Hu Shi and Guo Moruo (by far the most famous and widely read of the pioneers). The somewhat more obscure poet Xu Yunuo, whose work has only recently started to receive attention after fifty years of neglect, was more at ease with free verse. Interestingly, his work was the topic of a heated debate in the early 1920s. A number of critics assumed that his unrhymed free verse was prose poetry, even though the two forms are quite distinctly different. (Prose poetry is printed in sentences like a prose text and often written in a more prosaic style, while free verse is printed in lines and often employs poetic techniques like rhyme, though not in any systematic fashion.) These critics' confusion shows that, in these early years, unrhymed free verse was often associated with prose for the simple reason that in the Chinese tradition, poetry was by definition strictly rhymed and consisted of lines of a fixed length.

The most successful type of free verse published in this early period was the "little poetry" (*xiao shi*) of the young woman Bing Xin and others, written under the influence of Japanese haiku and the short verse of Rabindranath Tagore, the first Asian winner of the Nobel Prize for Literature, who famously visited China in 1924. In the following short poem, for example, Bing Xin renders a motif of classical Japanese haiku into *baihua* free verse.

From the bough she breaks the blossom
For a vase
        Then gazes, sighing
        At the empty branch.
(Bing Xin, *Myriad Stars*, 95)

Linked to this question of how to define New Poetry is the issue of printing the poem on the page with lots of blank space around it, like traditional Western poetry. With free verse being the form of choice, this way of printing poetry became essential; otherwise there would be no obvious distinction between poetry and prose at all. Some of the more avant-garde literary journals such as Guo Moruo's *Chuangzao jikan* (*Creation Quarterly*) also took to printing from left to right, as in Western languages, rather than from top to bottom, as in classical Chinese texts. Horizontal printing continued to be an avant-garde (and often a leftist) statement in literary writings (as opposed to in scientific writings, where it quickly became the norm so that Western mathematical formulae could be more easily reproduced) until the 1950s, when it became state policy.

"WESTERNIZED" CONTENT

The issue of content is more difficult to address, but it seems that for most of the pioneers it was a matter of principle that their poetry feature Western content. It is obvious in Hu Shi's poetry that he does his best to incorporate content based on his period of study in the United States and his readings in Western philosophy. Hu Shi also advocated a more "rational" approach to poetry, as opposed to the lyrical tradition of classical poetry. His footnote to "Dream and Poem," calling the poem his "poetic empiricism," emphasizes its source in Western empirical philosophy; his ideas about writing in the language of common speech and practicing efficiency and sparseness in diction echo the famous "Imagist Manifesto" of Ezra Pound and Amy Lowell, which was all the rage when Hu was studying in the United States. He always denied any direct influence of the imagist movement, but it is hard to take this seriously. Hu's manifesto that started the "Literary Revolution" of 1917 features a list of "eight don'ts" extremely reminiscent of Pound's "A Few Don'ts by an Imagiste." Hu called for flexibility of diction and structure ("do not avoid colloquialisms"; "do not use parallelisms") and for discarding classical models ("do not imitate the ancients"; "do not use classical allusions"). In his poem "Thought," for example, he replaces the typical classical allusions to the lakes and rivers of China with references to the Hudson River and Lake Cayuga, the settings of Columbia and Cornell, the two American universities where he studied.

These early poems fascinate because of their experimental nature and the willingness of the writers to go well beyond the native tradition. But later judgment of these works has been harsh. In recent years many critics, reasoning from postcolonial perspectives, have objected to the Westernized nature of these works. Postcolonial critics also condemn the vehement way in which these poets and critics actively suppressed other poets who tried to maintain more "Chineseness"; an example of such "suppression" is the alleged smothering of Huang Zunxian's use of *baihua* vocabulary within classical forms, and of his experimentation with native folk-song prosody. It is hard to establish when exactly the poets in this collection achieved canonized status and what their actual cultural power was in their own time. The fact is that in important recent anthologies like the ten-volume *Zhongguo xin shiku* (*A Treasury of New Chinese Poetry*), the bulk of the earliest New Poetry comes from these writers. In the present-day canon they are acknowledged as the beginning.

Hu Shi

(1891–1962)

The author of the first New Poetry to appear in print was a man of many parts. Poet, politician, diplomat, and philosopher, Hu Shi was born in Anhui Province, the son of an aged scholar-official and a countrywoman. After his classical education in the village school and four years of secondary school in Shanghai, he qualified for a scholarship from the American Boxer Rebellion Indemnity Fund to study agriculture at Cornell at age nineteen. He soon switched to philosophy and literature. After Cornell he enrolled for a PhD in philosophy at Columbia, where he was deeply influenced by his professor, the American pragmatist John Dewey. Hu returned to China advocating modernization along Western lines and cooperation with Western powers.

In America Hu came to believe that the history of Chinese poetry during the first millennium CE was one of constant evolution, repeatedly invigorated by the vernacular language, but that in the second millennium China's poetic tradition had become so rigid that by his own time it was ossified. Hu saw in the visual imagery and simple diction of Western imagist poetry a similarity to Song dynasty lyrics, and sought to transform what he found in the imagists into a modernized kind of Chinese verse. In January of 1918, after becoming a professor at Beijing University, he published nine poems of vernacular free verse in *New Youth*. They caused a furor. The rules of classical poetry were so deeply identified with the Confucian moral and social system that readers perceived Hu's poems as an attack on traditional Chinese culture – as Hu intended them to be.

Michelle Yeh notes that Hu sought to establish a new poetic canon with new language, new forms, and new content. In place of classical restraint, a poem like Hu's "Thought" was bursting with natural energy, celebrating the power of the untrammeled human mind. The poem embodies Hu's advocacy of individualism in the narrator's self-confident proclamation of his own powers, in deliberate contrast to the conventional self-effacement of the classical poet. "Dream and Poem" purports to explain in terms of

Western empirical philosophy how a poem comes to birth in the poet's psyche. The narrator in Hu's poetry tends to be impersonal and detached; this stance reflects the pragmatism Hu imbibed from Dewey at Columbia. Hu's 1920 *Experiments* was the first published book of vernacular poetry. Although most of his verse deals with his own experience and feelings, a few of Hu's early poems describe the plight of the poor and issue a call for revolution. He omitted these revolutionary pieces when he republished his works in Taiwan at the close of his life, after long years of service as a Guomindang official.

Hu took a leading role in the May Fourth Movement of 1919. This epoch-making event began as a student protest that quickly evolved into a movement for democracy, advocating vernacular writing and attacking Confucianism and classical literature. Hu's work of this period assailed the power of the privileged classes, whose cultural ascendancy rested on their mastery of the complex classical language. The employment of the vernacular to replace classical Chinese was intended to enable the ordinary educated person to read all forms of serious literature, poetry included. At this early stage of the cultural struggle Hu was actually an ally of Lu Xun, who later became Hu's political adversary as standard-bearer of the left.

When the Guomindang took power in 1927, Hu joined their ranks. From 1938 to 1942 he served as Chinese ambassador to America, a key role in the negotiation of American aid for China's resistance to the Japanese. In 1946 Hu returned to China as dean of Beijing University and subsequently became secretary of the national assembly. When the Communists took power Hu fled with the Guomindang government to Taiwan, where he became head of the Academica Sinica and editor of *Free China* journal. Denounced as a capitalist and oppressor of the common people under Mao, Hu has experienced something of a revival in the post-Mao era, when the Westernization he advocated became the order of the day under Deng Xiaoping.

Michelle Yeh notes Hu's emphasis on concrete imagery. He believed that the essence of a poem lies in its content and that its language should be natural. In a 1917 article in *New Youth*, Hu prescribed "eight don'ts." Hu enumerated the characteristics of traditional verse to be avoided: imitation of the ancients, classical allusions, artificial content (especially an assumed pose of melancholy), hackneyed expressions, the use of rhymed couplets, and pairs of lines parallel in syntax and meaning. Instead he advocated writing with real substance, and the use of vernacular in place of the refined, allusion-laden diction of classical poetry. Yeh observes that these rules for poetry derive from Hu's conception of the Chinese language. He rejected what he saw as the empty formalism of contemporary classical verse, together with the classical rhyme formulas which were based on pronunciations that were long out of date, so that many pairs of "rhyme words" did not, in fact, rhyme at all. Instead of classical verse's rhymed stanzas, he advocated free verse. In short, the New Poetry was to replace poetry in dead language and restrictive form with untrammeled poetry in living language. Hu himself was a translator, and he compared his own poetry to his translations of Byron and the ballads of Scottish poet Anne Lindsay. The similarity of his original verse to his translations of foreign poems served as a basis for the notion, which quickly became widespread, that New Poetry was related in style and language to poetry translated from Western languages.

In 1923 Hu joined Xu Zhimo and others to form the Crescent Moon Society – which would later advocate formally structured poetry, the very opposite of Hu's free verse. Hu turned his attention to politics. The Society's press began to publish anti-Communist political articles, many authored by Hu himself. He is quoted as defending Chiang Kai-shek's mass execution of Communists captured in Shanghai in 1927.

Hu's complete works, published in Taiwan after his death, comprise thirty-seven volumes. His vernacular poetry can best be viewed as a harbinger of things to come. He did not himself transform *baihua* into a literary language, but he pointed a way for poets after him who would create masterpieces in the vernacular.

Thought

Revolving planets, constrained to circle the sun,
Changing moon, orbiting the earth day and night,
Countless stars great and small, confined in endless rounds through
the sky,
Radio wave flashing thousands of miles in an instant –
I despise you!
You can't compare with my least thought!
This thought of mine:

From Bamboo Lane to Bamboo Peak[2]
From Cayuga Lake to Hudson's shore[3] –
If only I don't get snagged on love
    I can spin round the world a million times a second!

1918

Dream and Poem

Experiences common to all,
Images common to all
Welling up by chance in dreams
In strange new shapes.

Common feelings,
Common words
Striking the poet by chance
In brand new verse.

Only a drunkard knows wine;
Only a lover knows love's power.
I can no more dream your dream
Than you can write my poem.

1920

2 "Bamboo Lane was the street I lived on. Bamboo Peak was a mountain behind my home town." (Author's note.)
3 In America the author attended Cornell University, located on the shores of Lake Cayuga in Ithaca, New York, and Columbia University, on the shores of the Hudson River.

Liu Dabai
(1880–1932)

Liu was born in Shaoxing, Zhejiang province. He received a classical education and successfully passed the Qing dynasty imperial exams. When the Qing dynasty fell, he took work at a newspaper in his hometown. In 1913 he went to Japan, where he studied modern Japanese literature. After living for a short time in Singapore and Sumatra he returned to his home province, where he worked in a bank in the provincial capital, Hangzhou.

Liu's early classical verse imitated Huang Zunxian (1848–1905), who wrote poems in *baihua* vocabulary about modern ideas and inventions. Liu even invented words: to mention a telephone in one of his classical poems, he created the sound-alike term "delefeng" because there was no word for "telephone" in Chinese. All this was highly innovative. One did not write about Western-style leather shoes in classical verse. With the May Fourth Movement, Liu turned away from classical poetry to compose vernacular poems based on Chinese folk songs and on the *Book of Songs*, a collection of ancient popular songs.

As secretary of the Zhejiang provincial assembly in the early 1920s, Liu witnessed first-hand the conditions of peasant life. In response to what he saw, he composed poems in the folk-song structure: lines of equal length, rhymed, with simple vocabulary. Their theme was the sufferings of tenant farmers and the working poor. These poems became propaganda for the peasants' anti-landlord movement. From this period comes his "Turtle," a vitriolic satire on the figure of the warlord. But while Liu's student and fellow New Poet Feng Xuefeng was to become the associate of the leftist writer Lu Xun, Liu was to follow a more conservative path. After becoming a prominent academic, he was appointed an official of the Guomindang regime.

In several respects, Liu ran counter to the majority of pioneer poets. He eschewed free verse and Western models and sought a distinctively Chinese form. Following in the footsteps of Huang Zunxian, he experimented with the use of folk-song prosody. In this he was virtually unique among the New Poets. (We do not include any of his folk-song poems in this collection.) Liu soon turned away from revolutionary verse. "Spring in the Air" is a transitional piece, neither a folk song nor political, a depiction of contented peasants. In "Autumn Evening on the River" Liu echoes the contemplative mood of classical poetry. He eventually turned to composing short verse after the model of Rabindranath Tagore. His *Tracks of Tears* is a series of reflective poems of personal sentiment in imitation of Bing Xin's *Myriad Stars*.

Liu's first book of poetry was published in 1924. In that same year he became chairman of the Chinese department of Fudan University in Shanghai. He wrote no verse after 1926. The rapid change in his poetry from radical popular protest to personal sentiment and contemplative reflection was a harbinger of the conservative change in his public career. A radical champion of the common people in his youth, Liu was to become vice-minister of Education with the ruling Guomindang party.

Turtle[4]

The ancients revered you as a spirit,
Yet how dull you are,
And not only that,
But filthy too.

You have a pot belly
Like the God of Wealth.
For all that you're penniless.
And you call this prosperity?

Armored all over
Like a warrior,
At every turn you pull in your head.
Is this the victory you boast of?

A poised bearing, a stately tread,
Like a big spender from the country,
You drag your tail in the dust.
So this is your dignity?

4 Slang for "prick." The poem is a satire on the warlord.

You never toil.
You survive by happenstance.
Your fortuitous success
Is the luck of a bandit.

1921

from *Tracks of Tears*

21

Some tears flow openly –
Tears of joy;
Some flow invisibly –
Agonized tears.
Tears of joy –
How many times in a life do they flow?
Agonized tears –
How often can one hold them back?

1922

Spring in the Air

A little boat with no awning
Buoyed by the warm spring river,
A barefoot man in a short smock
Rowing at the stern.
A rough-clad woman, hair dishevelled,
Rowing in the middle,
Holding with one hand
A child in red and green.
Dipping oars and rowing,
One before, one behind,
They chatter,
They giggle.

The child gazes left and right,
Listening wide-eyed,
Babbling a song –
A boat with no awning,
Floating to the rhythm,
Dipping, rowing, chattering, giggling, babbling.

A boat
Full of life,
Love,
Vitality
That fill the river, the sky,
Embodying better than willows and flowers
The awakening of spring.

1923

Autumn Evening on the River

Weary as it is,
The homing bird
Bears the setting sun on its wings.

With a single flap
She drops the sunset on the river:
The pale-headed reeds
Rouge their faces in its fleeting crimson.

1923

Xu Yunuo
(1894–1958)

Xu Yunuo produced a large body of highly praised verse at the start of the New Poetry movement, then withdrew into silence. Unlike the other members of the Literary Research Association, Xu came from a peasant family. He was born in Xuying, Henan province. The rural region of Henan where he grew up was in a constant state of social turmoil. From the age of six Xu witnessed imperial soldiers, bandit gangs, and warlord troops battling for control of his home town. Bandits and local officials sometimes shared control of the local government. Warlord soldiers looted peasant homes, reducing whole families to poverty. This violence and political chaos formed the background of poems like "If I Weren't Such a Coward."

Xu's family still managed to give him an education. After seven years with private tutors he began formal schooling late, only graduating from the local primary school at the age of eighteen. Four years later he entered Henan No. 1 Teachers College in Kaifeng. Here he encountered the literature of the May Fourth Movement, read the poetry of Tagore, and began writing short stories and poetry. In 1919 he published a collection of verse, *The Garden of the Future*, after which he was invited to contribute to the Literary Research Association's anthology, *A Snowy Morning*. His poems drew considerable attention among those interested in the New Poetry. Fellow members of the association praised his verse for its expressive emotion.

As a member of the Association, Xu was an adherent of the Poetry for Life movement, which advocated idealism and humanism in opposition to the "art for art's sake" creed of Guo Moruo's Creation Society. Xu was not an active participant in literary meetings in Beijing or Shanghai since he lived in Kaifeng and identified with his native district, staying in contact with his fellow poets by correspondence. His peasant background provided Xu with tragic subject matter unavailable to gentrified fellow members of the Literary Research Association. The stark realism in Xu's poems is a far cry from the urbane humanism of other poets of the Association. His early work treated with skepticism the popular optimism that education could save China from its turmoil. This tone of pessimism was to be a keynote of poems like "The Cage of Reality."

Michel Hockx enumerates four themes in Xu's poems: memories, depression, homesickness, and nature. In certain poems, Michelle Yeh observes, Xu treats poetry as a kind of religion, establishing a world of its own values. Such a world takes shape in "A Child." In his introduction to Xu's poems, Zheng Zhenfang describes him as a poet who longs to write of a dreamlike beauty but refuses to let that dream obscure the blood and tears of the real world. "A Child" portrays a bucolic world of harmony and love, but in other poems this vision is overwhelmed by the horror of the warfare that surrounds the poet. These were scenes he had witnessed growing up in rural Henan.

After graduating in 1921 Xu took up a series of teaching posts, constantly moving from town to town, province to province. He stopped writing and disappeared from the literary scene. For the next twenty years he taught in secondary schools and normal colleges all over eastern China. He is said to have sometimes disappeared for months in the middle of the semester. He was often fired. At one time he accepted work as a tailor; at another time he managed a mill. He lived a solitary life with no active political affiliation, but he espoused Communist thought. When Lu Xun offered to publish Xu's youthful short stories Xu refused because, he said, they contained too much *petit bourgeois* individualism. In 1937 he worked with an anti-Japanese resistance unit. In 1940 he returned to his native province, taking teaching posts in a variety of cities and towns, returning home from time to time to farm.

The Communist takeover in 1949 provided new impetus for Xu the poet. He wrote in support of the Communist land-reform program, attacking in free verse the landlord class from whom his family had rented farmland. He wrote poems in support of China's military involvement in the Korean War. Later he worked with peasant drama groups and collected their plays. By the time he died of cancer in 1958 his youthful poetry had fallen into neglect, not least because it did not give voice to Communist policy, but today he is regarded as one of the most significant early New Poets.

Xu has been compared to his contemporary Li Jinfa. But Xu's is not the fantastic surrealism of Li Jinfa: it is the horribly real surrealism of war. While Li's language is complex to the point of obscurity; Xu's is plain, direct, and clear. Like Baudelaire's, Xu's poems explore the nexus between beauty and evil. They lay bare the darkness and at the same time embrace it. "A Child" is an exception, in that it celebrates a world of innocent freedom and beauty; much more often Xu presents a romantic image only to describe its suffocation by reality. In "The Cage of Reality," the harsh world traps the bird of the imagination. "If I Weren't Such a Coward" expresses a sense of nihilism at the scene of slaughtered innocents, while the narrator daydreams about joining in the very slaughter that drives him to despair. In "Conflagration" Xu portrays the world as a battlefield, yet paradoxically the narrator feels responsible for the chaos that engulfs him. The poem ends with the poet's self-accusation for his own "corrupt heart."

In evoking the despair that social turmoil causes its innocent peasant victims, Xu opens a new vista in modern Chinese poetry. His focus on the effects of political chaos anticipates the themes of communist poets of the thirties like Tian Jian and Ai Qing. On one level, Xu's poems can be read as an implicit lament for the dissolving social order of the dying imperial system. On a broader perspective they express the tragedy of all social struggle, a lament for the futility of human existence.

A Child

Our steps are lambs
Roaming the pasture,
Our songs are birds
Wandering the forest,
Our passionate hearts
        Run free.

We do not know
        Borders, possessions,
        Law or virtue.

        This world,
        This carefree, idle world
        Belongs to us.

1922

As the Sun Slides Down behind the Mountain

As the mournful sun
Slides down behind the mountain,
Birds steal into the woods,
And crabs scuttle one by one to the bottom of the lake.
Only I have no refuge.
Maybe something worth waiting for?
Yes,
Peacefully,
To realize I'm someone,
I await
The stars like fireflies
To shine on me,
And maybe
In the enveloping darkness
Some wolf with an edge to his appetite
Will come whisper in my ear.

1922

The Cage of Reality

Reality is humanity's cage;
Fantasy is humanity's wings.
A desperate tiny bird
With damp, broken wings
Struggles to fly
Only to fall back to earth:
Pitiful humanity, trapped in its cage.

1922

If I Weren't Such a Coward[5]

In my home town
Amid gunsmoke and splashing blood,
Bodies strewn all over the ground,
  Soldiers,
  Bandits,
  The mayor's gunmen,
Who can tell who's on whose side?
If I weren't such a coward
I'd take a gun
And annihilate them all.
Or else
They'd annihilate me
Which would be just as good.

1922

Conflagration

There is no terror, no lament
    For virgins and mothers
    Trampled like rice stalks
        To die in flames,
    Only hot blood spurting,
        Mad, bloodthirsty cries,
        Homes ablaze,
        Gunfire, neighing horses,
    A bedlam of confused wailing.

There is no night, no day.
Swirling ashes and dust blot out the sky.

5 This and the poem "Conflagration" reflect the anarchy in the poet's native Henan province. (See the author's bio.)

We are drunk, we stagger, we struggle
Over the dead beneath our feet –
        Bodies of friends,
        Corpses of brothers and sisters.
        We inhale the scent of our burning mothers.
                There is no poem, only the beating of a corrupt heart.

1923

Lu Xun
(1881–1935)

Lu Xun is the pen name of Zhou Shuren, the most prominent leftist Chinese author of the early twentieth century, considered by many the greatest modern Chinese writer. Lu Xun was born in Shaoxing, a small cultural center one hundred miles from Shanghai. His family belonged to the scholar gentry. While he received an education in the Chinese classics, an illiterate, superstitious nurse told him stories from Chinese folklore. Their grotesque imagery and bizarre incidents would be prominent in his works.

His formal studies were meant to prepare him for the imperial examination, but his grandfather was imprisoned for attempting to bribe a government official and the family's fortunes declined. He attended a series of minor colleges and institutes, sometimes sponsored by family members, sometimes attending free state schools. In the School of Mines and Railways he first encountered Western learning, including science, German, and English. He read Chinese translations of Huxley, John Stuart Mill, and *Uncle Tom's Cabin*. In 1902 he went to study in Japan, where he would spend the next seven years. After a brief return home for an arranged marriage, he returned to Japan to enroll in Sendai Medical Institute in northern Honshu, but medical studies bored him.

By then Lu Xun was involved in revolutionary groups among Chinese students. At this time an incident occurred which, according to his memoirs, changed his life. He was present at the showing of a slide which pictured a Japanese swordsman beheading a Chinese man for allegedly spying for Russia in the Russo-Japanese War (1904–05). What struck Lu Xun was the demeanor of the Chinese onlookers. They had gathered merely to see the spectacle. "Their expressions revealed all too clearly that spiritually they were calloused and numb." The incident, Lu Xun wrote, impelled him to abandon medicine for literature. "The best way to effect a spiritual transformation … would be through literature and art."

He left Sendai and returned to Tokyo, where the Chinese government continued to pay his monthly subsidy even though he was not enrolled in any program of study. He began to publish essays which reflect his reading of Nietzsche. One of these, "On the Power of Mara Poetry," calls for a "warrior of the spirit" to transform Chinese culture, and praises the power of demonic poets like Byron, Shelley, Pushkin, and Lermontov to shock a slumbering nation of out its complacency. In addition to Nietzsche, his reading at this time included works on idealism, democracy, and Darwin.

Abandoning a plan to study in Germany for lack of money, he returned to his home province in 1909 and undertook a series of teaching posts. After working as head of Shaoxing Normal College, he took a position with the Ministry of Education and moved to Beijing. When dictator Yuan Shikai assumed the title of emperor, the author recounts in his memoirs, he grew despondent over the political situation. In 1918 he published the short story "A Madman's Diary," one of the most influential early works written in vernacular Chinese. The "madman" begins to imagine that his fellow villagers and even his family desire to eat his flesh. He then envisions the words "eat people" written as glosses everywhere in texts of the Confucian classics. The story was interpreted as an ironic attack on the alleged superiority of China's Confucian civilization and as a call for a new culture. It exerted considerable influence on the May Fourth Movement, which began the year after the story's publication. Through the Movement, Lu Xun's writings gained a wide influence.

Two years after the Movement began he wrote his most famous piece of fiction, *The True Story of Ah Q* (1921–22). The novella is a tale of a wandering ne'er-do-well who is eventually beheaded for a petty crime. The protagonist's befuddled state of mind, cluttered with half-baked Confucian notions, represents the author's diagnosis of his degenerate country's social and political malaise. Each time he is humiliated, Ah Q employs some Confucianism to convince himself he is actually superior to his oppressors. This psychological self-deception represents Chinese people's false sense of cultural superiority to the foreign powers that humiliate them. The story epitomizes the May Fourth movement's anti-Confucian stance in reaction to foreign colonizers' exploitation of China.

In 1925, Lu Xun began a relationship with one of his students at Beijing Women's Normal University, Xu Guangping. She was to become his common-law wife, lifelong companion, and the mother of his son. In 1926 he was involved in public protests against the influence of the foreign powers on the local government, and as a result had to flee Beijing. He moved first to Xiamen, then to Guangzhou, where in 1927 he took a position at Zhongshan University. In April, Chiang Kai-shek began his purge of Communists from the ranks of the Guomindang. Lu Xun attempted unsuccessfully to secure the release of detained Communist students. In September 1927 he moved to Shanghai, which would be home for his remaining nine years.

By this time Lu Xun had produced a volume of prose poems and two books of essays. He was widely recognized as China's leading intellectual figure. In Shanghai he refused invitations to teach and became a professional writer, relying solely on royalties for his income. Although politically a progressive, he remained at first artistically independent. In a 1927 lecture at Jinan University, he expressed the conviction that a writer will always be in conflict with any political organization. Soon after he settled in Shanghai, however, his thought took a definite turn toward the left. He studied Marxist theory and formed regular contacts with leading leftist intellectuals like the novelist Mao Dun. When Feng Xuefeng arrived in Shanghai from Mao's base in Yan'an, he met with Lu Xun and the two became collaborators. In this final, radically committed phase of his career, Lu Xun engaged in polemics with liberals like Hu Shi, who advocated gradual change within the framework of the existing political system.

In 1930 Lu Xun joined prominent Communists in forming the League of Left Wing Writers, serving on its three-man directorate. His notion of the relation of literature to politics had evolved. "Politics leads the way," he wrote in 1929. "Literature follows in its wake." But he remained artistically independent, resisting the Party's demands. Michelle Yeh stresses that although Lu Xun accepted the Communist doctrine of an inseparable link between literature and socio-historical reality, he insisted on the separation of aesthetics and politics. Literature and propaganda, he believed, were inevitably distinct. Doctrinaire Communists attacked him in print for such convictions. An article by Guo Moruo accused him of being "an evil feudal remnant," a counter-revolutionary, and a "spokesman for the bourgeoisie." When the Party called for authors to write in support the struggle against the Japanese invaders, Lu Xun refused. The call to worldwide revolution remained his foremost theme. The dispute over whether to write about revolt or resistance against the Japanese led the Communist Party to dissolve the League of Left Wing writers in 1936, the year of Lu Xun's death.

How precisely Lu Xun understood Mao's objectives may be in doubt, but his commitment to the Communists was unambiguous. In the year of his death he telegraphed the Party's Central Committee to congratulate them on the successful completion of the Long March: "In you rest the hopes of China and mankind." A heavy smoker, Lu Xun suffered from tuberculosis. He died in October, 1936, widely regarded as China's leading literary figure. Although he never joined the Communist Party, it immediately claimed him as its intellectual godfather. In 1938 Mao established the Lu Xun Academy of Fine Arts in Yan'an. In 1956, on the twentieth anniversary of his death, the National People's Congress, China's legislative body, honoured Lu Xun. In 1966 Chairman Mao co-opted him for his newest campaign, calling him "the chief commander of China's Cultural Revolution." Lu Xun's name came to be invoked to condemn the very kind of satire and intellectual independence that typified his own writing. He has been more useful to the Party in death than alive. It is tantalizing to imagine what Lu Xun's destiny would have been had he lived to witness Mao's triumph. An equally outspoken author, the novelist Ding Ling, spent years in Communist prisons for refusing to write on dictated themes and follow prescribed norms – just as Lu Xun always refused to do.

Lu Xun wrote in a wide variety of genres: fiction, autobiography, essays, prose poetry, and verse both classical and modern. He specialized in what came to be known as the extempore essay, a short, polemical piece, didactic in its purpose, which begins with some incident involving the author, then goes on to set forth a controversial political principle. Although he was one of the earliest advocates of the New Poetry, he soon abandoned the form. His most important poetic works are prose poems, a genre which he effectively invented in Chinese. His vernacular poetry includes both folk ballads and six poems in free verse, the latter all written in 1918. Three of them appear below. Lu Xun eventually expressed some misgivings about the course of the New Poetry's development. Michelle Yeh notes his 1934 remark that the new verse had encountered "a stroke of bad luck." In poetic composition he reverted to classical forms. His negative assessment of the New Poetry is reflected in the opening lines of one of his classical poems, as translated by Jon Kowallis: "Forlorn and empty / The new literary garden."

Lu Xun puts into practice his notion of the writer as the physician of society, diagnosing its ills. But even though he was politically committed, Lu Xun was too perceptive to be doctrinaire. His work expresses the misgivings of one who perceives the ambiguities of life. His poem "Dreams" is not just a personal narrative or even a psychological analysis, although it may include both. Its theme is the distressing plight of the Chinese intellectual, wearing himself out in the effort to imagine (i.e. dream) some plausible future society.

Dreams

A mob of dreams runs riot at dusk.
One drives off the other,
And is attacked by the next.
The one that's gone was black,
The one here now is black as ink.
Both proclaim, "How fair I am!"
Their real colour, who knows in the dark?
Or even who is talking?
Who can know in the dark
With this feverish headache?
Come, some good dream, oh come!

1918

Humanity and Time

One person says, the future beats the present.
Another says, the present can't match the past.
Somebody else says, huh?
Time says,
  If the past is good, go on back.
  If the future is good, come along.
  What's all this supposed to mean?
  I'm not talking to you.

1918

The God of Love

A little baby, his wings spread in the air,
Fixes a shaft to his string, draws his bow
And – who knows how? – an arrow in the breast!
Master Baby, thanks for your haphazard assistance
But you'll have to tell me whom to love.
"Ai!" Flustered, the infant shakes his head.
"You've got a heart, so why ask me?
Anyway my arrow's shot home!
Love whoever you want, for all you're worth
And if there's nobody you love,
For all you're worth go hang yourself."

1918

Guo Moruo
(1892–1978)

Guo was born in the town of Shawan, Sichuan province. His father was a prosperous self-made merchant who had bought land and joined the landlord class. Guo was educated in the Chinese classics at home. In 1912, five days after an arranged marriage which he would soon repudiate, he went to study a modern curriculum first in Shanghai, then at Kyushu Imperial University in Japan. Here he eventually completed a degree in medicine although he never would practice as a physician. In Japan he began to devote his time to foreign languages and literatures, with special interest in Whitman, Shelley, Goethe, Nietzsche, and Tagore. In 1918 he decided that his calling was to be a poet. Enamoured of the Russian Revolution, he began writing verse in *baihua*, the language of the common people. In his early work he espoused an aestheticism that meant to change society by transforming readers' sensibilities.

Guo wrote his first vernacular poems from 1916 to 1918 while in Japan, with no knowledge of Hu Shi's similar endeavour in Beijing. Guo developed a new literary language from vernacular speech, with extensive introduction of Western vocabulary and even Western grammar to create a new poetic diction. He experimented with structure, writing some poems with lines of equal length and others with lines of unequal length; he wrote in regular meters based on Western poetics and in irregular meters, poems with rhyme and poems without rhyme. The last four poems by Guo printed below are in rhyming stanzas composed of lines of roughly the same number of characters. In contrast, his early "A Night Walk through Jurimatsubara" is in free verse influenced by Tagore, a pantheistic poem celebrating the vital power of nature.

Guo espoused the theory that poetry was self-expression and that artistic creation was by its very nature revolutionary; this was how he reconciled his contradictory beliefs in all-out individualism and social revolution. In Tokyo in 1921 he joined fellow Chinese students to found the Creation Society, dedicated to promoting modern vernacular literature. In this phase of his career he attacked everything traditional – in morals, philosophy, and poetics. He sought a prosody that would incorporate the rhythms of the masses' vernacular. His first anthology of poetry, *The Goddesses*, appeared in 1921. Of the New Poets of the May Fourth Movement, Guo enjoyed the greatest public popularity. After finishing his medical degree in Japan he returned to Shanghai, where he began to publish poetry which sounded the call for a revolutionary literature.

In 1926 he went to Guangzhou and lectured at the Peasants Revolutionary Institute, where Mao Zedong and Zhou Enlai were leading figures. In 1927 he served as General Secretary of the Communist faction of the Guomindang army. After Chiang Kai-shek purged the Communists from the Guomindang ranks on 12 April 1927, Guo served as general political secretary of the rebel Communist troops in the city of Nanchang. When Chiang's forces overwhelmed the Communists in Nanchang, Guo returned to Japan. He wrote almost no poetry for ten years but undertook research on oracle bone inscriptions, the earliest form of Chinese writing. His first book on this subject, published in 1935, endeavoured to prove in Marxist terms that these inscriptions reveal ancient China to have been a "slave society."

When the Japanese swept south through China in 1937, Guo returned there to take part in the resistance. He rejoined Zhou Enlai to serve as political cadre of the Communist troops fighting in alliance with the Guomindang against the Japanese. To support the resistance he wrote anti-Japanese plays and poems, including "The Iron Virgin." When, at the end of the war, his Japanese common-law partner came to China, she found him with a new wife, Yu Lichun, whom he had married in 1939.

After the Communist victory over the Guomindang in 1949, Guo became China's chief cultural statesman. He held a number of major government posts, including membership in the party's central committee. He is reputed to have polished Mao's classical verse for publication. In 1966 Guo was one of the first prominent figures attacked in the Cultural Revolution. He publicly confessed to misunderstanding Mao Zedong's thought and agreed to the burning of his own works. After their father's denunciation, two of his sons died at the hands of Red Guards. Guo Moruo himself was quickly rehabilitated, however, and reappointed to the National Party Congress in 1969.

Guo's poetry is self-consciously iconoclastic. He inverts the symbols of classical poetry in an effort to overthrow traditional thinking. He rejects its elegant pastorals because such poetry ignored the suffering of peasants oppressed by their landlords. "A Confrontation with the Moon" transforms a usual motif of classical poetry. In traditional verse the moon is associated with the melancholy longing shared by separated friends or lovers. Guo rejects this sentimental meaning. Instead he makes the moon an emblem of the bond uniting workers and peasants, celebrating their victorious revolution.

Guo emphasizes passion over logic. His poems reflect his study of Nietzsche in their depiction of the eternal cycle of destruction and creation. He eagerly espoused the democracy of Whitman at the same time as the classicism of Goethe, whose *Faust* he translated into Chinese. In early poems he denigrated Marx, Engels, and Lenin, only later to revise the same poems into panegyrics of them.

The various philosophies that Guo espoused during the course of his career would be impossible to reconcile. A rebel who shattered cultural idols, a pantheist who worshipped the divine force within himself, a romantic democrat who advocated absolute freedom of self-expression, Guo ultimately devoted his energy to Marxist-Leninist thought, announcing, "I am content to be a slogan man." An importer of European ideas in poetry and politics, he worked for the rejuvenation of Chinese culture. An advocate of Western culture who mocked the Japanese as cheap imitators of Western technology in "The Iron Virgin," he could also write nostalgically about "Snow on the Emei Mountains," the bucolic, tradition-bound region of his birth, which he fled. A Promethean poet who believed in Marx, a microcosm of unresolved contradictions, Guo Moruo personifies many of the paradoxes of what he celebrated: the modern world.

A Night Walk through Jurimatsubara[6]

The sea is slumbering, at peace.
Gazing far off, I see only a glow of misty white,
Hear not the least murmur of the waves.
O endless space, so lofty, so mighty – translucent and serene!
An infinity of stars open wide their eyes
To gaze down on this landscape of the night:

6 The Japanese place-name means, literally, "Three Miles of Pine-Covered Plain."

In Jurimatsubara countless ancient pines
Raise slender hands in silent praise of the universe,
Each branch trembles against the sky,
Within me every fibre of my nerves is trembling.

1920

Snow on the Emei Mountains

I think the snow that falls on the Emei Mountains
Must now cover the peaks,
And the mist that comes to linger
Snakes among the mountains as before.

Most of all I love the towering summits,
Melting into purple mist beneath the moon,
And – stretching endless – the silver fog
That wraps itself round my family's quiet courtyard.

So. This is my native place,
Already fifteen years since I departed,
And still the rapids in the Dadu River
Beneath the mountains must surge, as does my verse.

The Dadu rapids foamed, grand and mighty
Under the pure moon that rose above the eastern bank
Whose range of shallow hills remained always green,
But not awesome like the peaks on the western shore.

In youth I loved to wander
These distant, phantom banks beside the ferry crossing,
Standing in moonlight among shattered boulders,
Knowing a majestic desolation.

Yes, this is my native place.
It's fifteen years since I departed.
Beneath this evening's moon
The lofty summits must be melting into purple mist.

1928

A Confrontation with the Moon

Moon, you light the ground outside my window;
It's long since last I saw you face to face.
I have not returned
That pallid stare of yours for decades.

Now it is not Nature I observe.
A change came over me long ago;
Your world of silver-gray and mine
Have no common border.

I lack your transcendental emotion,
Am deaf to your twanging note of loneliness.
The only music I listen for is wild and triumphant,
Like drum-rolls rising, defying heaven,

Like the vastness of the ocean
Roaring through crests and breakers,
Crashing against a thousand feet of cliffs,
Crashing against the shore and exploding into spray.

Such is the resoluteness of my heart,
That nothing you can do will please me
Save when you shine on the peasants when the battle is over,
Singing and dancing, triumphant in their millions.

1928

Taking All by Storm

So, friends, you think this weather strange, oppressive?
It's but an omen of the coming storm.
And you think these times chaotic, extraordinary?
They are in labour, big with a new society.

The birth pangs are coming stronger, closer.
The motherland will not have long to endure them.
Already I have prepared a ceremonial cup,
Red, but not with grapes from the banks of the Seine.

That cup of new wine is waiting. Friends,
It is the hot blood coursing through my heart.
This night I have brewed a storm of blood
To capture the dawning sun, the dawning universe.

1928

The Iron Virgin

Medieval Europe built a cruel instrument of torture,
The Iron Virgin:
Outside, a girl who resembled the Blessed Mother;
Inside, a box with a spike.

The girl like the Virgin was the door of the box.
On its other side, where her heart should be, was the spike.
The torturer put you inside the box, shut the lid,
And the spike pierced your chest.

In Manchuria, the Japanese have a new invention.
From outside they pound nails into a barrel,
Then shut you inside, naked, seal both ends
And force some passerby to start the barrel rolling.

While it lacks the Blessed Mother's loving expression,
It has the Iron Virgin's bosom of steel.
The Japanese call it a nail box.
Ah, you Japanese, what skillful imitators you are!

1937

Bing Xin
(1900–99)

The author who first brought vernacular poetry to the attention of a popular audience is known by her pen name, Bing Xin (literally "Ice Heart" or "Pure Heart"). Xie Wanying was the daughter of a Qing dynasty naval officer who supported democratic reform. He taught his daughter to shoot, ride a horse, and row – all contrary to the traditional education of Chinese girls. Born in Fujian province, Bing Xin was tutored at home and began to write stories and poems at an early age. When she was fourteen her family moved to Beijing, where she was enrolled in Bridgeman Academy for Girls, run by American Protestant missionaries. In 1918 she entered Beijing Union College for Women, also founded by American missionaries and later incorporated into Yanjing University.

She originally intended to study medicine. The May Fourth Movement of 1919, with its debates on politics and language, sparked her to study literature instead. She later wrote, "This time of youthful patriotism and literary renewal swept me out the door of my family home and my school to behold semi-feudal, semi-colonial Chinese society with all its problems." At age twenty, she began contributing articles and stories written in the vernacular to the Bejing *Morning Post.* She rapidly became the best-known woman in the May Fourth Movement. *Stray Birds* (English edition, 1916), a collection of short poems by Rabindranath Tagore – the Nobel-prize-winning Bengali poet – validated her own brief poems, which she had thought too insignificant to publish. These appeared as *Myriad Stars* (1923) and *Spring Rivulets* (1923). The two collections were hailed as an innovation in vernacular literature and came to define a subgenre, the "small poem." As Michelle Yeh observes, Bing Xin's work in this form shows the influence of Tagore's pantheism as well as that of German romantic poetry, fashionable at the time. Bing Xin's short verse inspired numerous imitations, including those of Liu Dabai and Feng Xuefeng. Unusually for so young a writer, Bing Xin assumed the role of a moral guide; many of her short verses are explicitly didactic, while others use natural symbols to commend steadfastness, persistence, and sympathy.

In 1921 she helped to found the Literary Research Society, dedicated to the reform of Chinese literature through the study of Western literature. Graduating from Yanjing University in 1923, she won a scholarship to Wellesley College where she took her MA in literature in 1926. She described the countries she visited in *Letters to Young Readers,* published in the *Morning Post* and regularly anthologized in primary school textbooks throughout China from that time on. These, together with her numerous volumes of short stories and extempore essays, won her recognition as a master of twentieth-century Chinese prose. She wrote little poetry after she returned to China in 1926 to teach at Yanjing and Qinghua Universities in Beijing. In 1929 she married sociologist Wu Wenzao.

During the thirties and forties she began to write stories devoted to the description of social detail, adding a new dimension to her work. Stories like "Our Mistress's Parlour" satirize the figure of the new cosmopolitan woman, as portrayed by such progressive female writers as Ding Ling. A number of Bing Xin's stories, like "A Photograph," portray the Protestant missionary subculture with sympathy. As Japanese forces extended their southward advance through China in 1940, she moved with her husband and children to Chongqing, the wartime capital, where she served on the Nationalist government's artist committees.

At the time of the Communist takeover she was in Hong Kong. Her role with the Guomindang entitled her to move to Taiwan. She and her husband surprised many when they returned to the mainland in 1951. Premier Zhou Enlai personally welcomed her at an official ceremony at party headquarters in Beijing. She traveled abroad as a prominent member of delegations and political committees and sat as a member of the National People's Congress in 1954. In Mao's China, where the creative arts were expected to glorify the Party program, she turned like other major writers to translation, producing Chinese editions of the works of Tagore and of Khalil Gibran's *The Prophet,* both writers of nonsectarian religiosity. Her works came to be treasured during the bleak cultural years of the fifties, sixties, and seventies. That neither her writing nor her translations were ever banned testifies to the high degree of respect accorded her in the People's Republic of China. During the Cultural Revolution, Premier Zhou Enlai issued orders to protect her. The continued publication of her works through the Cultural Revolution is evidence of her political shrewdness. "Don't Trample This Flower," published during the Hundred Flowers Campaign of 1957, demonstrates her discretion. The flower in the poem represents individual political opinion, which Mao had invited people to express openly, only to arrest many who expressed ideas contrary to his policies. Bing Xin's poem symbolically commends personal expression – just as Mao had done – but refrains from expressing any personal opinion of her own. Her husband was not so lucky; he was denounced as a rightist in 1957 and banned from teaching.

In an age of enforced ideological orthodoxy she devoted her writing to the nurturing of human relations, a theme branded by some Marxist critics as "escapist." Marxist critics like Mao Dun dismissed her "philosophy of love" as mysticism, but in fact her poems express not a philosophy but concrete love of individuals, especially within the family, like the narrator's love for her mother in "Paper Boats." Moreover, a poem like "No Forgetting" explores the spiritual anguish of a relationship in crisis.

MacDougall and Louie suggest that the anguish and doubt of other Chinese writers of her time fail to trouble Bing Xin because her expectations differ from theirs. Bing Xin envisions the role of the writer as communicating with common people to give expression to their simple emotions, like the herd-boy's "mute praise" of the cosmos in *Spring Rivulets*, 153. At the same time, she feels it is the writer's duty to face the mystery of the universe, its unanswered questions, standing as a bulwark against psychic chaos, "a sentinel in the dark" (*Spring Rivulets*, 112). Her literary reputation and her work on behalf of Chinese women made her a revered figure in late twentieth-century China.

No Forgetting

Rip the top page off the calendar –
What day is this?
A sheet of black cloud
Sweeps across my eyes.

"Tranquil one!
Philosopher!"
I try to stop thinking of him,
But think of nothing else.

This is me, this is how I am!
I can't pretend to be serene
Or a philosopher. I don't deserve the name.
I only understand
That if someone loves me, I love him in return,
But if he doesn't, then ...
This place, as tiny as a leaf,
Is home.

How can I forget him?

1922

A Token of Remembrance

For my little brother Bing Ji

His right hand gripping a slingshot,
    His left hand ready with a chunk of clay,
He sits, his back against a pillar,
    His two feet together, flat on the ground,
His dark eyes gazing up toward the sky.
    Was he spying on the crows
    That steal grapes from the trellis?
His intent was murderous, but now his expression is full of affection.

I catch sight of him from the window,
And before I realize it, I'm staring,
    My eyes full of tears!

1922

from *Myriad Stars*

10

Tender green shoots
Tell the young,
"Prepare yourselves!"

Pale white flowers
Tell the young,
"Dedicate yourselves!"

Crimson fruit
Tell the young,
"Sacrifice yourselves!"

28

Waves of the sea by my native town,
As once your spray
　　　　Struck the rock I stood on,
　　　　Now – drop after drop – you strike my heart.

48

Delicate blades of grass,
Stand proudly!
　　　　None but you grace the whole earth.

95

From the bough she breaks the blossom
For a vase
    Then gazes, sighing,
    At the empty branch.

1922

from *Spring Rivulets*

24

Little island,
    How do you stand so firm
When so many mountain peaks
    Are lying in the chasms of the ocean?

25

It blows! And snowflakes are blossoms –
    Even the north wind is gentle.

33

Flower in the cranny of a wall,
While you enjoy your fragrance in solitude
    Heaven and earth are crowding close around you.

66

This absolute solitude –
Is it my loneliness or is it Qingming?[7]
Only the city wall standing frozen
And the willows blanketed in snow!
What matter the cold?
Through this vast expanse of white, I walk into a painting.

105

O Creator,
If in eternal life
You grant one bliss,
I implore you,
Grant me to lean against my Mother's breast,
Together with her in a tiny skiff
On a moonlit sea.

112

The higher the waves,
The greater the joy
Of the steadfast rock,
A sentinel in the dark.

7 Qingming: literally "clear and bright"; the period in the solar calendar – generally around the 5th of April – when the Chinese pay respect to the dead.

118

Purple wisteria fall on the pool.
Beneath the arbour
        No one all day long,
Only the rustle of the wind that stirs the leaves.

153

In his little bamboo hat,
        Riding on a cow,
Little herd boy
                Totally at ease,
        Bathed in the spring light that sweeps the earth –
                A culmination of mute praise –
What poet can compare with you?

169

The unborn child
Clambers to the window-sill of birth,
And vaguely glimpses
Death's cavern.

182

Farewell,
        Spring rivulets!
My thanks to your murmuring currents
        For bearing my thoughts all season long.

I bid you good-bye.
        Flow off slowly, without hurry, among humanity.
        As for me, I will sit here at your source,
        Listening quietly to the echoes.

1922

Paper Boats

For Mother

I never carelessly throw away a sheet of paper,
        But save them all. Page by page,
I fold them into little boats,
        To throw them from the railing to the sea.

The wind rolls them up, blows some into a porthole;
        Some, soaked by waves, stick against the prow,
But undeterred, I keep on folding, day after day,
        Hoping that one will float off as I wish.

Mother, whenever you see a small white boat
        Floating into your dreams, don't be surprised.
It is your beloved daughter who folded it in tears,
        To send it to you over ten thousand leagues of ocean –
        A record of her love and grief at parting.

1923

Thoughts of Love

To escape thoughts of love
I throw on my fur-lined cape
        And rush out of a bright room full of silent people.

The secret moon spies on my path.
Crisscrossed from above on the snowy ground
          Dry branches scrawl
                    Thoughts of love.

1925

Don't Trample This Flower[8]

Look here, children –
There by your feet,
A tiny yellow flower!
Let's all
          Walk around it.
Don't trample this flower!

One day last autumn
When the sky was clear and bright
And the wind cool,
Its mother gave it
A soft, downy jacket
Like a parachute
On which it floated here beside the road.

The snow of winter covered it
          With a heavy overcoat
And it slept here silently,
Waiting for news of spring.

Today it felt
          Its body grow moist;
It smelled the fragrance of the soil
And happily rose,
Stretching its golden wings.

8 The poem was written at the time of the Hundred Flowers Campaign during which Chairman Mao briefly encouraged the expression of political opinion under the slogan, "Let a hundred flowers bloom, let a thousand voices contend."

Look how brave it is
To make its home so near the road,
Not frightened by the tread of passing feet,
Nor frightened by the busy traffic.

O young friends full of joy,
        So merry in the first days of springtime,
With your new skirts and jackets
Fluttering in the spring breeze,
And your heads so high
And your steps so firm –
Be careful lest without thinking you snap
This yellow blossom's life.
I know you understand my meaning!
In our boundless springtime joy,
        This flower, too, has its place.

1957

After the Rain

The tender green tips of branches shine like gold.
The square has become an ocean.
Barefoot, the children flock to the water,
Happy as Immortals.

My brother[9] races ahead,
Splashing grandly,
Shouting, "Sister, look out! It's slippery!"
And sliding as he shouts.

Patting his muddy, dripping trousers,
He mutters, "Phooey, oh phooey!"
His face is flushed and joyful,
Beaming with excited pride.

9 The terms "brother" and "sister" can be used between siblings, between playmates, and also between lovers.

Little sister grasps her thick, short braids
And follows Muddy Trousers,
Biting her lips.
She holds up her skirt,
Running lightly and carefully,
Secretly hoping she too may have
Such a joyful fall.

Published 1960

Liu Yanling
(1894–1988)

Liu was born in Jiangsu province in 1894. Although his family was not well off, he managed to win various scholarships enabling him to continue his education until he graduated from Fudan University in Shanghai in 1919. He taught for a year at Hangzhou No. 1 Teachers College, where he met Zhu Ziqing. The next year he returned to teach in Shanghai where he worked with Zhu and Ye Shaojun, joining them in the Literary Research Society and serving as editor of its magazine *Poetry Monthly*.

Liu did not remain long on the Chinese literary scene. From 1923 on he suffered from a complex of nervous and physical maladies causing severe headaches and extreme fatigue. He continued a sporadic career of teaching at Jinan University in Shanghai, publishing the occasional poem or essay. When in the 1930s the Japanese bombed the Shanghai classrooms where he taught, he moved to Malaya, then to Singapore. Here he achieved a modest literary reputation among the local Chinese community. He took up Singaporean nationality during the 1960s.

Until the late 1980s Liu was entirely ignored by mainland Chinese literary criticism. His reputation as a poet today rests almost entirely on "Sailor," which appeared in the first edition of *Poetry Monthly* and is still anthologized today. The poem turns on the interplay of landscape and feeling, a common device in classical poetry. Modern critic Li Lin observes a stream-of-consciousness quality in the way Liu exploits this interplay. Another modern critic, Sun Qin'an, notes the simplicity of the poem's language and of its rhythm and rhyme: of its eleven lines, seven rhyme together in the original Chinese.

Liu's comments on contemporary Western poetry illuminate his intention in "Sailor." He praises American poet Vachel Lindsay for beautifying the life of common village people and peasants, as Liu beautifies the image of the girl in "Sailor." Liu also commends John Masefield as a poet of the common people; Masefield wrote widely about English sailors and the sea.

Finally, Liu lauds French poets of his day for centering their poems on the self, as expressed in symbols, just as "Sailor" develops a sequence of images that reveal the protagonist's inner consciousness.

Sailor

A moon in the sky,
A ship on the sea.
He hides by the helm in the dark,
His face in his hands.

He fears the glimmering moon,
                    The swell of the sea,
That lure his eye to where sea meets sky, his home,
Recalling
Pomegranate blossoms by the well
Where she is propping up a bamboo pole
To dry her black cotton clothes in the sun.

1922

Ye Shaojun
(1894–1988)

Author, educator, and publisher, Ye was born in Jiangsu Province in 1894, the son of a landlord's bookkeeper. After graduation from high school in 1907 he became a schoolteacher. After losing his job at the age of twenty he began writing fiction. He wrote at first in classical Chinese but with the advent of the May Fourth Movement he turned to the vernacular. In 1921, with Zheng Zhenduo and Mao Dun, he founded the Literary Research Association, the first organization expressly dedicated to the New Literature. In fiction he advocated realism under the slogan, "Literature is for life." With Zhu Ziqing he cofounded the journal *Poetry* in 1922. Throughout the 1920s he published many short stories recounting the lives of poor people and of intellectuals. His novel *Ni Huanzhi* (1929), the chronicle of the life of a teacher from 1911 to 1927, is recognized as a masterpiece of the new vernacular fiction. Throughout the twenties and thirties he wrote essays, novels, and poems, also working as a journalist.

At the same time Ye was involved in publishing and education. He was a leading figure in the movement to reform the Chinese language, which introduced the pinyin system of romanization which has become standard both in mainland China and globally. After the establishment of the People's Republic of China in 1949 he held various posts in the Communist government, serving at one point as vice-minister of education. Ye is best know today for his novels and stories, many of which have been translated into English, published under his pen name Ye Shengtao.

A Small Fish

The mouth of a small fish floats on the river,
Ceaselessly opening and closing.
Ripples spread.
A rod jerks up,

The fish is gone.
Widening ripples
Expand to infinity.

1922

Zheng Zhenduo
(1898–1958)

Zheng was a journalist, poet, critic, fiction writer, and archaeologist, born in Wenzhou, Zhejiang province. In 1918 he enrolled in the Beijing School for Railway Management. When the May Fourth Movement began in 1919, he involved himself in various literary groups and was a founder of the Literary Research Society. In 1921 he moved to Shanghai, where he took a job as an editor for the Commercial Press and worked with a number of *baihua* literary journals. He was one of the translators of Tagore's short poetry into Chinese, helping to popularize the short poem as a genre. Tagore's influence appears in his series of short poems, "Distraction."

Zheng saw literature as a driving force for social change. Many of his poems of the twenties give voice to a zealous revolutionary commitment. It was his belief that emotions were the core of literature. This focus is evident in "Distraction." The sequence portrays the inner conflicts and self-questioning of a lonely young man.

Zheng produced a wide variety of fiction, poetry, and criticism. Although he never joined the Communist Party, after 1949 he held many posts in the Chinese Academy of Sciences, including directorship of the archaeological research institute. He died in a plane crash in the Soviet Union in 1958.

from *Distraction*

1

Already on the bus
        And don't know where I'm going.

3

Empty heart floating like a spider web in the wind
Yearning to stick to something.

4

Wanting to erase my heart's longing
Only deepens the scar.

7

A long, drawn-out siren
Wailing again tonight.

9

Deathly still. Why have I awoken?
Elbow on the pillow
Listening to snores from the next room:
What could be more absurd?

12

Misty drizzle blown in on the spring breeze
Too late for the shriveled bud.

1923

Zhu Ziqing
(1898–1948)

Poet, essayist, and scholar, Zhu Zihua, who wrote under the pen name Zhu Ziqing, was the son of a minor Qing dynasty official in Jiangsu province. His education included both traditional and modern learning. After completing high school in his family's native town of Yangzhou in 1916, he enrolled in Beijing University, from which he graduated in philosophy in 1920. To support his family's declining income, he then undertook a series of teaching posts in his home region, Jiangsu and Zhejiang.

During the May Fourth Movement he began writing short vernacular lyrics. In 1922 he joined the Literary Research Association and helped to transform its magazine, *Poetry Monthly*, into the leading journal of the New Poetry movement. His long poem "Annihilation" appeared in 1923. The poem displays the influence of the classical *Songs of the South* in its elaborate emotions and its near-mystical quality. The work was originally printed without line-breaks, resembling prose in its layout. "Annihilation" embodies Zhu's prescription that a long poem should be an all-embracing complex of modulated sounds and rhythms, employing torturous, complex sentences, while at the same time concise in its expression of thought. It is a mark of Zhu's skill that he is able to balance these apparently antithetical requirements.

In its content, "Annihilation" represents Zhu's conviction that a poem should portray the author's individuality by expressing sincere, humane emotions. Michel Hockx identifies as the poem's central idea that one should shun decadence, taking life one step at a time, without trying to fathom the intricate connection between its succeeding moments. Hockx points out a distinct similarity of this idea to the Confucian doctrine of the mean (*zhongyong*).

After 1925 Zhu turned from poetry to the prose of the *extempore* essay. Pieces like "Moonlight on the Lotus Pond" have become classics in this genre. Zhu is considered one of the foremost prose-masters of twentieth-century China. In 1925 he joined the staff of Qinghua University in Beijing.

Here he traced the development of the New Poetry in critical essays. A collection of his verse, published in 1937, was the first of a single author's New Poetry. In his notes to this volume he divided modern poetry's development into three succeeding movements: free verse, formalism, and symbolism. Without siding with any of the three, he characterized his own writing as free verse, an attempt to liberate the New Poetry from the residual strictures of classical verse. In the 1940s his criticism began to turn against the esoteric quality of symbolism in favour of a realism more accessible to the common people. As the war against Japan raged on, Zhu issued essays that espoused patriotism in literature, justifying slogans in poetry while still insisting that popular verse need not be vulgar.

Zhu's widely acclaimed studies of classical Chinese literature and his *extempore* essays have won him a lasting reputation as a scholar and prose stylist. His criticism, together with "Annihilation," places him among the foremost figures in the development of modern Chinese poetry. He died in 1948 from complications of a stomach ulcer, exacerbated by his refusal on principle to eat relief food shipped to Beijing by the Americans. Because of the manner of his death, some have honoured him as a martyr.

Annihilation

Last June I was in Hangzhou.[10] *After three nights in pleasure boats on the lake, I felt like a wisp of smoke, like a drifting cloud, with no solid ground beneath my feet, so broken and worn out by entangling temptations that I longed for self-destruction ... After returning to Hangzhou in September, I completed the first draft of this poem ... Luckily my general mood had not changed so much, and I was able to recapture, however imperfectly, my original feelings. Tentatively I leave this poem as a personal record.*

9 December 1922, Hangzhou

Loitering halfway down the road,
Hanging my head,
It's me! It's me!

10 One of China's ancient scenic attractions, West Lake in Hangzhou is surrounded by forested hills, landscaped gardens, and ancient pagodas.

All colours arrayed near at hand:
Here, beauty for the eye,
There, for the ear,
Lush fragrance,
Delicate savour,
All that I touch, my body yields to,
Lustrous,
Soft, smooth,
Intoxicating!
How to resist this rapture?
Pushed,
Pulled,
Transformed in the twinkling of an eye.

When was I ever master of myself?
In dreams,
In fever,
Never of sober mind;
I am in the clouds,
In the wind;
I am in the abyss,
Swept by an undersea current,
But never on the green, green earth.
Where have I left the faintest footprint?
I wander,
Drift,
My feet tread,
But never on my home soil.
Aging, weakening in swirling dust,
Nothing left of me but a spent body
And dismal shadows.
I brood on omens of annihilation.
My beloved, distant, hazy, homeland,
My home –
"Go home, go home!"

Hazy moonlight shrouds the silent lake.
The spectral hills prepare for sleep.
Fireflies wander in the fog,

Flitting sparks.
Who is lighting that lotus blossom lantern?
"Ha
Ho."
Laughter broken by the low notes of a flute.
Nearby frogs begin to croak.
Swayed,
Spirited off,
I sleep in the arms of Sister Moon.
Yes, who would not be wafted away?
But the real moon is lonesome.
What have I to do with fireflies?
That hearty laughter must be theirs!
Nothing is mine
But the flute's disconsolate melody.
And even that is irrelevant.
It is just a flute.
Only the swaying,
The bewitchment are mine.
Everyone departs, each his own way.
Who notices you?
They have never been your friends.
Where does all this melodious pathos lead?
Loneliness,
Desolation,
Tedium, tedium.
Wend your homeward path.
Return! Return!

Snowy gowns have fluttered away
Like ashes of paper money burned on the graves of the dead.
Those eyes – vibrant brooks
Replete with words so full of meaning
Have run dry as a desert under a blazing sun.
The lacquer-black hair
Is transformed to tangled autumn weeds.
That delicate, sensitive face
Has become a waxen mask.

Its flowery smile has vanished,
Not a trace of that pearly voice.
Before my eyes, a void.
Toss it away!
What else is left to cast away?
Return! Return!

I have whiled away the days
With clouds of friends,
Mutual comforters,
Mutual flatterers,
Bombastic,
Bold imbibers,
Boon companions,
Like luxuriant blossoms,
Scarlet flames.
The same words on many tongues,
The same thoughts in many hearts –
Who could forget?
But once parted,
All changed.
They came as clouds,
They departed as rain.
They glance away,
Turn their backs,
They cannot recognize yesterday's you!
It was just a whim.
Who took you to heart?
Nothing left but vague names beneath the vast blue sky.
You are abandoned,
A void wherever you look.
Grope back home.
Perhaps brothers and sisters
Await you anxiously.
Return! Return!

Profundities floated down like flowers from heaven
Blossoming before my eyes

A vista of hazy expectations
Lured me off, floating, floating me up
To seventh heaven
Shrouded in rainbow clouds.
Beneath my feet the ashen earth
Shrank,
Distant, out of mind.
But the winds of these heavens
Swirled into my flesh,
I was cradled, rocked –
Plummeting
Like a deflated blimp,
A trampled balloon,
A hollow swoosh!
Shall the whirlwind of these heavens
Sever my flesh
Like a two-edged sword,
Cleave me inside my rainbow cloud
Into a wisp of smoke,
Dissolve me?
With a shudder
I recall "How high the sky, how vast the earth ..."
Return! Return!

My ravenous stomach,
Spasmodic hands,
Hair tangled like autumn weeds,
Sunken eyes,
Slack feet
And above all my feeble heart
All lure me down,
Entice me to smoke,
Drink,
Eye women.
In the midst of this dissipation
My sense of the degradation of my body,
And the drifting of my mind,
Augments imperceptibly –
My degenerate self!

Though I have muddled away time,
My present self has not yielded.
I defy you!
I can endure this degenerate man no longer!
Can I so frivolously let myself decay?
No! No!
Before you are completely ruined
Use the little strength left you.
Return! Return!

Death like a maiden robed in white
Beckons ahead, lantern in hand.
Like a black-clad giant,
Death pursues me from behind, iron hammer aloft –
I brood over the dissipation of my family's fortune,
A year of hostile looks among my blood kin,
Glaring at each other from bloodshot eyes –
Life's burdens weigh me down,
Suffocate me.
I survey my accomplishments,
A mist among clouds …
When I confront the future, a black mass, a blank expanse,
Ignorant which road to choose,
Wavering, confused,
Then he, she, dimly emerge
Seeming to be there
And not there –
Death's elusive spirits draw me:
Go, go
To her, to his bosom.
Yes, she beckons,
He nods to me,
But, but
They are strangers.
I am wary.
Their hands float in the air,
Nebulous,
Impossible to grasp.
How shall I clasp them?

Besides, death is an alien land.
Who knows its soil?
Only on the plains of life
Am I on familiar ground.
My memory of home blurs,
But I know its contours so well!

Ah! Does my homeland not open its arms to me?
Ripe fruit is luscious,
Old friends and familiar hearths are sweet.
Maiden in white,
Black-clad giant,
I must go home.
Return! Return!

Returning, I struggle to raise the curtain of smoke
And to behold my homeland.
Visions disappear,
Radiances fade.
I am disentangled,
I am my old self again!
I shall never again stare at the sky,
I shall never again gaze at pale water.
I shall mark my steps with care;
I shall tread the soil
And leave clear footprints.
And though my tracks be small
And soon obliterated,
And my tardy steps
Trace no transcendent journey,
Insignificant as I am,
I will note each new step with joy.
All that is remote and distant
I cannot and I shall not notice.
Delay no more!
Go! Go! Go!

1922

PART TWO

Formalists

Introduction

MICHEL HOCKX

Wen Yiduo and Xu Zhimo, the key figures of the so-called "formalist school" of modern Chinese poetry, were contemporaries of the poets dubbed "the pioneers" in the previous section. Yet conventional accounts of the history of modern Chinese poetry treat them as a kind of "second generation" of modern poets, whose vernacular verse with strict rhyme schemes and meters acted as an important corrective to the overly free expression of the earliest experimenters. It is undoubtedly true that Wen Yiduo, who besides being a poet was also a prolific and outspoken critic, had little sympathy for most early free verse and dismissed its representative works in a series of influential articles beginning in the early 1920s. Yet he was an admirer of Guo Moruo's romantic expressionism and praised the raw poetic talent of Xu Yunuo. Despite their disagreements with exponents of other styles, poets of the formalist school who were members of the Crescent Moon Society, which published an influential literary magazine, frequently interacted with their more experimental contemporaries and in the process developed a poetic style of their own which was to have a lasting influence.

The basis of Wen Yiduo's theory about poetry is the concept of beauty – as distinct from the concept of "freedom" that was fundamental for many of his contemporaries. This idea he inherited partly from his reading of the English romantics and their definition of formalist poetry as "dancing in chains." Yet in light of Wen's later career as a revolutionary and his martyr's death, it is interesting that his ideas about poetic beauty are tinged with nationalist elements. Wen was probably the first to advocate the idea that modern vernacular Chinese poetry should not be in free verse but that it should adopt a "national form." Wen believed that languages possess particular characteristics that demand the use of particular poetic forms, and that the unique nature of Chinese made it imperative for poets to write with strict prosodies. After all, modern spoken Chinese has many homophones, facilitating rhyme, and its words are rarely more than two or three syllables long, making it easy to create lines with regular "feet." For Wen therefore, formalist poetry was more "Chinese" than free verse. Wen also differed from Hu Shi – who emphasized the need for a vernacular poetry that followed the "natural cadences" of the *baihua* language – an implicit denial of the notion that language can dictate a regular form. Wen was convinced that Chinese *baihua* must have its own prosodies, and that the language would not permit the easy use of either "classical Chinese" or "non-Chinese" forms.

The content of Wen Yiduo's poetry has often been presented as patriotic or nationalistic, although this reputation is not entirely of his own making. His most famous poem, here translated as "Stagnant Water," is always read (and still taught in Chinese schools) as a metaphor for the degradation and misery of warlord China. This is despite the fact that the word "China" is never mentioned in the poem and there is no textual evidence to suggest that the poet is doing anything other than painting an image of "beauty amidst decay," as in lines like these:

Let the ditch water ferment to a green wine
Bubbling with fine froth, white as pearls,
Small pearls growing larger, chuckling
Until burst by gnats drawn to their odour.

Considering Wen Yiduo's emphasis on preserving the national character of modern Chinese poetry, it is surprising he became such good friends with fellow poet Xu Zhimo. Having spent two years in England, and having fallen in love with Cambridge, Xu returned to China in 1922 filled with an astounding and probably somewhat affected disdain for all things Chinese. Ironically, however, he did state explicitly what is implicit in Wen Yiduo's "Stagnant Water." When asked to give a lecture in English at the Qinghua School in 1922, Xu launched into a damning indictment of Chinese civilization, forging the image that Wen Yiduo would make famous three years later in his poem:

> If the Westerners are being dragged along by their own machinery of efficiency, all bustle and hustle, nobody knows whither, my almost brutal imagery of the society we know, would be a stagnant pool of water, dark with mud and noisy with base insects and worms swarm-

> ing over and about it; it smacks only of decay and lifelessness. Indeed it would not require an extreme cynic to aver that, here in China, one finds a magnificent nation of physical weaklings, intellectual invalids, moral cowards and withal, spiritual paupers. In a community like ours, where one experiences but extremely rarely, if indeed ever, thrills of music, excitements of the intellect, delights and sorrows of worthy love, or raptures of religious and aesthetic moments, where idealism of any kind is not only unacceptable, but doomed to be misunderstood and laughed to scorn should ever any such thing appear, one possesses a body without a soul joined to it or is, as the poet Shelley would say, spiritually dead.[1]

The two men were united by their love of poetry written in beautiful, regular forms and their preference for the English romantic poets. In the second half of the 1920s, Xu and Wen, together with a few like-minded Anglophiles, including the "pioneer" Hu Shi, used privately raised funds to set up a publishing venture, launching a literary magazine called *Crescent Moon Monthly*, as well as a series of books. The *Crescent Moon Monthly* was published from 1928–33, advocating aesthetic autonomy and artistic integrity, and actively opposing the left's attempt to politicize literature. This earned them criticism from left-wing circles, who accused them of fostering "upper class" habits – which is, of course, exactly what they were doing and what most serious writers tend to do, but in late 1920s China, it was not always appreciated.

Characteristic of the *Crescent Moon* style is a type of stringently prosodic verse that was sometimes jokingly referred to as the "bean curd style" because the poem's appearance on the page resembled a block of tofu. Both Wen Yiduo and Xu Zhimo enjoyed striving for perfect formal regularity with poetic lines consisting of equal numbers of characters and equal numbers of "feet" (or *dun*, a unit of two or three syllables of which only one is stressed) and rhyme occurring at the end of each even line. In terms of visual appearance on the page, they preferred the four-line stanza. In terms of content they preferred expressions of romantic love, nostalgia, and languor. Xu Zhimo, especially, was a master at striking the romantic pose, not only

1 Tsemou Hsu, "Art and Life," cited as printed in *Chuangzao jikan* (*Creation Quarterly*), 1.

in his poetry but also in his personal life, which saw him become a celebrity. His rather sentimental but rhythmically and melodically brilliant "Farewell to Cambridge" is, to this day, the most popular modern Chinese poem ever composed, known by heart by many Chinese, both young and old, and even turned into a popular song.

"Farewell to Cambridge" also epitomizes the Anglophile character of the Crescent Moon group. This is evident both in terms of the poem's subject matter and its language. Xu Zhimo was particularly fond of transplanting English-language rhetorical constructions into Chinese verse. The penultimate stanza of the poem is translated here as follows:

> But now I cannot sing;
>   Hushed is the departing flute.
> For me the crickets are still;
>   Silent is Cambridge tonight.

As reflected in this translation, the original Chinese text of the second and fourth lines imitates the reversed word order of English poetic convention, bringing the predicate adjectives ("hushed" and "silent") to the beginning of the sentence in violation of normal Chinese word order. In some of his other writing Xu overdoes this to such an extent that his Chinese appears foreign to the native reader, as is typical of the "translation style," in which the poet intends his verse to read as if it has been translated from a European language.

Others who developed the formalist style in the context of the *Crescent Moon* included Chen Mengjia and Zhu Xiang. The latter was another romantic personality of the tragic variety, who committed suicide at the age of twenty-nine. Although later poets shied away from the formulaic structure of the *Crescent Moon* poets, the use of "feet" as a rhythmic device was to have a lasting impact and can easily be discerned in the work of two younger poets also included in this section: Feng Zhi and Wu Xinghua, both of whom excelled at writing in the sonnet form. Wu Xinghua's wartime work, only recently rediscovered by critics in Mainland China, is remarkable for its ability to blend classical Chinese imagery and sensibilities into modern poetry.

The popularity of formalist writing throughout the 1920s and 1930s, and to some extent also in later decades, demonstrates the continued importance attached to poetry as a *craft*, and as a higher form of writing that requires training and knowledge of "rules." However, it should not be forgotten that free verse also continued to flourish throughout this period, and was not replaced by the arrival of the formalists.

Xu Zhimo

(1897–1931)

Xu Zhimo's reputation has seen radical ups and downs over the eighty years since his death. His family background contributed to the denunciation of his poems under Mao: he was a native of Haining, Zhejiang province, the only son of an industrialist and banker who was part owner of the Shanghai-Hangzhou Railroad.

In 1915 Xu married the daughter of a prominent financier in a match arranged by their fathers. After attending the preparatory academy of Beijing University, he enrolled in its department of politics and law in 1917 to prepare to manage his father's businesses. In 1918 he studied banking at Clark College in the US. At the time of the May Fourth Movement he wrote in his diary that his ambition was to become a great Chinese financier, "So what is the point of my talking about poetry?" After completing a master's degree in political science at Columbia, he moved to Cambridge, England, to study political science and economics. Here he met and fell in love with fifteen-year-old Lin Huiyin, who would herself become an important New Poet. Lin's father opposed Xu's proposal of marriage to his daughter; Xu was still married to his first wife, who was living in London at the time. Xu's poems "Coincidence" and "Go" are said to represent his poetic farewell to Lin.

At Cambridge Xu discovered the English romantic poets and the French symbolists. Like the young Shelley, Xu devoted himself to recording in poetry a life of experience untrammeled by social or moral constraints. In 1922 he divorced his wife, who was pregnant with their second child. After traveling through France and Germany, he returned to China in 1923. He soon embarked on an affair with Lu Xiaoman, the wife of a friend. Lu divorced her husband – a rare thing for a woman to initiate in China at that time – and married Xu in 1926. Xu and Lu's publication of their love letters created a literary sensation.

In 1923, together with Hu Shi, Xu founded the Crescent Moon Society in Beijing. (The group's name comes from the title of a poem by Rabindranath Tagore, for whom Xu had served as translator on the Indian poet's tour of China.) In 1926 the society moved to Shanghai, where members met in rented premises paid for by Xu's father. They published collections of some seventeen members' poetry as well as their own journal.

Like most of the earliest New Poetry, Xu's first poems were almost entirely free verse, but he soon began to search for stricter forms. The Crescent Moon's stated objective was to develop the New Poetry by introducing structured stanza and meter. They espoused "freedom of ideals." As the Crescent Moon's informal leader, Xu had written in 1926 that reform in poetry was an integral part of the spiritual revolution taking place among the Chinese people. Development of new patterns and prosodies was crucial, he said, because perfection of form was essential to perfection of spirit. The source to which the society's members turned for poetic structures and meters was European verse. Michelle Yeh suggests that Xu's stress on a poem's organic unity derives from his reading in post-romantic Western criticism. One of Xu's greatest innovations is his prosody. He creatively adapted many Western poetic forms. "Beggar, It Serves You Right!" is a sonnet. His love poem "Coincidence" is in the form of a limerick. (Our translation does not attempt to reproduce the rhymes.)

In classical Chinese poetry, words are all of one syllable. Xu wrote that European languages offer greater elasticity to the poet because words are several syllables in length, with some syllables stressed and some unstressed, in contrast to the rigidity of classical Chinese in which every syllable is stressed. The prosody Xu developed in conjunction with Wen Yiduo is based on a "foot" of two syllables, one stressed and one unstressed, analogous to the two-syllable foot of European poetry. This innovation was intended to bring greater verbal flexibility to Chinese poetry while maintaining a strict stanza form. In a poem like "Farewell to Cambridge," each foot is divided into an unstressed syllable followed by a stressed one. There are an equal number of feet per line and a fixed pattern of rhyme in each stanza. Like Wen, Xu employed Beijing Opera's "Thirteen Tracks" system of rhyme.

Xu's public readings of his love poetry – and rumours about the affairs which inspired them – made him a celebrity. After his marriage to Lu Xiaoman, Xu took up a career as a professor of literature and English, eventually holding down two jobs, shuttling by airplane between lectures in Nanjing and Beijing. Besides poetry, he published *extempore* essays on a variety of subjects. One of his essays, "Flying," describes his airplane travels. On 19 November 1931 his life came to a sudden end when his plane crashed on route to Beijing, where he was reportedly going to attend a lecture by Lin Huiyin.

Hu Shi observed that Xu's poetry explores the conflicts between love, freedom, and the search for beauty. Some of his early poems like "The Paradise of the Poor" follow Wen Yiduo's call to make that which is ugly in real life into something beautiful in poetry. This poem's description of scavengers on a garbage heap reads like social realism. "On Hearing the Ritual of Prayer at Tianning Temple" records the narrator's search for nirvana. This Whitmanesque poem embodies in its free verse the Buddhist flight from the mundane that the narrator yearns for. The desire to escape the fleeting world is expressed again in "Farewell to Cambridge" as the narrator longs "to pole upstream" into the world of imagination like Keats's narrator in "Ode to a Nightingale," but now the desire for escape is expressed no longer in free verse but in strictly patterned stanzas. While the poem displays English romantic influence, Michelle Yeh points out, the farewell poem is a commonplace of classical Chinese poetry. Yeh notes the poem's circular structure. As in Keats's ode, the flight into the realm of the imagination proves to be fleeting, and the poet ends up where he began, entangled in the realities of the everyday world. In Xu as in Keats, the romantic impulse has tragic implications.

Soon Xu abandoned both religious and social themes for the theme of love. His verse owes much of its appeal to its spontaneity. Yeh notes his conviction that the essence of poetry is emotion. "He makes you feel that all the world is fresh and vibrant," wrote Zhu Ziqing. Xu's dynamic narrative voice confides to the reader the vitality of his intimate experiences. The protean complexity of Xu's narrator emerges in poems like "Acknowledging Sin." His poems dramatize their author as an amorous celebrity, entangled in the conflicts of his real-life love relationships. Michelle Yeh points out that love between a man and a woman was relegated to a minor theme in classical poetry. In Confucian ethics the sole purpose of the relation between a man and a woman was to perpetuate the family, the fundamental institution of society. Xu promoted sexual romance to a central theme, an innovation in Chinese poetry. Even more innovative was his idealization of the romantic relationship as the goal of life. But as Michelle Yeh also notes, Xu simultaneously insists on love's transience. His poetic narrator struggles for courage to face the evanescence of the sexual relationship. Poems like "The Oriole" and "I Cannot Tell" sketch the trajectory of romantic involvement from ecstatic infatuation to painful parting. In a farewell poem like "Go," the world and all its landscapes are cold, alien. The lover's predicament is tragic.

Xu's combination of formal structure with the freedom and unconstrained tone of vernacular speech was something new to Chinese poetry. Written in a period of intense social conflict, Xu's work was regarded as irrelevant by politically committed contemporaries. Leftists criticized his disregard for social issues. The association of the *Crescent Moon Journal* with conservative politics was a further black mark on Xu. In Marxist China his verse fell into obscurity thanks to his "individualist" morality and his capitalist family background. His grave was desecrated during the Cultural Revolution. When Mao died, the poetry of Xu Zhimo was virtually unknown to the Chinese reading public. Today he is regarded as one of China's greatest twentieth-century poets.

On Hearing the Ritual Chant of Repentance at Tianning Temple, Changzhou

As though lying face up in sunlight beautiful as fire, amid long, tangled clumps of weeds, hearing the cry of the first partridge of summer resounding from the horizon to the clouds, from the clouds to the horizon;
As though in a moonlit desert, as the soft fingers of the moon gently stroke each scorched grain of sand, hearing on the down-like tropical air the bell of a camel – ethereal, ethereal, resounding far away – then nearer, nearer, then once again resounding in the distance;
As though in a desolate valley, as the bold evening star comes out to shine on a universe from which all the sunlight has departed, and wild grasses and trees pray in silence, hearing the gong of a blind fortune-teller led by a child's hand ringing through a world of heavy darkness;
As though on a rock in the sea amid waves that rush madly like tigers beneath the closed, heavy curtain of black clouds, hearing the sea in a soft voice repent all its sins to the threatening storm;

As though on the summit of the Himalayas, hearing the sound of the wind's urgent footsteps beyond the horizon, as it drives the clouds into view, hearing it resound amid countless snowy, glittering peaks and gorges;
As though hearing from behind life's curtain the laughter of the void, the cheers that greet despair and suffering, the roaring carnival of slaughter and depravity, the clamorous song of world-weariness and suicide, all of them performed on life's stage,
I hear the ritual of prayer at Tianning Temple!
From where did these gods come? Humanity does not live such states of being now!
This drum, this bell, this chime, the sound of the wooden fish[2], of the Buddhist horns and the chant, of the temple music – distant, leisurely, resonant, prolonged – the beating of countless waves harmonized, the clash of countless colours stilled, of countless opposites reconciled;
The horns, the bell, the drum, the wooden fish, the chant – a harmony echoing throughout the universe – has freed a single grain of time, and gathered together incalculable centuries of fate.
What creates this harmony? The radiance of the sea of stars, the sounds of the universe, the flooding tides of actuality, all motions and all tumults cease;
At the ends of the earth and the borders of the universe, among the temple's golden pillars, in the middle of the stone Buddha's forehead, in my sleeves, at my brows, in my senses, in my soul, in a dream –
In a dream, in a fleeting revelation, the blue sky, the pale water, the green grass, this soft maternal breast of earth – can this be my native place? in truth, my native place?
Feathered wings of light flutter through the infinite!
The ecstasy of enlightenment wells up as self dissolves in this boundless, solemn, harmonious trance.
O, praise, Nirvana; O, praise, Nirvana!

1923

2 Wooden fish: a Buddhist percussion instrument, shaped like a fish.

The Paradise of the Poor

At the mouth of the alley, a pile of garbage, newly dumped,
No doubt from inside those crimson gates.
Not all ashes; there are bits of unburned coal.
Not just bones; there may be some marrow,
Or, clinging to them, shreds of meat.
Half-frayed cloth and untorn newspapers,
Two or three lamp wicks, half a cigarette butt.

The garbage pile is a mountain of gold
Covered with prospectors bent over –
A squad of dirty rags, shabby trousers, blue jackets in tatters.
They come in ones and twos, numberless hunched backs,
Small girls, middle-aged women, ancient grandmothers,
A basket on one arm, a stick in the other hand,
Bent double, not coughing, not chatting,
Not quarreling, just poking through the heap,
Rummaging ahead of them, rummaging behind, rummaging on both sides,
Shoulder to shoulder, head to head, poking and pulling.
A grandmother finds a strip of cloth, top quality!
Some search only for bits of coal that litter the ground.
A girl cries, "Mama, I found a bone with fresh meat!
Let's take it home and stew it – can we?"

A squad of rags like a magic lantern show,
Passing this way then that, and back again.
Housewives, little girls, grannies – and among the heaps of humanity,
Joining in the excitement – a few yellow dogs.

1923

Beggar, It Serves You Right!

"O, kind Madam, generous Master" –
Like a knife, the north wind cuts into his face –
"Give me a crumb from the leavings of your table."
So cries a shadow, huddled against the gate.

"Have pity, prosperous Sir, I am starving!"
Inside the gate – laughter, a glowing stove and cups of jade.
"Have pity, wealthy Master, I am freezing!"
"Serves you right, Beggar!" the north wind laughs.

I too am a trembling heap of shadow
Crouching before humanity's house.
I too seek only a little charitable warmth
To shield what's left of my slashed body,[3]

But the massive gate stays shut: who takes notice?
On the street – only the cold wind's taunt: "Beggar, serves you right!"

1923

Sayonara

For a Japanese woman

Above all – the warmth of her bow,
Lithe and delicate, reluctant as the water-lotus bending in the breeze,
As she says, "Take good care, Take good care" –
A phrase, so unexpected in our language, so heavy with tender sadness.

1924

3 A reference to "the death of a thousand cuts," an ancient form of execution, here metaphoric.

Beside a Mountain Path

One misty morning beside that mountain path
The first buds of the violet peeped from the thicket.
I was seeing her off, there to say good-bye
As her pure white dress came rustling over the grass.

I spoke not a word, she did not say farewell.
We stopped beside the path. Silently, I thought:
"Out with your secret; this is your chance."
The dewy violets deplored my hesitation.

"Why delay? This chance won't come again.
Now! This misty morning beside this mountain path!"
Gathering my courage, I turned to her –
But why were her eyes brimming with distress?

I lowered my head, swallowing my words.
Fire burned, ice froze my heart by turns.
I knew my fate and sensed her anguish
In the thick mist, on that isolated path.

That morning by the misty mountain path,
The violets looked at me askance from the thicket.
I watched her walk into the distance, and left her forever
As her pure white dress went rustling over the grass.

1925

Coincidence

I am a cloud in the sky
Quite by chance reflected in the heart of your wave.
        No need to be surprised,
        And still less to rejoice;
In the blink of an eye my image will disappear.

We met by chance one dark night at sea,
You were voyaging your way, I mine.
        It is well enough to remember,
        But still better to forget
The light we shed, each on the other, crossing paths.

1926

I Cannot Tell

I cannot tell which way
The wind is blowing
For I am in a dream
Spun round in gentle waves.

I cannot tell which way
The wind is blowing
For I am in a dream
Of her tenderness and my dizzying enchantment.

I cannot tell which way
The wind is blowing
For I am in a dream
Whose sweetness is its Glory.

I cannot tell which way
The wind is blowing
For I am in a dream
Of her indifference and my emptiness.

I cannot tell which way
The wind is blowing
For I am in a dream
That breaks the heart.

I cannot tell which way
The wind is blowing
For I am in a dream
Whose desolation is its Glory.

1928

The Rebirth of Spring

Last night
And also the night before,
In the mad frenzy of thunder and rain,
Spring was reborn in the carcass of winter.

Don't you feel the earth spongy beneath your feet,
The gentle warmth on your forehead?
Green is floating in the treetops,
Pond water ripples into infinite yearning.
And then there is this strange pulsation
In your body and mine, in our breasts.

Peach blossoms bloom in your cheek,
And I savour, keener still,
Your alluring charm, I drink
Your laughter, flashing like pearls.
Don't you feel my arm
Urgently seeking your waist,
My breath on your body,
Like a swarm of fireflies immolating themselves in flame?

All these things, and so much more that cannot be spoken,
Share the passionate ecstasy of the birds,
Joining to praise
The rebirth of spring.

1929

Dusk: Six Views from a Car Window

1

How could I fail to praise this afternoon
In early May, now melting into evening,
These paddies, so delicately, so ingeniously laid out,
Embraced by clouds and trees?

2

Across an empty sky white clouds are sweeping:
White swallows above the isle of the Immortals.
Now the clouds glow with sunset,
White feathers in a frame of gold.

3

Evening cooling on his back, his labour ended,
The ox stands quietly and dreams.
Children crouch beside him, playing hero,
O, to be mounted on his back!

4

Through the soft shadows of a stand of trees –
A running brook, a white stone bridge.
Beneath the stone arc, the dark comes early,
Stars flashing in the stream.

5

Green are the patches of beans, shadow-dark the mulberry groves,
Fragrant and lush the grassy thicket by the stream,

Secret, silent, the fields as dusk comes on,
But listen – the insects' flitting hum.

6

Dusk. The moon is powdering her cheeks.
Abashed, the sun flees toward the horizon,
Afraid to see her, afraid she'll see him
And laugh in his face, so flushed, so coarse.

1930

Acknowledging Sin

This is a crucial moment in my life – perhaps:

The silence is ending as birds in a nearby garden,
Cuckoos, sparrows and the rest, are greeting dawn,

And I cannot resist my troubled weariness,
Heavy as the winter ice that loads the branches.

Now a vision flits before my inward eye
Wavering like a tree-top in the winds of daybreak.

No circumstance outside the everyday
Demands that I choose between a lie and truth.

I must force myself to stay awake and thrust away
The seductions of the comfort-world of dreams,

For this moment is my one chance
To arraign myself, acknowledging this sin –

Acknowledging what? But if it is not sin, what is it?
I can find no words for how I pass my nights.

1931

The Oriole

A flash of colour is streaking toward the trees.
There – someone says – an oriole!
It lifts its tail and makes no sound.
An alien beauty shines amid dense green –
Like the light in spring, like flame, like passion.

We watch in silence, waiting for its song,
Afraid to scare it. The oriole spreads its wings
And, bursting from the foliage,
Dissolves into a blur, vanishing as it flies –
Like the light in spring, like flame, like passion.

1931

Farewell to Cambridge

Quietly I leave Cambridge,
        As quietly I came,
And gently wave, in parting,
        To the evening clouds.

A golden willow on the bank
        Marries the setting sun,
And shadows tinged with sunset
        Ripple in my heart.

Sedge blooms from the muddy depths,
        Flamboyant, free –
I'd gladly be such a water-plant,
        In the ripples of the Cam.

That pool in the elm tree's shadow
        Is no spring but a rainbow fallen,
Scattered among the plants,
        A sinking, many-coloured dream.

O, to dream and go poling upstream
        Where the banks are greener still,
The punt laden with brilliant stars,
        And then to break into song!

But now I cannot sing;
        Hushed is the departing flute.
For me the crickets are still;
        Silent is Cambridge tonight.

Quietly I leave Cambridge,
        As quietly I came.
I wave farewell; my sleeve shakes off
        The smallest thread of sunset.

1931

On the Train

In this car sit passengers of all ages and classes:
Bearded old men, nursing infants, teenagers, merchants, soldiers,
Each with his own pose, sitting close together or lying back –
Wide-eyed, eyes closed, or gazing out into the darkness.

Over and over the wheels utter the same sound.
No stars shine in the sky, no lights outside,
Just a dim light in the car falling on their faces,
Young and old, exhausted by the journey.

Suddenly from the darkest corner a song arises
Like a mountain spring, a bird at dawn,
Sweet, high and clear, as if the sky were lighting up a desert,
It golden rays shining on a distant mountain pass:

A child raises her voice in joy
At this dark hour of the blind journey;
Like a surging mountain stream, like a tiny bird in rapture,
Her song fills the car with profound sweet music.

One by one the passengers look up, surprised,
And gradually their faces shine with wonder;
Merchant, soldier, old and young,
Even a nursing infant opens tiny eyes.

The girl sings until light kindles and shines on the route.
Clouds part to reveal an exquisite moon, the Dipper's great stars,
Flowered branches vie in beauty like coloured lanterns,
And the slender grasses sway to the nimble flight of fireflies!

1931

Wandering Cloud

That day you wandered at your ease, like a cloud near the horizon,
You were graceful, unconstrained, with no thought of lingering

At this curve of sky, that corner of the earth,
Enjoying freedom from all care and all constraints.

Still less did you think that below in a narrow gully
Flowed a small brook whose simple spirit

You had dyed in passing with your seductive colours,
Startling him awake to bear your reflection.

What he embraced was constant sorrow,
For beauty never pauses.

He longs for you, but you fly beyond the mountains
To grace the grander lakes and seas with your reflection.

Because of you he dwindles to a trickle,
Hoping in vain that you'll fly back.

1932

Go

Leave, and I'll go too. Let's part here.
Go down that street. Don't worry, go.
See, lamps are lit as far as the horizon.
Go. I'll stay here watching you.
Step softly, don't raise the dust.
I want to see you clearly
Until you're so far I can't see you at all.
Otherwise I'd have to call out your name
To remind you I'm still here,
Dispelling the desolation of the street
And the bleakness of the night,
Watching as you return
To where you came from.

There's no such place for me. Mine is within,
The place that I return to. No need to worry. Go.
Just take the main street. I'll go down that alley.
See that tree stretching up to heaven?
I'll walk there and turn the corner
Into a desolation of murky swamps and stagnant ponds
Scattered through the night like incoherent tears
And over rocks and vines that wait to trip and bruise.
Don't worry. I take courage with me.
I won't grieve. The treacherous road won't daunt me.
When you are far away, I'll stride ahead.
There is a freshness in the wilderness at night.
Black clouds won't distress me for the wind is sure to rise,
And the mercury of stars will flow out and illumine the abyss of my heart –
And more – I have this nightless pearl: I love you.

1932

Wen Yiduo

(1899–1946)

Wen Yiduo and Xu Zhimo are frequently mentioned as China's two greatest twentieth-century poets. For a short time they were close collaborators, but their backgrounds and personalities were entirely different. Xu's father was a rich capitalist, while Wen was the fourth son of a scholar-gentry family. Xu was a romantic who wrote about love affairs; Wen was a scholar-patriot who wrote about China.

Wen was born in Xishui, Hubei province, and educated both in the Chinese classics and in the modern curriculum, learning English from the age of ten. At fourteen he went to study painting and literature in Beijing, where he later entered Qinghua University. During the May Fourth Movement he turned from composing classical verse to writing New Poetry. His early interest in the visual arts is reflected in the vivid colour imagery of a poem like "A Gathering of Chrysanthemums." In 1920 he published a study of "Rhythm in Poetry," its original title written in English. He graduated from Qinghua in 1921.

In 1922 he married a schoolteacher from his native town. Five months later he sailed alone for America where he would study art, literature, and drama, first at the Chicago Art Institute and later at Colorado College. His arranged marriage was by all accounts a success, as witness "Red Beans," a cycle of short poems that Wen wrote to his wife while he was in the US. But Wen was to face a conflict between family love and political duty: in his posthumously published "Silent Night" he sets forth the dilemma of one who is called to abandon his happy home to serve his country in crisis.

While studying in America, Wen read an article in a San Francisco Chinese newspaper about battles between warlords in east China. Among the dead and wounded were members of his family. "These last few days I feel as if I have lost my mind. They say I'm crazy, but whoever isn't driven crazy by these questions is simply numb, unfeeling!" It was not, he wrote, merely that his own family members were among the victims. He was "not thinking of family in the narrow sense of the word. No! I'm thinking of ... the homes of China, the people of China." Warlord troops looted peasant homes, reducing families to poverty, forcing whole communities to become refugees. Four years later, in 1927, Wen took up the theme of civil war in his "Deserted Village." He describes a prosperous village the peasants have fled. Wen does not mention civil war, but wonders with assumed naiveté what could possibly have made them leave home. The contemporary reader could have guessed that the inhabitants had fled ravaging Guomindang troops, who were capturing villages held by enemy loyalists. Wen's masterpiece, "Stagnant Water," likewise leaves its theme unstated. Written in reaction to the social decay of China under the warlords, the poem develops the image of contemporary politics as a sewage ditch.

Wen became an ardent nationalist, espousing an end to internecine struggle. "I have my people, I have five thousand years of culture. In what way am I worse than an American? Shall I say that because we can't stop the warfare, we are not as intelligent and upright as they are?" Wen's attitude to the West was complex: he admired Western poetry and democracy, but he loathed Western imperialism and other aspects of occidental culture that he saw as crippling China. Written in America, his "Laundryman's Song" implies that the Americans are filthier than the Chinese laundryman who washes their soiled clothes. But China's problems remained. MacDougall and Louie point out the complexity of Wen's attitude to his own culture. He admired classical poetry, but he believed that China had to modernize in order to resist conquest by Western powers. Wen would become increasingly obsessed with the problem of how to employ China's cultural tradition to heal the sufferings of his people. Written after his return to China, "Stagnant Water" implies that China's future salvation can only emerge from the ferment of corruption that was her present condition.

In 1923, while he was still in America, Wen's first book of poetry, *Red Candle,* was published in Shanghai. In 1925 he returned to China without a degree and took up a series of teaching posts. Soon he joined Xu Zhimo's Crescent Moon Society, helping to edit its monthly poetry magazine. In 1927 he engaged in propaganda work for the short-lived leftist uprising in Wuhan. When it was suppressed by Guomindang forces, Wen had to lie low for a time. In 1928 he rejoined Xu Zhimo in Shanghai, where the two would work together with Chen Mengjia and Zhu Xiang in editing *Poetry*. In 1928 Wen's influential volume, *Stagnant Water*, was published by the Crescent Moon Society Press.

Wen's 1920 essay "Rhythm in Poetry" anticipates his introduction of a metrical structure based on traditional English verse, in which lines are grouped in patterned stanzas with each line made up of a fixed number of feet. In poems like "Stagnant Water," Wen developed this prosody to a sophisticated level: in that poem, each line has three feet of one unstressed and one stressed syllable and one foot of two unstressed and one stressed. Groups of four lines form stanzas with patterned end-rhyme. Abandoning rhyme in Chinese poetry, said Wen, was like starving yourself with gold under your bed. He advocated a rhyme system derived from the Beijing Opera's "Thirteen Tracks" system, which grouped all sounds into thirteen rhyme-groups. These metric innovations, together with those of Xu Zhimo, were the cornerstone of the formalist school of New Poets. In 1931 Xu wrote, "I think over the past five or six years, all of us poets [of the Crescent Moon Society] have been influenced by the author of 'Stagnant Water.'"

In addition to English metrics, Wen was deeply interested in English poetic forms like the quatrain and the ballad. He spoke of the poet's need to create a form to fit the content of the poem. In "The Laundryman's Song" he employs ballad devices. In the original Chinese, each stanza's second and fourth lines rhyme. The poem's basic form is the quatrain, with a fifth line added like a ballad's refrain. In this way Wen creatively employs restrictive, fixed devices to achieve a complexity in structure that animates his verse. Wen's innovations in rhyme and meter had a wide influence on the New Poetry. The free verse of writers like Hu Shi and Bing Xin had abandoned rhyme altogether, rejecting both regular meter and the artificial rhyme of classical poetry. But, Wen said, in the New Poetry one is free to create new stanza forms and rhyme patterns to reflect the content of the poem. In his 1926 essay "Form in Poetry" Wen wrote that form was an aid to artistic expression, not an obstacle. "The stronger the poet is, the more he revels in dancing in shackles, and the better he dances."

Michelle Yeh suggests that his notion of the integral relationship between a poem's form and content may derive from the Western romantic doctrine of a work of art as an organic unity. In "The Laundryman's Song" Wen tailors the ballad form, traditionally associated with themes of the common folk, into a fitting mode of expression for a poor laundryman's complaint. Wen translated some Shakespeare into Chinese, and wrote modern poetry in English. He acknowledged the Western influence on his work but he rejected the translation style, in which New Poets wrote verse that was intended to sound as if it was a translation of a European original. Rather, he strove to root his content in the Chinese people and their culture. "The Laundryman's Song," for example, may be written in Western ballad form but its subject is the exploitation of a Chinese man in America.

Wen opposed Guo Moruo's innovative expansion of the subject matter of poetry. He felt that poetry should be restricted to the traditional themes of love, nature, death, and the sufferings of the common people. His earliest poems from America express a longing for China. The illness and subsequent death of his infant daughter while he was in the US inspired "I Wanted to Come Home." "A Gathering of Chrysanthemums" expresses nostalgia for the classical beauty and harmony of Chinese culture. As he developed his mature style, Wen came to believe that the poet should describe things both modern and specifically Chinese, avoiding allusion either to classical or to Western literature.

Wen began his poetic career as a devotee of aestheticism. MacDougall and Louie summarize Wen's aesthetics, developed in the mid 1920s, under three headings: architectural beauty (regular stanza form), musical beauty (rhyme and rhythm), and pictorial beauty (image and symbol). Wen's early poems show the influence of the classical Chinese *Songs of the South*, of the late Tang poet Li Shangyin, and also of John Keats, whose richness of diction and profusion of natural imagery can be seen in Wen's "A Gathering of Chrysanthemums." Wen's pursuit of the aesthetic ideal is no less devoted that Xu's, but in Wen the ideal beauty is inseparable from the ideal of the nation and her people. This fusion is typified in "A Gathering of Chrysanthemums," where the poet identifies the complex, intricate beauty of the flower with the multifold beauty of the motherland. But as his sense of horror at the anarchy of a China torn by feuding warlords increased, Wen changed his conception of the pictorial, drawing beauty out of ugliness in the mode of Baudelaire. "Stagnant Water" describes Chinese society as a ditch choked with garbage which takes on a grotesque splendour. His country is no longer a panorama of chrysanthemums but a tormented land of downtrodden victims. Wen turned to stark realism. His description of his dead daughter's corpse in "Perhaps" is shocking in its detachment. "Deserted Village" describes a rural scene – the lotus leaves, the rotting fishing nets, the rusted hoe – a landscape of bleak detail coolly captured by his painter's eye.

Wen gradually dissociated himself from Xu's Society. Its increasingly conservative politics clashed with his democratic populism, given voice in "One Phrase" with the cry "Ours, our China!" The Crescent Moon poets admired and imitated Wen's innovations in formal structure and meter, but Wen was struggling to make his poetry a catalyst for social change. Poems like "The Laundryman's Song" and "The Deserted Village," with their sympathy for the downtrodden, were poles apart from Xu Zhimo's poems about amorous adventures.

Yeh identifies a recurrent theme throughout Wen's poems of the transcendent ideal of beauty for which the poet expends himself and is even willing to die. His posthumous poem "Silent Night" develops the inner conflict of a dedicated family man who feels himself called to sacrifice himself for the sake of his country. By 1931 Wen concluded that poetry could not rescue China from its cultural and political malaise: it was powerless to resolve the sufferings of the common people. He stopped writing and embarked on an in-depth study of the Chinese tradition. Essays like "Confucianism, Daoism, and Banditry" search for the roots of China's social turmoil in its classical culture. After intense study, Wen identified an ancient figure who embodied integrity and compassion for common people in Qu Yuan (340 BCE?–278 BCE). As Michelle Yeh points out, Qu's fate embodied the plight of an individual pitted against the collective might of an unjust ruler. A government minister, Qu committed ritual suicide in protest against the unscrupulous regime under which he lived.

Wen's own death bears a resemblance to that of Qu Yuan. When the Japanese swept south in 1937, Wen set off – accompanied by many of his students – on a trek of over a thousand miles to Kunming in the southwest, where he resumed his classes as a professor at Southwest United University. In 1943 he joined the Democratic League (Tongmeng), a left-of-center "third force" political party. In 1946 civil war was breaking out between the Guomindang and the Communists. Chiang Kai-shek set about to wipe out the Democratic League along with the Communists. In spite of death threats, Wen continued to call publically for peace and national unity, denouncing the brutality of the Guomindang's sham democracy. On 15 July 1946 he addressed a public meeting in memory of Li Gongpu, a Democratic League leader shot by the Guomindang secret police: "Reactionaries, you killed one man, but hundreds and thousands carry on ... We have the martyr's spirit!" Later that same day Wen himself was assassinated. Wen was a well-known as a scholar, poet, and patriot. It was public knowledge that he was not a Communist. His assassination was widely attributed to the Guomindang authorities, and was the subject of public protest throughout China.

Wen's work is a striking amalgam of aestheticism, formalism, and the ardent patriotism of a reformer. His influence on subsequent Chinese poets is all the more remarkable since his career as a poet spanned only ten years of his tragically short life. He is one of those rare writers who can be admired equally by readers loyal to antagonistic schools of thought.

A Gathering of Chrysanthemums

Standing in a long-necked vase of enamel green as shrimps,
Or in a hexagonal vase of crystal – chrysanthemums.
Or preserved in a purple wisteria maiden's-basket, basket of
  the Immortals,
Or kept in a wine-pot – chrysanthemums,
Or with pincer-petals clasped around the center – chrysanthemums,
Unopened, about to open, half-open, fully open – chrysanthemums.

Chicken's-claw chrysanthemums, crimson set in gold,
Embroidered silken balls of pink chrysanthemums, their petals ragged,
Listless, luxuriant January blooms
Hanging upside-down like bee-hives, a vase of yellow hearts in
  purple sunflowers,
Long petals embracing the blossom's heart,
Dense-petalled, flat-crowned chrysanthemums.
Soft, richly coloured white chrysanthemums, their sharp petals clutching
  the pistil
As a beautiful woman's fist
Grasps a handful of golden millet.

Under eaves, by stairs, along fences, in the midst of gardens,
Enveloped in light mist – chrysanthemums.
Chrysanthemums washed in fine, thread-like rain,
Golden yellow, white-jade, the green of spring wine, the purple
  of autumn mountains.

Like slices of fall radish – tiny red chrysanthemums.
Chrysanthemums from goose-down yellow to old bronze.
Slightly greenish, with a purple stem – the "true chrysanthemum,"

Its tiny tubes of jade stitched together
So that the little Flower Spirit
Can steal away, and the flower become the pipes of his *sheng*[4] singing in the night.
The king chrysanthemum, big as a peony, bold and luxurious,
His claret-red petals, like armour,
Half concealing – every one – a silver-white lining;
Chrysanthemum buds like tiny stars
Crowding about a brown calyx, sleeping.

All nature's beauty harvested,
The masterpiece of Mother China's autumn!
O Flowers of the East, like great ministers retired and now poets in seclusion,
Are not these poems of the Orient the metamorphoses of your spirits
Refining the inborn wisdom of the soul?
Is not our double-ninth day[5] a celebration of flowers, mountain-climbs and wine?
Is it not also the auspicious day of a celestial spirit born among us?

You are not like the hot roses of carnal desire,
Still less like the lowly violets,
But rich in history and long observance;
O celebrated flower, nobility's emblem over four thousand years,
Yours is a lofty past, an unsurpassed elegance of ceremony.

Poet's flower, I always remember you,
And my heart blossoms like a flower opening,
Like you radiant,
Remembering the motherland we share,
Noble, resplendent China,
My hope, a flower, blossoming like you.

4 Sheng: a Chinese wind instrument consisting of a cluster of tubes.
5 The ninth day of the ninth lunar month, when families traditionally sweep and decorate the graves of their dead.

Gently murmuring autumn wind, blow on!
I shall praise the flower of my motherland,
I shall praise my motherland, itself a flower.
May my words blossom into bright bouquets,
Golden-yellow, jade-white, wine-green, the purple of autumn
mountains …
Then, autumn wind, scatter them all in wild profusion,
Filling the heavens, blanketing the earth!

Whispering autumn wind,
I shall praise my motherland, itself a flower!

1922

Pondering

In the deep silence of twilight
Strange thoughts emerge
From this desolate brain of mine –
Half-formed, disordered thoughts,

Strange little monsters, neither bird nor beast,
Like timid anxious bats flying
Out of a rain-soaked, mud-encrusted bell tower
In front of an old temple.

Like wild bats, my thoughts
Refuse merely to crawl on the ground
But wheel constantly through the air
In loops, ellipses, circles.

Out of this desolate brain of mine
In the deep silence of twilight
Bizarre thoughts emerge
That resemble a flock of bats.

1922

A Little Brook

Leaden gray, the tree's shadow
Like a long nightmare
Presses down on the breast
Of the little brook, entranced in sleep.
The mountain brook struggles, struggles
To no avail.

1923

from *Red Beans*[6]

9

Beloved,
Let me be the warp,
And you the woof.
Destiny has woven our marriage:
A palindrome in brocade.
Horizontally it is *longing*,
Vertically it is *longing*,
Forwards it is *longing*,
Backwards it is *longing*,
Aslant it's *longing*, level it's *longing*,
However we read it, we never find *reunion*.

6 The title is an allusion to the idiom *hongdou xiangsi* – "Red beans remind me of the one I love." This series of short poems was written for his wife while the author was separated from her while he was studying in America.

10

We two have become one body.
At least our union
Is as round and ample as the globe –
Two hemispheres,
You are the Orient, I the West,
And the tears we shed
The vast Pacific
That keeps us from each other.

14

I send you these poems.
Though you may not understand each word,
No matter.
With your fingertips
Caress them gently
Like a doctor taking the pulse of one sick.
Perhaps you will discover they are
Anxiously throbbing
In time with the rhythm of your heart.

1923

The Laundryman's Song

The most common job among Chinese living in America is washing clothes. Americans often ask students from China, "Does your father work in a laundry?"

One shirt, two shirts, three shirts,
Wash them clean!
Four shirts, five shirts, six shirts,
Iron them smooth!

Handkerchief soaked with sorrow – wash it clean;
Undershirt black with sin – scrub it white,
Greasy scum of greed, ashes of desire …
Everything filthy in your family –
        Give me it to wash, give me it to wash!

Copper corrodes, blood stinks.
What gets filthy has to be washed.
What's been washed gets filthy again.
My indifferent customers, won't you ever pay attention?
        Wash it for them! Wash it for them!

You say that laundries are a dirty business,
That only a Chinaman would stoop so low.
But one day your minister told me
That Jesus' father was a carpenter.
        Do you believe it? Do you believe it?

If scrubbing with soapsuds can't wash out a stain,
How much better to work at building battleships.
I agree this job has no future,
Shedding my sweat and blood to wash out yours.
        Would you want to do it? Would you want to do it?

Year after year I shed my homesick tears:
Midnight in the laundry, a solitary lamp.
You well-off folk just can't be bothered
Searching for wrinkles, searching for stains.
        Let that guy do it, let that guy do it.

Handkerchief soaked with sorrow – wash it clean!
Undershirt black with sin – scrub it white,
Greasy scum of greed, ashes of desire …
Everything filthy in your family,
        Give me it to wash! Give me it to wash!

One shirt, two shirts, three shirts,
Wash them clean!
Four shirts, five shirts, six shirts,
Scrub them clean!

circa 1925

Stagnant Water[7]

This ditch is rank with the water of despair.
A brisk wind cannot stir it to ripple.
Why not toss in more scrap copper and iron?
Might as well add soup and rotten vegetables.

Maybe the red copper will turn green like jade
And the rust on pots bloom into peach blossoms.
Its greasy surface might thicken into damask,
And toxic germs send up mist like evening clouds.

Let the ditch water ferment to a green wine
Bubbling with fine froth, white as pearls,
Small pearls growing larger, chuckling
Until burst by gnats drawn to their odour.

This ditch full of desolate, stinking water
Certainly has an aura of distinction.
If local frogs cannot bear their solitude,
This stale muck can gurgle them a tune all its own.

This ditch is rank with the water of despair,
Hardly picturesque, or a national treasure.
Now let's leave it to stew in its own juice,
And see what devilish world it can produce.

1925

7 The poem is usually interpreted as a socio-political metaphor, the ditch of stagnant water standing for China.

Perhaps: An Elegy

Perhaps you've only cried yourself to sleep.
Perhaps, perhaps you need a bit of rest.
May the heron now forget to call,
The frog to croak, the bat to leave its roost,

The sun not raise the curtains of your eyes,
Nor the cooling breeze of dusk disturb your brow.
May no one – no matter who – awaken you,
And may the pine's umbrella shield you now.

Perhaps you'll hear the worms turn in the earth,
Or grasses groom their bearded roots with rain.
Perhaps such music of the realm below
Pleases more than curses and cries of pain,

So tightly shut your eyes against the light,
And I'll lay you to rest. I'll make your bed
And lightly blanket you with yellow earth
As paper money swirls above your head.

1925

The Last Day

Dew sobs in the choked bamboo water-pipes,
        The green tongues of the plaintains lick at the window.
The walls around me, chalk-white, recede.
        Alone, I cannot fill the enormous room.

I light a brazier in the chamber of my heart
        And wait in silence for a visitor from afar.[8]
With spiderwebs and mouse droppings I feed the flame;
        For kindling, a scaly mottled snakeskin.

8 Cf. Confucius: "Friends come from afar. Is it not a joy?"

The cock crows to hurry me. The brazier fills with ash.
        A chill wind passes, tearing at my mouth.
So, at last the caller stands before me!
        I close my eyes, departing with this stranger.

1926

I Wanted to Come Home

        I wanted to come home
When your small fists clenched like unopened orchids,
When your hair was as fine as silk floss,
When the light of your soul was glowing in your eyes,
        I wanted to come home.

        I did not come home
When your footsteps seemed to flutter in the wind,
When your soul was like a fly vainly battering the window pane,
When the sound of your laughter was a silver bell,
        I did not come home.

        I should have come home,
When lethargy flitted through your eyes,
When a chill breath blew out a fading light,
When a cold hand came and snatched you away,
        I should have come home.

        I did come home
When a firefly struck the lantern that shone on you,
When the katydid cried at your ear,
When you'd fallen asleep, your mouth filled up with earth,
        I came home.

1927

The Deserted Village

For sixty miles around Liangyuan town in the region of Linhuaiguan the population has vanished. The residents have fled from the villages on both sides of the road. The peasants have tied their wooden tools and furniture together with cords and submerged it all in the ponds and rice paddies so it won't be burned. They've taken away all the doors and windows, and stopped up the gaps with coffins or rocks. When night falls there is not a single light. Pigs, dogs and chickens search for food in the fields with nobody to look after them. Here and there roses and peonies still bloom by themselves in the corners of walls. Newly sprouted rice seedlings are a charming green. Is this not because the plants are ignorant of it all?

The sixteenth year of Guomindang rule: Xinwen Daily, *May 19th, 1927*[9]

Where have they all gone?
Why is a toad squatting on the rice steamer,
And white lotus blooming in the water dipper?
Why are tables, chairs and benches floating
In the flooded paddies, and below the weir?
Why do bridges of spiderweb lead from room to room?
Why a coffin jammed in the door frame, rocks wedged in the window?
So strange a scene, so desolate!
A rusting scythe, abandoned, crumbles into dirt
And fishing nets rot on an ash heap.
O God! Couldn't even such a village keep them –
A village where roses bloom and lotus leaves grow large as parasols;
Where the tips of the rice seedlings are so sharp, the lake so green,
The sky so blue, and the songs of birds as round and full as dew drops?
Why are the seedlings so green, the flowers so red?
Whose blood has mingled with this earth, whose sweat?

9 In 1927 Guomindang forces advanced northward from their base in Guangzhou to defeat the southern warlords. The poem may allude to the effects of warfare on regions in the countryside, from which peasants fled approaching armies.

Those who are gone left with such resolution, so deliberately.
Was it some grievance, did they make some vow?
Someone should tell them that now
Pigs roam the road and ducks crowd after the pigs,
The cock scratches up the peonies, the cow munches vegetables –
Tell them that when the sun has set, the cattle won't leave the hill,
And each black silhouette lingers on the knoll, waiting.
Hillocks crouch all around like jackals,
Closing in. The livestock stare and shiver,
Lower their heads, afraid to look.
This too, tell them: the cattle remember the old days.
When the evening cold came on and poplars trembled in the wind,
The mountain trail was treacherous
But they had only to low from the hilltop and the master would guide them home.
The tune of his flute would lead them through the gate into their pen.
How fragrant was the rice straw, how warm the barn!
When they remember this, they shed hot tears.
They press together, face against face.
Go, tell their masters,
Tell them everything, omit nothing!
Tell them to return, tell them to come back!
Ask them how they can neglect even their own cattle.
Don't they know that beasts are like little children?
Poor animals, so frightened!
You there! Messenger, where have you been?
Quick, go and tell them – tell Third Wang,
Tell big Zhou and his eight younger brothers,
Tell all the Linhuaiguan farmers,
Tell Old Li, the red-faced blacksmith,
Tell One-Eyed Dragon, tell old Xu the Sage,
Tell Auntie Huang and all the village women –
Tell them all these things, one by one.
Make them come back! Make them!
The scene is so pitiful, so tragic!
Even such a fine village could not hold them;
Such a paradise, and now no smoke from the hearths!

1927

One Phrase

One phrase – to speak it is disaster.
One phrase – it can ignite a conflagration.
Forget that no one has said it aloud for five thousand years.
Are volcanoes always dormant?
Who knows when, possessed by a spirit,
Out of the blue a thunderbolt will suddenly
          Explode:
          "*Ours, our* China!"

How shall I say those words today?
You doubt that an iron tree can bloom,
But here is a phrase for you:
Wait till the volcano inside can't be restrained.
Don't tremble, raise your voice or stamp your feet.
Out of the blue a thunderbolt will suddenly
          Explode:
          "*Ours, our* China!"

1927

Statement under Oath

I won't fool you; I'm no kind of poet –
Even though what I love is white stone, chaste and steadfast,
Green pines and the sea, a crow that carries sunset on his back,
A dusk thickly woven with the wings of bats.
You know I love a hero, and also a lofty mountain.
I love our nation's flag flying in the wind,
And I love chrysanthemums – from the light yellow to the old bronze,
And remember, my chosen food is a pot of bitter tea.

Yet there is another me – does this scare you?
A me with thoughts like flies crawling in a garbage bin.

1928

Silent Night

This lamp and these four walls bleached by the lamplight,
This desk, these chairs – my ready, virtuous servants,

This fragrance that clings to the pages of old books,
My companionable cup, white and chaste as a bride,

My infant son, now nursing at his mother's breast,
My elder son, whose hearty snores proclaim his health,

This eerie, silent night, this round of perfect peace,
This song of gratitude that rises in my throat –

And at once the song of thanks changes to a curse.
Silent night, I cannot, will not, accept your bribe!

Who can be happy with a peace inside four walls?
My world is greater; it reaches far beyond.

These walls cannot keep out the roar of battle.
Can they still the furious beating of my heart?

Better stuff my mouth with mud to choke me
Like others who knew only how to sing.

Best give my skull to the field mice as a burrow,
And feed this clump of blood and flesh to maggots,

If merely for a cup of wine, a book of verse
And an eye-blink of comfort in the silent night

I grow deaf to neighbours groaning on all sides,
Blind to shivering widows and orphans,

The dead in trenches, the madman gnawing his cot,
And all the tragedies of those ground down by life.

Good Fortune, I cannot accept your bribe;
My world cannot be locked inside these walls.

Listen! Cannons! Roaring spirits of the dead!
Silent night, how can you hope to still my pounding heart?

Published 1948

Zhu Xiang
(1904–33)

Zhu was born in Yuanling, Hunan province. After being tutored in the Chinese classics, he went at the age of thirteen to Nanjing, where he studied engineering and learned English. At eighteen he resolved to concentrate on poetry and entered a special program at Qinghua University to prepare students for study in America, but was expelled, reputedly for defying a regulation that required all students to attend breakfast.

He remained in Beijing and joined the Literary Research Association. In 1926 he and some poet friends approached Xu Zhimo to publish their work in the poetry supplement of the *Morning Post*, where Xu served as editor. A friend subsequently arranged for him to return to his studies at Qinghua. The university awarded him a grant to study in America, first at Lawrence College in Wisconsin, then at the University of Chicago, where he studied Latin, French, Old English, and English literature. Zhu returned to China in 1929 to teach foreign languages at Anhui University.

While still in America in 1927 he published his second volume of poetry, *Rank Weeds*, which was to remain his most important collection. The reviewer in Xu Zhimo's *Crescent Moon Journal* wrote, "The poet's painstaking technique and strict meter are in harmony with what this magazine advocates." His emphasis on regular meter, with alternating stressed and unstressed syllables, on patterned stanza form, and on aesthetic beauty as the object of poetry all accord with the Crescent Moon Society's norms and objectives. However, Zhu had hardly any personal connections with the society beyond a brief period of service on their editorial committee, and later publicly denied any connection with the group.

Neglected under the Communist regime, Zhu has since been recognized as an important figure in the New Poetry. His poetic line does not, like Wen Yiduo's, employ a flexible version of feet with varying numbers of syllables; Zhu employed a fixed number of syllables per line. Indeed, Zhu's meticulous attention to stanza structure and meter exceeds that of Xu Zhimo and Wen Yiduo: he criticized Wen and Xu for carelessness of technique. He experimented with a wide number of Western poetic forms, including the couplet, the quatrain, the villanelle, and the ballad. Zhu authored a sequence of seventy-one sonnets, some in the Elizabethan and some in the Petrarchan form. His rhyme schemes follow the "Thirteen-Tracks" system employed by Wen Yiduo, which would become common in vernacular poetry.

Zhu's professional career was stormy, punctuated by conflicts with colleagues and superiors. Dismissed from his university in Anhui province, he lived a hand-to-mouth existence in rooming houses, pawning his possessions. Finally he moved to Shanghai, where he managed to locate his wife, who undertook to support him by doing embroidery. All the while he continued to write poetry.

In his "Bury Me," Zhu's narrator longs for water burial. On 4 December 1933, he borrowed the fare for a steamer ticket from Shanghai upriver to Nanjing. At six o'clock the next morning he took a bottle of liquor from his small suitcase, drank half of it, then jumped overboard and drowned. He was twenty-nine years old.

Luo Niansheng described his dead friend as having a "proud nature, irascible and oversensitive ... too credulous, overpoetic, and so he was taken in at every turn." Chaotic in his personal affairs, Zhu was preoccupied with poetic form. Oversensitive in his dealings with other people, he wrote poems in a tone of extraordinary detachment, like "The Pawnbroker." In this respect, Zhu's aestheticism is a form of escapism. As Shu Xuelin suggests, Zhu sought to create in formal verse the elegance and structure that he lacked in his personal life.

The Pawnbroker

Beauty runs a pawnshop,
        Accepting men's hearts as collateral,
But when you try to redeem your property,
        The sign reads: "Closed."

1925

Bury Me

Bury me in a pond of flowering lotus
With water creatures stirring past my ear
And on the lotus leaves, the light
Of glow-worms flashing – now dark, now bright.

Bury me under red lantana flowers
Eternally dreaming a fragrant dream,
Or on the holy summit of Mount Tai
Where the winds cry through solitary pines.

Or burn me to cold ashes
And scatter them in springtime on a swollen river
To drift away amid the fallen flowers
To a place no one knows.

1925

Shao Xunmei

(1906–68)

Shao consciously personified the decadence of Shanghai. He was the offspring of an established family, the grandson of a high-ranking imperial official. As a child he received a classical Chinese education. He was also given a solid grounding in English, which his father spoke.

In 1923, at the age of seventeen, he left Shanghai to study at Cambridge. Landing at Naples, he was entranced by a fresco of the Greek poet Sappho; her elegant eroticism was to set the tone for Shao's own poetry. From Sappho, he said, he came to discover Swinburne, and from Swinburne the pre-Raphaelites, and from them Baudelaire and Verlaine. His 1928 manifesto *Fire and Flesh* includes essays on the Western poets who served as his masters in the aesthetics of erotic sensibility. Baudelaire's verse, he would later write, was the work of a genius with the power to liberate a culture shackled by "religious, ethical and social mores." Shao's hedonism resembles Baudelaire's in its self-conscious nihilism: "The Soul of Shanghai" concludes its portrait of the City of Pleasure with the invitation, "Come, here is your graveyard." But Shao's hedonism differs from Baudelaire's in its lack of metaphysical dimension, and of any critique of modernity. In this respect, at least, he remains an heir of the classical poetic tradition.

At Cambridge Shao made the acquaintance of Xu Zhimo and other prominent Chinese intellectuals. When he returned to Shanghai in 1927, he began publishing verse, joining Xu and Wen Yiduo at the Crescent Moon Society. Shao claimed to have written his earliest verse without ever seeing the poetry of Wen or Xu; rather, he affirmed, his introduction to New Poetry came through reading vernacular Chinese translations of Western verse. However this may be, Shao's poetry is in the "dried-bean curd" form of Wen and Xu: patterned stanzas of set length, with a regular meter consisting of feet of one stressed and one unstressed syllable. Like Xu and Wen, Shao showed meticulous care about metric structure. He praised the sonnet for its full expression of a particular emotion within a small space. The contrast between strictness of form and utter abandon in content is just one of the fascinating paradoxes in his poetry. After Xu's untimely death, Shao carried on as editor of the *Crescent Moon Journal* until its final edition in 1933.

The amorous adventures Shao describes in his poems had gossip-column interest for his Shanghai audience – as Shao no doubt intended they should. He even became a figure on the pages of *The New Yorker* in the guise of Mr Pan, the Chinese protagonist in the stories of the American writer Emily Hahn, whom he informally married in the mid-thirties – violating a Chinese taboo against sexual relations with a white person. Contemporary critics denounced Shao's verse for its neglect of social and political issues, for its aestheticism, and for pornographic content. When the good-time twenties gave way to the desperate thirties, Shao fell out of fashion. The luxurious sensual abandon which permeates his verse was anathema to the Communists: Lu Xun refused to contribute to any magazine associated with him.

It is probably not surprising that a hedonist like Shao went bankrupt; short of cash, he tried to reverse his fortunes as a publisher of glitzy magazines, supplementing his dwindling income by writing as many as three cheap detective novels in a single month, and publishing pornography at his moribund press. After Mao's takeover in 1949, this son of a privileged family became a street vendor. He also taught night school. He was jailed during the Anti-Rightist Campaign of the late fifties on charges of having collaborated with the Japanese during the war. Four years of imprisonment broke his health. When released in 1962, he was suffering from a severe heart condition. The author who once personified the elegance of Shanghai spent the last six years of his life selling off his deluxe library, book by book, in order to make ends meet.

Shao's volume *Paradise and May* (1927) portrayed the extravagant passions of a voluptuous, perverse persona. Its verse proclaimed Shanghai the Paris of the Orient, the cultural twin of the decadent French capital, an image that Shao cultivated in poems like "The Soul of Shanghai." In the preface to his *Twenty-five Poems* (Shanghai, 1936) he quoted William Morris: "I do not believe in any soul. I only believe in technique." In the same preface Shao spoke of the possibility of having two conflicting feelings at the same time. Shen Congwen summarized Shao's calculated ambivalence of feeling: "He praises the beauty of life, the beauty of love. But in describing the aesthete's enjoyment of the world, and praising the allure of this world, he does not lose sight of the world's emptiness." Shao reissued *Paradise and May* in 1928 under the title *Flowerlike Sin*, an allusion to Baudelaire's title *Les Fleurs du Mal*. In Baudelaire, physical beauty attracts the narrator in tandem with the dark pull of evil. The same ambiguity underlies Shao's finest poems. "May," a celebration of sexual desire, concludes,

> Heaven's portals open wide.
> God frightens me – I am not one to enter.
> I have found consolation already in hell,
> Awake and dreaming through this brief night.

Shao's verse develops tensions: between strictness of form and libidinous abandon; between dreamlike sensuality and the ascetic rigour of a religious consciousness which the narrator in "May" rejects, but cannot forget.

The Serpent

From palace steps and temple roof-tiles
You dangle your tender length
Like a woman's sash, undone,
Awaiting the male shudder.

Which of my lips will your red
Forked tongue penetrate with agony?
Both of them await, await
A simultaneous double exhilaration.

I cannot forget how that slipperness which no one can hold
Has polished many a bamboo joint.
I know there is hurt in pleasure,
And I know still better that in ice there's fire.

O, if only you would entwine me in your length,
Tightening it round my irrepressible body
As the peal of bells slips under the delicate netting,
And warmth crawls beneath the brocade quilt in the cold palace.[10]

c. 1928

10 The cold palace is that part of the imperial harem where rejected imperial concubines resided.

Sweet Dream

Lovable, horrible, infuriating –
The tip of a virgin's tongue, a lizard's tail!
I do not understand; perhaps you can tell me
If happiness can be found between pairs of lips.

Oh, for a bed the colour of rose and ivory!
This sweet dream goads my soul
For I am a faithful acolyte of sin
And long to see a yearning nun disrobe.

1928

May

Lusty May – back again, rekindled!
Sin revives with a virgin's kiss.
Sweet tears tempt me
To feel between her breasts with trembling lips.

This earthly life is infinite as death,
As the terrified raptures of a wedding night:
If she is not the white blossom of a rose,
Then she will be redder than fresh blood.

Ah, this flamelike, fleshlike
Radiant darkness, these laughing sobs,
Are soul of my love's soul,
The enemy of my enemy!

Heaven's portals are open wide.
God frightens me – I am not one to enter.
I have already found consolation in hell,
Awake and dreaming through this brief night.

1928

The Soul of Shanghai

I stand atop this seven-story building:
Above, the unscalable heavens;
Below, cars, power lines, the racetrack,

The door of a dance show, a whore's backside.
Ah, these are the spirit of the metropolis,
These are the soul of Shanghai!

No need to fret about whether it's rainy or clear,
Whether it's dying autumn or burgeoning spring.
What summer could warm better than those offered lips?

Here are real fantasy and illusory passion,
Here are wakeful twilights and smiling neon;
Come, here is your graveyard.

1928

Chen Mengjia
(1911–66)

Chen was born in Shangyu, Zhejiang province. His father and his mother's father were both Christian pastors. The author did not embrace his family's faith. His "Spring Landscape with a Small Temple" satirizes religiosity in the person of the idle monk – in this case a Buddhist one.

Chen's parents had thirteen children. Because they could not afford to care for them all, Chen was sent to his sister's family in Nanjing. Before he finished middle school he was admitted to Nanjing Central University. Here he met Wen Yiduo, who taught on the English staff. Wen introduced Chen's poetry to the editors of the *Crescent Moon Journal*, which began to publish his work in 1928. In 1929 Chen met Xu Zhimo when the latter began teaching in Nanjing. In 1931 Xu arranged for the Crescent Moon Press to publish Chen's first collection of poetry while the author was still an undergraduate.

In Shanghai Chen wrote for Shao Xunmei's magazines. He published further poetry collections in 1934 and 1936. Chen writes in a version of Wen Yiduo's "dried bean curd" poetry: lines of an equal number of feet, each foot composed of one stressed and one unstressed syllable. He also employs a strict rhyme scheme.

In the preface to his 1931 volume of poems Chen wrote, "Everyone dreams of some heaven, some way. But I have none. I have never been able to grope toward a clearer view of myself, much less of the world. Like a gust of wind, I cannot find a place for myself." The author projects this rootlessness onto the subject of his poem, "An Old White Russian," an opponent of the revolution who fled Russia after the victory of the Reds. In his selection of such a subject, the author of this starkly realistic piece hints at his own reactionary political sentiments. Chen's sympathy with the counter-revolutionary figure in this poem foreshadows his own future plight as an anti-revolutionary "rightist" during the Cultural Revolution.

When the Japanese attacked Shanghai in 1932, Chen briefly joined the army and served at the front, describing his experiences in a series of war poems. After Shanghai fell he entered Qingdao University, where Wen Yiduo was teaching. In 1934 he joined Yanjing University in Beijing and began what was to become a lifelong study of ancient Chinese artifacts, especially bronzes and oracle bones.

In 1944 he went to the University of Chicago where he wrote articles, some in English, on ancient Chinese bronzes. He also compiled a catalogue of Chinese bronzes in Western countries. The catalogue was eventually published in Mao's China in 1962 as evidence of foreigners looting China of its cultural artifacts, but by this time Chen had been denounced, and his book appeared without its author's name.

Chen returned to China in 1947 to work at Qinghua University. In 1952 he began work at the Chinese Academy of Sciences' archaeology department. In the mid fifties he was revising his poems for a new complete edition, but withheld them from publication when the Anti-Rightist Campaign began. Soon he was denounced. Persecuted by Red Guards at the start of the Cultural Revolution, Chen hanged himself in 1966.

An Old White Russian[11]

Once splendid, grand, heroic,
Feeble now. How many gales and frosts has he endured?
He coughs, gasps, then falls again as silent
As the Siberian tundra.
A typhoon has ripped away his tent,
Scattered his men, his herds, his familiar constellations,
And blown him to this alien shore.

As always, he is stern as a mountain peak
In autumn, hoary and quiet.
Now and then a knot catches in his chest,
Makes him wheeze and gasp.
The spasm gently vibrates
The tiny drops condensed on his yellow beard.
He only shakes his head and does not speak.

11 Many Russians who fought with the Whites against the Reds in the Russian Revolution fled to China after their defeat.

Ever taciturn, he sucks his pipe.
As he glances back and forth over the newspaper,
Something disturbs his thoughts.
He stops, raises his eyes,
And his quick glance falls on the portrait
Of his dead Czar Nikolai. Perhaps it is the cold
That makes him cough and cry out – "Tanya!"

1932

Spring Landscape with a Small Temple

Let the sunlight reach the young grass
That sprouts between the tiles on my roof,
Let rains come when needed, let winds be gentle,
Seasonable weather all the year long.

Let prayer-flags sleep
Round this collapsing courtyard wall,
Let the tiger-lizards climb the wall's back,
One after another.

I hunt for fleas in my patchwork robe,
As beneath the sun I bask at ease
For I am a bodhisattva
Reincarnated as a monk.

1935

Shen Congwen
(1902–88)

As an author of fiction, Shen was one of the most respected figures of twentieth-century Chinese literature. A prolific novelist and respected scholar, he belonged to the Miao (Hmong) minority, an ancient racial group spread over southern China, Thailand, and Vietnam. In China the Miao inhabit remote mountain regions, where they subsist on slash-and-burn agriculture. Shen was born in western Hunan province. After attending the local county school, he went off at sixteen to serve as a soldier. Over the next five years he traveled with his unit, meeting a wide variety of people, coming to know the bravery and cruelty of army life. His experiences in the military and his intimate knowledge of the customs and traditional values of China's racial minorities provide the material of his fiction. Many of his novels and stories tell of a hero's struggle to lead a life of moral integrity in a world of poverty and turmoil.

In 1923, at the age of twenty-one, he traveled to Beijing to establish himself as a writer. He audited classes at Beijing University. Here he formed a relationship with Ding Ling and her lover Hu Yepin. Beginning in 1924 his fiction, plays, essays, and poetry began appearing in journals and newspapers.

In 1928 he moved to Shanghai, where he joined the Crescent Moon Society. Fellow member Hu Shi helped Shen find work as a university professor. His prosody is a loose version of the meter developed by Wen Yiduo and Xu Zhimo, alternating one stressed syllable followed by one or more unstressed ones. Shen uses rhyme in a casual way, composing verse without the strictly patterned stanzas of Chen Mengjia or Wen Yiduo.

Shen taught Chinese literature at several institutions of higher learning, including Beijing University. After the Japanese extended their control down the Chinese coast, he joined Wen Yiduo at Southwest United University in distant Kunming. Like most creative writers in China, Shen abandoned literature after 1949, when writers were required to serve party policy. His works were banned. He turned to the study of ancient Chinese costume. His book on this subject, published in 1981, is recognized as a landmark in its field.

Panegyric

They said the day would surely come
When your body would become my private landscape –
Those twists and turns, those little mounds, those levels and rises –
That I would know each plant and tree by heart
So in the dark I would not lose my way.
Now – suddenly – the day has arrived.

I have grown familiar with the fragrance of your body
Just as a snipe used to eating cherries
Can distinguish the cherry's fragrance.
It also knows the difference between cherries and mulberries
  or strawberries;
Though it has never eaten mulberries or strawberries,
The snipe knows.

You are a willow.
You move in the wind, and when the air is still you also move,
But after gale winds rock and shake you,
You can stir no longer.
I yearn to be a never-ending wind – your wind.

1928

I Delight in You

I delight in you.
Your intelligence is like a deer,
Your other virtues like a lamb.
I would be gentle and attentive with the lamb
But fear the deer might needlessly take fright
So in your presence I must study silence
(A silence almost bordering on gloom).
  How could you know?

I lack everything.
I have no shiny coat or glossy feathers
Nor skill with words to clothe my feelings.
I can't wear an attentive face like some
Nor hang a smile on my lips.
Besides, my eyes have such a stupid look –
  I can't catch what's on your mind.

When someone unexpectedly mentions you
My heart trembles, I break out in a sweat.
I'm not equal to others.
It's only when the evening sky is filled with stars that I dare
To whisper your name.

1928

Fang Lingru
(1897–1976)

Fang and Lin Huiyin were the two most significant women associated with the Crescent Moon Society. Fang was born in Tongcheng, Anhui Province. When she was nineteen her family married her to the son of a prominent Nanjing family. In 1923 she went with her husband to study at Washington State University. In 1927, leaving him and taking her two daughters, she went to study at the University of Wisconsin. After returning to China in 1929 she separated from her husband. That year she began to write poetry. A year later she joined the Chinese department of Qingdao University. Her department head was Wen Yiduo, who encouraged her writing. In 1932 she had to abandon her post because of an illness which lasted more than a year. She returned to live temporarily with her husband's family in Nanjing. Here she became a literary hostess, entertaining avant-garde writers, including the famous woman novelist Ding Ling. When Ding Ling moved to Mao's base at Yan'an in 1936, the two maintained a correspondence.

After working as a government translator in Chongqing, she moved to Shanghai in 1943 to take a position at Fudan University. She joined the Communist Party in 1956 and was named secretary of the Zhejiang writers' committee. When the Cultural Revolution arrived, she was dismissed from her post and suffered persecution at the hands of Red Guards.

Fang employs the "dried bean curd" meter of Wen Yiduo and Xu Zhimo in stanzas of patterned rhyme, with lines of equal length. She later turned to the writing of *extempore* essays. This is the first appearance of her work in English.

Sailing Past Zhenjiang Pavilion

Oh, to linger here beneath Mount Jiao
And listen to the current pulsing
Like a whisper from the River-Spirit,
"How long may I ripple in your heart?"

Zhenjiang Pavilion, my soul is tethered;
My lamp, the setting sun through the elms.
River wind, upon this tranquil scene
Be still. Boatman, lower your sail.
1920

A Stone

Love, take me for a stone.
Offer me no more
The lily's tenderness,
The heat of incense,
A Yellow River of tears.

Look, that calf on the hill
Walks into a strange new world;
Don't call him callow, foolish,
He's just natural,
Preserving solemn silence.

1931

Fleeting Vision

Beneath the blue haze of stars
One night I walked the familiar mountain road
Where delicate springs trickled in the hollows of the rock,
And white dew soaked my hem and sandals.

A will o' the wisp lit up the hazel rows.
Scarlet-crowned, two tiny pythons wound ahead in anticipation,
Leading me up the cliff-face by a thousand white steps
To find the words cut in a crumbling ancient stele

Engraved in stone! At once the beloved name
Transforms itself into white doves, diving, rising nimbly.
On those small white wings ride all my hopes,
The substance of my faith and life eternal.

Full of wonder, I long to hold you fast,
O spiritual sign. You elude my grasp,
And I grope in the black night, whose stillness
Invades my heart in a cold wind.

1931

Feng Zhi
(1905–93)

Feng Zhi is the master of the sonnet form in Chinese. He was born in Zhuozhou, Hebei province, attended middle school in Beijing and entered Beijing University in 1921. One of his literature professors sent his poetry to Guo Moruo's Creation Society in Shanghai, which published twenty-seven of his poems in their journal in 1923. In 1927 he sent a copy of his first volume of poems to Lu Xun; the standard-bearer of leftist intellectuals replied with praise.

Feng spent 1930 to 1935 in Germany at Berlin and Heidelberg Universities, where he studied Nietzsche, Kierkegaard, German romantic philosophy, and the poetry of Rilke, whose sonnets were to have a deep effect on his work. He returned to China in 1936 and taught German at Tongji University in Shanghai, where he joined Bian Zhilin and Dai Wangshu in publishing the journal *New Poetry*. When the Japanese occupied Shanghai in 1937, he set off with colleagues on a trek of thousands of kilometers to Southwest United University in Kunming. Here for seven years Feng taught German and wrote the poems for which he is best known today: twenty-seven sonnets influenced by Rilke's *Sonnets to Orpheus*. Many contain oblique references to the turmoil of the war years, as in Sonnet 18's description of wayfarers trekking across unfamiliar countryside like Feng and his colleagues on their way to Kunming. When the Japanese were defeated, Feng joined the staff of Beijing University.

Feng's poetic career falls into three stages. His early work shows the young poet's search to escape the rigid classical tradition. His meter and form are flexible, his images sometimes shocking. In "Snake," the "indecorous" use of the serpent as an image for amorous desire was a drastic innovation for Chinese poetry. The sonnets represent a second phase in Feng's work; his form becomes strict, his meter regular. Each sonnet's rhyme scheme is a variant of the Italian or English sonnet pattern. Feng's metrics are a bit more flexible than Wen Yiduo's. His lines usually contain the same number of syllables, but with some variation. In the fifties he began a third phase, writing "down to earth" Marxist narratives like

"Hanpo Chops Wood," the poetic narration of a group of peasants' struggle against a landlord. Influenced by the folk narrative tradition, this poem follows Mao's 1942 dictum that poetry should be written about the masses, for the masses.

Michelle Yeh notes Feng's conviction that a poem should not require external explanation. His goal was profundity of thought and feeling without obscurity. Like a piece of sculpture or a painting, a poem's only interpretation is itself. The concrete language of his sonnets reflects his study of Goethe, who also wrote sonnets, and whose work like Feng's explored the relationship between objective phenomena and personal experience. Like the sonnets of Rilke, Feng's sonnets fuse concrete symbols with spiritual reality: "Our growing, our grieving / Become a pine on a particular mountain slope." Michelle Yeh draws our attention to Feng's notion of the meaning of a life focused in a single all-encompassing moment, as captured in the poem. The landscape viewed out a window in Sonnet 18 can "hold our forgotten past, our dim future."

"Some experiences reappear eternally in our consciousness," Goethe wrote. Yeh also points out that Feng's sonnets assume a circular development, returning again and again to the same central ideas. In German idealist philosophy, the forms of nature correspond to forms in the human psyche that structure our perception and shape our experience. Feng's sonnets become a celebration of such a concept of form. The vase in Sonnet 27 that gives shape to the water it contains is a paradigm of the forms through which we both experience the world around us and express that experience. Yeh remarks on the influence of the romantic philosophy which Feng had studied in Germany on his preoccupation with the organic unity of a poem. Without the vase, the water would be shapeless; without a formal structure, the poem's content would be inexpressible. In Sonnet 27, the banner-vane gives form to the otherwise formless wind. Feng's concern with the concept of form as integral to expression of content explains why he likes the highly structured sonnet. His sonnets treat the unity of life and poetry on the epistemological level, and at the same time treat the unity of content and form on the literary level. In Feng's work, suggests Yeh, poetry is the vase or banner-vane that structures and gives existence to fleeting, elusive experiences such as the passage of time and the metamorphoses of nature.

Feng maintained a long-term literary relationship with Lu Xun, the foremost revolutionary writer of his day. The leftist implications of Feng's sonnets might not be evident at first reading. The sonnets' theme of constant change subtly alludes to the revolutionary political change the author espoused. The banner-vane (a pennant used as a weathervane) in Sonnet 27 was a frequent communist symbol for the "historical trend" that directs the people toward the future "New China" of the revolution. The bridges between the islands of Venice in Sonnet 5 evoke the solidarity of the masses, a frequent communist motif. Such deft use of symbol permitted a leftist poet to treat revolutionary themes in a code that evaded censorship. But in Feng's sonnets such contemporary political symbolism is a single facet of a broader meaning that transcends the controversies of his age. Many of the sonnets are meditations on the ephemeral nature of temporal and spatial forms that give shape to the world and our experience of it. His focus on the vicissitudes of earthly existence reflects the displacement suffered by so many people during the war. A number of the sonnets involve the motif of journeying though unknown territory just as, fleeing the Japanese, Feng and his colleagues trekked thousands of kilometers to Southwest United University in Kunming.

Feng's notion of transformation of forms involves the poet's contradiction of what he has said previously. In the course of the artist's development, his later work negates his earlier works. The poet is like the moth and cicada in Sonnet 2, in a state of constant metamorphosis. And so Feng, like Goethe, is a poet whose meaning cannot be encapsulated within the concepts of any particular philosophical school or political movement.

The sonnets were not included in the 1955 edition of *The Selected Poems of Feng Zhi*, which focused on his revolutionary verse. They were restored in the 1980 edition, which established Feng as one of the foremost proponents of the New Poetry.

Snake

My loneliness is a snake,
Speechless, silent.
If you should see it in your dream,
Whatever you do, have no fear.

The snake is my faithful companion,
Stricken with my feverish nostalgia.
It yearns for that luxuriant meadow,
Your hair – thick, raven-black.

Soft as a shadow in the moonlight
The snake moves gently beside you,
Its fangs bearing your dream
Like a crimson flower.

1926

Sonnet 1: Deep Down We Are Preparing

Deep down we are preparing
To endure miracles we cannot foresee.
In the round of endless months and years, suddenly
A comet appears, a whirlwind rises.

At such moments in our lives,
As at a first embrace,
Past joys and sorrows coalesce before our eyes
And tower above us, solid images.

We praise those tiny insects
That survive a single copulation
Or endure a single peril

In order to consummate their wondrous lives:
Our fate lies in abiding
A sudden gale, the appearance of a comet.

1941

Sonnet 2: Whatever We Can Shed

Whatever we can shed from our bodies
We allow to turn to dust:
We make arrangements for ourselves in this life
Like trees on an autumn day, one after another

Bestowing their leaves and a few late flowers
On the autumn wind, thus stretching out their limbs at ease
Into the depths of winter. We make arrangements for ourselves
In nature, as moths and cicadas, transformed,

Abandon their shells in the mud.
We make arrangements to bestow our futures
On death, as fleeting as a song.

The body of the music sheds the song,
And what remains at the last is the music's form,
Metamorphosed into a horizon of blue, silent hills.

1941

Sonnet 4: Edelweiss[12]

Often, when I think about human life,
I can't help saying a prayer to you,
O small clump of downy grass.
You never betray your name

But shun all names
To lead a marginal, sequestered life,
Sullying neither your nobility nor your immaculate whiteness,
Silently fulfilling your destiny.

In your presence all spectacle
And tumult wither,
Or transform themselves into your stillness.

This is the great glory
You achieve by self-denial.
I pray to you for the life of humanity.

1941

12 In several different European languages, shuqucao (lit. mouse-song grass) is called edelweiss, from the German for "noble white" (author's note). The poet associates the plant with the ethos of the Daoist masters who left the world to retain their purity of soul.

Sonnet 5: Venice

Never shall I forget
That water-metropolis of the West,
Symbol of humanity,
Conclave of a hundred thousand solitudes.

All solitudes are islands
Joining together in archipelagos of friendship.
Your hand stretches out to me
Like a bridge across the water.

When you smile
A window opens
On the island opposite.

I worry only lest in the deep still of night
All the windows close
And every sign of life cease across the bridge.

1941

Sonnet 12: Du Fu[13]

You starved in a deserted village,
Constantly foreseeing your own death in a ditch,
Yet without stop you sang a lament
For a magnificent world in ruins:

On the battlefield the valiant lay wounded or dead,
A brilliant star fell to the horizon,
Ten thousand horses vanished with the fleeting clouds –
You sacrificed your whole life to their memory.

13 Du Fu (c. 712– c.770) the great Tang dynasty poet, who was sympathetic to the suffering of the common people, recorded the devastation of the An Lushan rebellion, which plunged Tang dynasty China into chaos at the time of its greatest glory.

Your poverty illuminates and gleams
Like the tattered garments of a saint.
Its smallest fragments, scattered among mankind,

Glow with the power of a deity.
Before its brightness, all crowns and pomp
Are nothing but paltry shadows.

1941

Sonnet 16: We Stand on a Lofty Mountain Peak

We stand on a lofty mountain peak,
Transforming ourselves into the boundless panorama,
Into the broad plain opening before us,
Into the footpaths that crisscross the plain.

What paths, what waterways are not connected?
What winds and clouds do not echo one another?
The cities and landscapes that we have traveled
All have merged into our lives.

Our growing, our grieving
Become a pine on a particular mountain slope,
Dense fog over a particular city.

We are blown in the wind, we are borne on the water,
We are the footpaths that crisscross the plain,
The lives of travelers on the paths.

1941

Sonnet 18: Occasionally We Have Spent an Intimate Night

Occasionally we have spent an intimate night
In a strange room. We have no way of knowing
Its appearance in the daytime,
Let alone its past, its future. Wild, open country

Stretches from our window to the horizon.
Only vaguely can we recall the road we took here
Through the twilight. That is all we know,
And we leave next morning, never to return.

Close your eyes! Let these intimate nights
And strange places weave themselves into our hearts:
Our lives are like the open country outside the window.

In those mist-filled wilds we recognize a tree,
A light glinting off a lake. That land stretching to the horizon
Hides our forgotten past, our dim future.

1941

Sonnet 26: We Tread Our Daily Path

Each day we walk the same familiar path,
Returning to where we live,
But hidden in the forest depths
Are narrow paths, strange, obscure.

To set off in new directions is alarming;
We fear we'll go so far we'll lose our way –
Until the forest thins and we gaze beyond it,
And suddenly, surprised, catch sight of home

Rising like a new island over the horizon.
How much more around us
Calls out to us for discovery!

Don't imagine that all things are familiar.
When death comes, we will touch our skin, our hair,
And wonder – whose body can this be?

1941

Sonnet 27: From a Stretch of Formless, Overflowing Water[14]

From a stretch of formless, overflowing water
The drawer of water fills his oval vase,
And a mass of water takes definite shape.
Look! The banner-vane[15] is fluttering in the autumn wind;

It holds fast what cannot be held fast.
Let something of the far-off light, the distant dark,
The glory and the withering of distant grass and trees,
And a thought that launches itself toward infinity –

Let something of these be captured in this way.
Empty, we have listened to the sound of a whole night's wind,
In vain watched a day's grass turn yellow, a day's trees red.

How shall we focus and hold our thoughts?
May these poems, like banner-vanes in the wind,
Hold something of what cannot be held.

1941

14 This is the concluding sonnet of the series.
15 Banner-vane: a banner that serves as a weather vane.

Wu Xinghua
(1921–66)

One of nine siblings, Wu was born in Tanggu, Tianjin Province. His father studied medicine in Japan, then returned to China to practice as a doctor in various cities in the Beijing-Tianjin region. At the early age of sixteen Wu enrolled in the foreign languages department of Yanjing University in Beijing, where he excelled as a student of European languages, especially English. Still in his teens, he published poems in newspapers in Beijing, Tianjin, and Shanghai. The peak period of his poetic creativity was the late thirties and early forties. He remained at his department (which had been merged into Beijing University) to become a member of the teaching staff and eventually head of the English department. In 1957, after expressing disagreement with the opinion of a visiting Soviet professor, he was branded a rightist, demoted, and banned from publishing.

When the Cultural Revolution began he was denounced again, subjected to public "struggle sessions," and put to forced labour. His health deteriorated. On 3 August 1966, while he was labouring on the university campus, Red Guards shoved his head into a ditch containing waste from a nearby chemical factory and forced him to drink. Then they pushed his face in a bucket of ink and again made him swallow. Collapsing, he was accused of faking. He was carried home and died.

Besides New Poetry, Wu wrote essays on a wide range of literary subjects, combining the critical approaches of the classical Chinese tradition and modern Western literary scholarship. His verse employs the *baihua* diction of the New Poetry, but the form of his poems is traditional. It employs the patterned stanza and rhyme found both in classical Chinese poetry and traditional Western verse. Michelle Yeh suggests another similarity of Wu's verse to classical verse: a poem addressed to an intimate beloved is a common device in classical poetry. Wu is also one of the rare New Poets who tried his hand at writing classical verse on themes from modern life. He translated several of Shakespeare's plays into Chinese, including *1 Henry IV*. The work reputed to be his masterpiece, a translation of Dante's

Divine Comedy into Chinese terza rima, remained unfinished at his death. A relatively complete collection of his verse appeared in 2005.

Wu's greatest influence as a poet has been outside the People's Republic of China. A manuscript of his work found its way to Hong Kong where his verse was published under a pseudonym and attracted the attention of a small but important group of poets both there and in Taiwan.

Red Guards chose Wu as their victim because his writing utterly ignores Communist norms. "In Dedication 1," addressed to a lover, hardly fits the socialist formula of revolutionary poetry. Wu resembles Li Jinfa and Ji Xian in his disdain for the political struggles that engrossed China in the thirties and forties. But while those two poets fled Mao's rule, Wu remained, to suffer the retribution reserved for one who ignored the regime's standards for art and culture.

In Dedication 1

Through your thick, fragrant hair, your glance
Falls on me like a white dove from who knows where;
But you gaze further, beyond what's in this room,

Beyond the window decorated with lush snow flowers,
Beyond the trees outside, the long river of horses and carriages,
Beyond the new moon and the constellations in their ranks,

Beyond the blind pond rippled by rainstorm,
Encircled by the tragic rushing wind and deer trampling the dried leaves.
As you sit here with your head bent, wrapped in silence,

Slender as a wisp of smoke without matter or substance,
Your soul unfolds, hurling itself against these walls in song.
Ah, such a beautiful shape cannot contain its fire!

You voyage off to follow the trembling melody
To the miraculous land where the light of the setting sun is buried
And innumerable poets can only melt their waxen wings.

Like a knife in my heart your milk-white hands
Melt into the piano keys. I cannot hear
The noise of the universe. All I want is to call you mine.

1945

Translated by Michel Hockx with Herbert Batt

PART THREE

Symbolists

Introduction

MICHEL HOCKX

The poets whose work is brought together in this section are among the finest to appear during the first half of the twentieth century in China. Emerging slightly later than the generation of "pioneers" and "formalists," these poets took full advantage of the efforts of their predecessors. They also borrowed quite heavily from foreign styles, but most of them were equally interested in the literary heritage offered by the Chinese tradition. They generally displayed considerably less anxiety about "nationalist" issues: they neither felt the weight of tradition as something to break away from (like the pioneers did), nor did they feel the need to establish national forms (like the formalists did). For most of these writers, poetry was an intimate endeavour, one that was highly personal and not intended for large readerships or to chime in with wider cultural or political movements. The symbolists advocated a doctrine of art for art's sake, and saw the poem as creating an imaginative cosmos unto itself, apart from the real world. It is no wonder that most of these poets flowered during the early 1930s, a brief respite in the Republican period when non-political literary writing in China enjoyed unprecedented freedom and displayed extraordinary variety.

If the formalists were largely Anglophiles, inspired by English romantic poetry, it should come as no surprise that important representatives of Chinese symbolist poetry, Li Jinfa and Dai Wangshu, were self-declared Francophiles and had spent considerable time in France. France, after all, was where the symbolist movement in poetry had flourished in the late nineteenth century with poets like Verlaine and Mallarmé. The poems of Dai Wangshu, especially, were marked by the typical symbolist attempt to hint at "correspondences" between concrete imagery and transcendental ideas. Dai's poems were written in free verse characterized by carefully orchestrated musical cadences. That is to say, they were neither as formally unfettered as the works of the "pioneers" nor as strictly prosodic as the works of the "formalists," but they carefully considered beauty of form and content, without adhering to any singular prescriptive format. They were also much more eclectic in borrowing from various cultural traditions, including the Chinese tradition. As the scholar Gregory Lee has pointed out, Dai Wangshu's most celebrated symbols and cadences, such as those in his famous poem "Rainy Lane," are indebted as much to classical Chinese poetry as they are to the work of French poets, especially Francis Jammes.[1]

In literary histories, Dai Wangshu is usually identified as a member of a group of Shanghai-based writers, many of them educated at the city's French-language Catholic university (Université l'Aurore). They founded the journal *Xiandai*, which bore the French subtitle *Les Contemporains*, and are renowned not just for symbolist poetry but also for so-called "Neo-Sensational" fiction. It was named after a similar trend in Japanese literature, which in turn claimed its origins in French writing of the 1920s and 1930s, especially in the work of Paul Morand. Not all poets represented in this section were ardent Francophiles, however, and in fact not all of them are outspoken symbolists. The Beijing-based group of friends consisting of Bian Zhilin, He Qifang, and Li Guangtian produced difficult, hermetic poetry that can appropriately be called "modernist." Whereas "modernism" is a highly elastic and overused term, these poets' works seem to me to live up to one of its strictest definitions, as provided by Douwe Fokkema and Elrud Ibsch:

> The Modernist interpretation of the world is provisional, fragmentary. The Modernists do not believe in definite explanations; they are sceptics rather than enthusiasts. They are interested in the various ways in which knowledge of the world can be worded and transmitted, but consider the actual transfer of knowledge as something of secondary importance. They detest every form of dogmatism, and instead propound their careful hypotheses.
>
> In short, they do not trust the attempts at a comprehensive description and explanation of the world which characterizes the great Realist novels of the nineteenth century. They also lack the belief in a higher, absolute truth that underpins Symbolist poetry. The Modernists present their intellectual hypotheses in arguments which some moments later they may be eager to qualify or even revoke. They emphasize the value of the intellectual consideration and reconsideration.[2]

1 Gregory Lee, *Dai Wangshu*, 140–9.
2 Douwe Fokkema and Elrud Ibsch, *Modernist Conjectures*, 4.

It is important to stop here and realize how far Chinese poetry travelled in less than twenty years, from the classical form that essentially had defined poetry in China for centuries, to a style that could be considered emblematic of twentieth-century European modernism. The idea that poetry is not meant to communicate any kind of "truth" about the world or to represent any kind of value system, and that its aim lies in putting forward deeply personal and skeptical "hypotheses" emphasizing the "fragmentary" nature of modern existence, is far removed from everything held dear by Chinese poets and poetry-lovers until the early twentieth century.

Bian Zhilin, especially, was a master at juxtaposing fragmentary images (or images of fragments) on the basis of free association (another hallmark of the modernist school), as in the opening lines from "Let the Current Take It":

> With the autumn leaves
> The street cleaner sweeps away
> The photograph of a girl.
>
> Is it the rain, or is it tears
> That blur her cheek?
> Who knows? But it reminds one
> Of the anxious look on a face one can't recall
> Glimpsed in a clouded mirror hanging in an old house.

Reflections, vistas, and different perspectives of the same fragmented scene or object also feature in Bian's most famous short poem, "Disjointed Lines":

> You stand in a pavilion gazing on the scenery,
> Someone on a balcony gazes down on you.
>
> The bright moon embellishes your window,
> You embellish someone else's dream.

As the war approached, the autonomous, apolitical stance taken by poets such as Bian Zhilin was considered less and less appropriate, especially by critics on the political left. In a foreshadowing of things to come after 1949, Bian Zhilin famously found himself forced to "explain" one of his own poems, in order to counter the charge that it was too difficult. He published an article in which he cited some of the criticism of his "obscure" poetry and then proceeded line-by-line to explain one of the criticized works. The discourse of "difficulty," another defining characteristic of modernism, soon lost most of its attraction for Chinese poets, although some, such as Ji Xian, carried it forward through the war and later to Taiwan, where it was to have a profound impact on debates about poetry in the 1950s.

Li Jinfa
(1900–76)

Published by the Literary Research Association in three successive years in the mid-1920s, Li Jinfa's three books of poetry startled and shocked Chinese readers. Then, just as suddenly as he appeared on the literary scene, he vanished.

Li Jinfa is the pen name of Li Yu'an, a native of Mei county in Guangdong province, south China. Li attended an English-language high school in Hong Kong, then at age nineteen entered a French-language academy in Shanghai to prepare for study in France. He arrived there in 1921 to study chemistry and aeronautical design. His choice of the pen name Li Jinfa ("Golden-haired Li") was inspired by a dream of a golden-haired angel who appeared to him when he was suffering from a fever in Paris. When a teacher suggested he study at a sculptor's studio, he readily agreed. In 1922 he went to study sculpture in Berlin, where he completed the first two volumes of his strikingly surrealistic poetry.

In 1925 he returned to Shanghai where he set himself up as a Western-style sculptor, one of China's first. After trying unsuccessfully to attract sculpture students, he served briefly as professor of literature at Zhongshan University in Wuhan, then moved to Hangzhou in 1928, where he taught sculpture for four years at the Hangzhou College of Fine Arts. In 1932 he moved to Guangzhou, where he began work casting a series of bronze statues of Chiang Kai-shek. By now his sculpture was thoroughly traditional in style, and his poetic output was reduced to the occasional poem.

When the Japanese occupied Guangzhou in 1941 he moved to Vietnam, where he worked for a Chinese import-export company in Haiphong. When the Japanese cut off trade between China and Vietnam, he made his way to the Guomindang capital, Chongqing, where he worked for the foreign ministry's European Affairs Department and wrote simple poems in plain imagery to support the war effort. In 1945 he was assigned as secretary to the Guomindang ambassador in Iran and wrote books introducing Chinese readers to modern British and Persian Literature. In June 1946 he was transferred to Baghdad.

Unwilling to live in a China under Communist rule, he emigrated to the United States in 1951. Here he wrote a novel which was published in the People's Republic of China. In 1960 he moved to New York City, eventually settling on Long Island. He retired from sculpture in 1971 and died on Christmas Day, 1976. Besides poetry and literary essays, Li also published a number of books on the visual arts, including *Michelangelo the Sculptor* (1928).

There is no evidence that Li had any connection with any of the associations dedicated to the New Poetry. His poems were completely unlike anything else in the early years of *baihua* verse. At the time he published them, there was no symbolist school among Chinese poets. His books drew waves of negative criticism. Bian Zhilin said he lacked a feel for the Chinese language and critics have since had trouble classifying Li's style. He is sometimes called China's first symbolist; more precisely, he is her first surrealist. Li's radical use of symbol exerted limited influence on the poets who came after him. He appears at the start of this section simply because historically he came first.

Surrealism explores the irrational. In the words of André Breton, the surrealist movement of Paris in the twenties sought to "express ... the actual functioning of thought ... in the absence of any control exercised by reason." The surrealist poem dislocates its imagery from all realistic context. The poet uses symbolic language to create a world outside ordinary human experience, fraught with mystery.

Li wrote that the purpose of his poems was to encourage sexual freedom in his conservative homeland. He claimed that his disjointed syntax, illogical thought, and bizarre imagery were intended to contribute to that end. The communist poet Ai Qing described the world of Li's poems as café society, populated with beautiful women in red shoes, redolent of perfume, the artificial paradise of decadent *fin de siècle* Paris. Li called his poems "a young man's literary toys," a remark that echoes the playfulness of French surrealist poet André Breton. His reader's first challenge is to figure out how the surrealist metaphors apply to their referents. To interpret Li's poem as a whole, the reader must seek a coherent pattern in a welter of irrational images. What connects these images? What do "spurts of fresh blood" have to do with the cast-off woman's facial expression? "Casting Her Aside" consists of a series of images that portray the rejected woman's emotions – from wild grief to anxiety to withdrawal to cold, silent dejection – as the man who rejects her watches her face through the curtain of her hair. Li's poems are rendered still more obscure by his occasional irony. Surrealism, as Breton proposed, disregards moral concerns. In "Casting Her Aside," the narrator's reference to his "pure ears" and his withdrawal in company with the "spirit of God" are hard to take seriously in light of the suffering he has caused the woman he abandons. The masochistic undertone in the narrator's cold, detached account of the woman's anguish recalls the Marquis de Sade's influence on the surrealist movement.

The influence of Baudelaire can be seen in Li's preoccupation with the voluptuous, with art for art's sake, erotic longings, and the lure of forbidden pleasure. The French poet's influence appears too in Li's nihilism: in the closing lines of "Cherished Desires," the narrator characterizes the paradise of his passion as an illusion, without forsaking it. Such subject matter, conveyed in such arcane imagery, was highly distasteful to Marxist critics, who characterized Li as decadent if they bothered to mention him at all. Li's work was deliberately ignored during the Mao era. Old guard Communist critics view his resurgence among young readers with bafflement and a certain degree of indignation.

Casting Her Aside

Slowly spreading out her hair to avoid my eyes,
Fending off, one by one, my reproachful glances,
And spurts of fresh blood, and the sleep of dry bones.
Without hurry, night and mosquitoes approach in step,
Surmount the corner of the courtyard wall.
My pure ears hear a mad cry behind me
Like the raging howl of wind in the wilderness;
Countless nomads tremble.

Lean on a blade of grass; withdraw to an empty valley with the spirit
  of God.
Even my distressed wasp-brain can register a deep impression:
The long pour of a mountain spring down a precipice,
Then all is gone with the red leaves.

Anxieties weigh down the abandoned woman, crippling her gestures;
The fire of the setting sun cannot burn doubt
To ashes, to spew them out a chimney

To sully the feathers of the first crow
Alighting with the flock on the crags,
Listening to the boatman's song amid the sea's roar.

A wail rises; a shabby gown
Wanders listlessly beside the grave,
With never a hot tear
Dripping on the grass
To adorn the earth.

1925

Cherished Desires

If only the palm of your hand
Were a boat
On which I could sail distant seas to ancient ruins
Until the slight bending of your arm
Drew me back to your heart's chamber!

O, if I could voyage in your eyes
Searching for the self-abandon of a poet's love,
A smile rising like a fierce wind through a forest,
The counterpoint of evening sun and reddening cloud!
Crisp night air
Brings the chirp of crickets in the autumn twilight,
Yet you bring me nothing but tears.

O, if only your curls were clusters of magnolia,
And I could slumber in peace among them!
Faintly humming my dream, the bee returns from wandering.
The bronze wine-cup
Bears the imprint of our lips,
But the love-ecstasy of springtime
Passes quick as a drunkard's elation.

c. 1927

Yao Pengzi
(1891–1969)

Yao Pengzi's verse remained under an unofficial ban for almost two decades after the end of the Cultural Revolution. The reason for this ban has less to do with the author himself than his son, Yao Wenyuan, one of the Gang of Four. Yao the son served as the cultural czar of China during the Cultural Revolution, Chairman Mao's literary hatchet-man. Under his aegis many writers in this volume were persecuted and at least two, Li Guangtian and Wu Xinghua, were murdered.

Yao Pengzi was born in Zhuji county, Zhejiang Province. The surrealist imagery of his volume *The Silver Bell* (Shanghai, 1929) distinguished him as a symbolist of the school of Li Jinfa. In 1930 he joined the League of Leftist Writers in Shanghai. In 1934 Yao was jailed by the Guomindang government and forced temporarily to renounce his Communist party membership. In 1938 he fled the Japanese occupation to Chongqing, the wartime Guomindang capital, where he edited the *War of Resistance Literary and Art Review* together with the famous novelist Lao She.

Yao's surrealist poetry bears the mark of Li Jinfa's influence. "Your Face" plays on a latent misogynistic undercurrent in Li's work.

Your Face

On your face I catch the scent of rotting leaves,
The odour of brick from a ruined sarcophagus,
Of dead snake and stagnant pond,
Of a rainy day at dusk;
In every kiss of your blood-red lips
I taste whiskey's bitter tang,
Smell the thorny rose, the scent of honeyed arsenic,
The savour of flawed love.

Every whiff of your face, every kiss of your lips
Exhausts half my springtime.

1929

Lin Huiyin
(1904–55)

Lin Huiyin was born in Hangzhou. Her father was a graduate of Japan's eminent Waseda University who served in the senate, courts, and diplomatic service of the Guomindang government. He was an advocate of women's education and began his daughter's schooling when she was four. In 1916 she enrolled in a British-run secondary school where she became fluent in English. At sixteen she accompanied her father to England, where she enrolled in St Mary's College, Cambridge. Here began her lifelong interest in architecture. In Cambridge she met Xu Zhimo, who proposed marriage. Her father disapproved of their attachment; Xu's wife was living in London. He took his daughter back to China where she became engaged to Liang Sicheng, son of prominent reformer Liang Qichao. Xu Zhimo's poems "Coincidence" and "Go" reputedly represent his poetic farewell to Lin Huiyin. Her "Do Not Forget" could be read as a reply to "Coincidence," repeating as it does Xu's image of passing ships.

In 1924 Lin accompanied her fiancé to America. Because the University of Pennsylvania architecture department did not admit women, she had to enroll instead in the fine arts department and attend architecture classes as an external student. After graduation, she studied set design at the Yale School of Drama. Lin and Liang married in Canada, then returned to China in 1928. Lin Huiyin is recognized as China's first female architect. During the 1930s, while she was raising a family, she designed buildings and traveled throughout China to study ancient monuments for a history of Chinese architecture which she and her husband coauthored.

The high-water mark of her poetic production was 1931, when she wrote poetry and stream-of-consciousness short stories while recovering from tuberculosis in a sanitarium in the Fragrant Hills, west of Beijing. When the Japanese occupied Beijing in 1937 she and her husband left the city and lived a nomadic existence until they eventually settled in Kunming. Harsh living conditions exacerbated her lung condition. In 1946 they returned to Beijing, where Lin took up a post at Qinghua University. Here she continued to work after the Communist takeover and helped to design the emblem which appears on the Chinese flag. She died of her lung condition in 1955.

Writing was not Lin's regular profession. She sometimes set aside completed poems without publishing them; manuscripts were lost in the years when she moved about during the Japanese occupation. An anthology of her verse finally appeared in 1985.

Some of her poems appeared in the *Crescent Moon Journal* founded by Xu Zhimo, but unlike most of the journal's other contributors, Lin pays little attention to formal structure. She employs a flexible pattern of meter and rhyme. Lin conceived of poetry as the expression of an uncanny process of association that captures the fleeting union of the subjective with the objective. In a single object appears an implicit principle of deeper unity present in all nature: the girl's expression in "Smile" encompasses natural forces of clouds and sea. This unitary principle which the poet captures is not unlike the Confucian concept of *qi*.

A Smile

What is smiling? Her eyes, her lips,
Their deep corners,
Delicate as dew.
The smile hides in these flashes of mother of pearl –
An incomparable smile,
The smile of a goddess –
The reflection of water, the quiet song of the wind.
What is smiling? Her hair in drowsy curls,
Falling around the ears,
Soft as a flower's shadow –
They smile too.
A warm shudder, sweet as honey,
Flows into your heart.
This is the smile of a portrait, the smile of a poem,
A wisp of cloud, a swell of wave.

1931

Do Not Forget

Do not forget
this fleeting closeness
like the comforting recognition of passing ships in the night.
Now the moment flows away like water,
swiftly, quietly,
like the distant cold of a mountain spring,
bubbling in a grove of pines at night –
vague as a sigh.
Remember the moment truly, as it is,
as in the night sky you would remember
the brilliance of the moon amid the stars,
though all is hidden behind a mountain –
unchanging,
invisible,
hanging dreamlike.

Call back from the night
that single phrase.
And stay to hear
its echo from the unseen valley.

1936

Fei Ming
(1901–67)

Fei Ming (literally "without a name") was the pen name of Feng Wenbing, a writer known during his lifetime for fiction rather than poetry. He was born in Huangmei, Hubei province, a town noted for its Buddhist culture. Fei Ming graduated from a local normal school in 1916, then went to Wuhan to study in Hubei Province Normal Institute. The May Fourth movement of 1919 sparked his interest in the new literature.

In 1924 he enrolled in Beijing University's English department where he read Shakespeare as well as Chekhov, whose realism influenced his fiction. For six months during a student strike in 1927 he studied Buddhism and Confucianism, subjects which were to mark his work. He began to receive notice for his short stories, which deal with the local folk customs and Buddhist culture of his home town. His narratives evince the "ordinary" and the "natural," as advocated by the prominent critic Zhou Zuoren (1885–1967). Upon graduation in 1929 he became a lecturer at Beijing University. After 1932 he turned his attention to social issues and stopped writing fiction, but continued writing the occasional poem, sometimes no more than one a year. They appeared in a variety of minor journals. No definitive collection of his verse has yet appeared.

In 1939 Fei Ming fled the Japanese occupation of Beijing to return to his home town, where he lived in straightened circumstances. He returned to Beijing University in 1946 to teach in the department of foreign languages and literature. In 1952 he moved to Changchun in northeast China, where he would become chairman of Jilin University's Chinese department. He also held various political posts, including a seat in the provincial legislature. Fei Ming died of cancer in 1967.

Michelle Yeh treats Fei Ming's "Street Corner" as a primary example of the difference between classical and modern Chinese poetry. In this poem the objects – the automobile, the post box – are recent technological innovations from the West. Autos were still relatively rare in China in 1937, when the poem was written. The speed with which the car vanishes embodies the rapid transformation of China by Western technology. Classical poetry plays on the inherent bond between human feelings and nature. It uses symbols from the natural world to express emotion. By contrast, Fei Ming's narrator stands isolated in his technological surroundings. The loneliness in this poem stems from the narrator's bewilderment at the changes of the modern world.

Yeh further observes the absence in Fei Ming of any formal conventions whether of rhyme, rhythm, or traditional imagery, implying a new notion of poetry. The reader of classical poetry is called upon to recognize conventional motifs that unify the poem; in "Street Corner" there is no such unity. The transition from line one to line two is introduced by the word "thus," but the implied logical connection is unclear. The reader of a modern poem like Fei Ming's must supply those connectives. The reader is thereby drawn into the creative process in a way that is unknown to classical Chinese poetry.

Fei Ming rejected any notion of a special poetic language. He advocated verse written in the diction and syntax of the *extempore* prose essay, free in expression. Taken individually, the details of Fei Ming's poems are "natural" and "ordinary," as they are in his stories: a woman's dressing table, a tree beside a pond, a passing car. But their effect is far from natural. Why, for example, should the gardener want to take "A Pot of Flowers" into his grave? Could this be a reference to some Buddhist folk custom such as Fei Ming described in his fiction? There is no explanation.

Yeh cautions the reader against the notion that Fei Ming imports Western poetics into Chinese. Although he studied English literature in university and was familiar with Shakespeare and *Don Quixote*, he relied for his notions of poetry exclusively on the traditions of Chinese classical verse. His writings on poetry display little interest in Western poetics. "If the New Poetry today is to establish itself," he wrote, "it must be a kind of Chinese poetry." A practitioner of Zen meditation, he was influenced by Buddhist and Daoist teachings. "Some people say my writing is obscure, that they can't understand what I mean," he wrote. The poem, Fei Ming said, should maintain a distance between poet and reader. "My intention is to set forth my state of mind gradually. I am even suspicious of the horror that lies in being too clear." His poetry represents one of the first examples of a studied synergy of Eastern anti-rationalism and Western anti-rationalism, blending the mysterious symbolism of Mallarmé with that of Daoism and Buddhism.

Bian Zhilin calls Fei Ming's verse free association, as distinct from stream of consciousness. Bian notes that this same kind of free association can be found both in modern Western poetry and in Chinese classical poets like the Tang Dynasty poet Li He. In Fei Ming we encounter, as in the symbolists Lin Geng and Bian Zhilin, the traditional Chinese notion that to express reality too distinctly is to fail to express it at all. Fei Ming's horror of the too-explicit echoes the dicta of the *Dao de Jing* that "The five (basic) colours make one blind, the five (basic) tones make one deaf."

The crux of Fei Ming's verse lies in the tension between the craving to verbalize the real and the impossibility of verbalizing it. His work anticipates Bei Dao and the calculated obscurity of the "Obscure Poets" who appeared the late 1980s and nineties.

from *Assorted Poems*

1

A noise from the street:
The voice of my father, calling my baby-name, then silence.

3

As I sit reading
I hear from the street the blind beggar's cry
Then the laugh of my friend mimicking him.

1923

The Dressing Table

I dreamed that I was a mirror:

So even under the sea, he still would be a mirror
That a young woman picks up

And sets on her dressing table.
Since she makes herself beautiful here
No sorrow is allowed.

1931

A Pot of Flowers

The spring grass has sprouted beside the pond,
And a tree on its bank
Says, "Once I was a seed."
"We are all of one life," says the grass.
Then the gardener who planted the tree comes by.
"How tall you have grown,"
He says to the tree.
And then, "Will I be buried here?"
As though, perhaps, he wanted to take a pot of flowers
Into his grave with him.

1931

Street Corner

Walked to the corner;
A car sped past.
Thus the desolation of the postbox,
And the emptiness of forgetting the X on the license plate,
And the loneliness of Arabic numerals.
The car is desolate,
And the street,
And all humanity.

1937

He Qifang
(1912–77)

He Qifang was a protean poet. More than once in the course of his career he remade himself, changing style, content, audience, and political affiliation, from romantic symbolist to social realist to Communist. His response to the political vicissitudes of his age have made him a controversial figure in Chinese literary history.

The author was born to a wealthy landlord family in Wan county, Sichuan province, a region beset by political turmoil during his childhood. Bonnie McDougall suggests that his childhood experience of the violent clashes between warlords inspired him with an early loathing of politics. After receiving a classical education at home, he enrolled at the age of fourteen in a modern curriculum school in Shanghai, where he encountered the poetry of the French symbolists. In 1930 he entered the foreign literature department of Beijing's Qinghua University. "Night Scene (i)" describes Tiananmen Square with a bleakness and desolation redolent of T.S. Eliot. Poems like "To a Friend at the End of the Year" contrast the northern China landscape of the Beijing region with the southern landscape of his Sichuan home.

In 1931 he switched to Beijing University, where he enrolled in the department of philosophy. His purpose, he later wrote, was to understand Western philosophical idealism, which he then believed to be the foundation of Western culture. But the dryness of Kant repelled him. In retrospect he was to describe himself as a student sitting in philosophy class staring out the window at the sunlight falling on the trees and grass.

In 1934 He Qifang published a volume of verse, *Prophecy*. His first poems were written in patterned rhyme modeled on the poetry of Xu Zhimo and Wen Yiduo, his early mentors. Some poems like "Autumn" have a balanced stanza structure as in the poems of Xu and Wen. The young author also joined fellow students Li Guangtian and Bian Zhilin in publishing a volume of poetry, *The Han Garden*, in 1936. During his years at Beijing University the Japanese took control of Beijing, but his poems of this period give no hint of the historical circumstances in which they were written. Rather, as McDougall suggests, he enclosed himself in a world of literary beauty, sealed off from China's political troubles. At this time he described himself as an individualist.

After graduation in 1935 he took a job teaching in a secondary school in Tianjin. The following spring the Japanese took control of this city too. He would later record his dismay at their occupation in "North China Is Ablaze." The poem gives voice to his indignation at the Japanese creation of an "autonomous region" out of their newly conquered territories in north China. He soon moved to teach in Shandong province.

The Japanese forces swept southward in 1937. The full implication of the occupation now struck He Qifang with all its force. He could no longer isolate himself from the political crisis. He had come to think that poetry "must have its roots deeply planted in the world of men" and professed the belief that whoever refused to renounce individualism had only one course left to preserve his integrity: suicide. The poet's duty was to "flog the back of the unjust society." He maintained his use of symbols, but abandoned the exquisite style for simple diction to exhort the public to action. In August, 1938 he moved to Mao's base at Yan'an.

Here in the remote Northwest He Qifang joined the Communist Party and did his best to turn his back on the world of imagination and feeling as he had depicted it in Western-style poems such as "Prophecy." During 1938–39 he visited Communist guerilla units as a reporter. He participated in the 1942 "Talks on Literature and Art at Yan'an," where Mao set forth the manifesto that the role of the arts was to serve the Communist political agenda in works addressed to soldiers and peasants. He Qifang developed a concrete, colloquial style aimed at a broader, less sophisticated audience. When the Communists took power in 1949, his diction had come to reflect the party's vocabulary and his content to echo the party's agenda. During the anti-rightist campaign he attacked fellow Communist writers like Feng Xuefeng, who took the liberty to deviate from Mao's line.

He Qifang's earliest published poetry appeared in Xu Zhimo's *Crescent Moon Journal*. Although he did not employ such strict metrical patterns and rhyme schemes as those advocated by Xu, his early poems nevertheless tended to have regular metrics with equal numbers of syllables in each line. He also published some of his early poems in Dai Wangshu's *Modernist Journal*. Like Dai, he at first admired and imitated the French symbolists. He Qifang's early verse shows the influence of Baudelaire both in its use of symbol and its love-melancholy. Like Bian Zhilin's, his verse is structured by a flow of images, often evoking the world of the unconscious. In "Cypress Grove," he espouses poetry as "paths through dreams." His early work is deeply evocative of the melancholy mood of the poetry of Paul Verlaine and its lonely, abandoned narrator recalls Verlaine's narrator.

Works like "Cypress Grove" also reflect his close reading of the English romantics. His longing to escape from the painful world of reality into the realm of the imagination shows the influence of Keats. The author's "Autumn" is reminiscent of Keats's great ode on the same theme. Michelle Yeh points out that the impact of "Autumn" arises from the order in which the images appear, invoking autumn's passing phases just as Keats's poem does. "A Prophecy" is reminiscent of Keats's dense, evocative imagery. As McDougall and Louie point out, the prophecy is the poem's symbolic foretelling of the passing of youth's spirit of eager expectancy: the god of youth visits the narrator fleetingly, then vanishes.

With his espousal of communism, He Qifang abandoned Keatsian aestheticism for concise poetry written in simple language accessible to the ordinary reader. His transformation is already under way in a poem like "Night Scene (i)," with its laconic, concrete description of Beijing after dark. The focus of this poem is the experience of simple workmen. The author formally announces his poetic metamorphosis in "The Clouds," a reply to a prose poem of Baudelaire of the same title: the narrator abjures the dreamy escapism of staring up into the clouds in favour of the clear-cut, down to earth theme of "honest peasants."

But though he proclaims his rejection of Baudelaire, the poems of his Yan'an phase still echo the French symbolist master. The "City" section of "North China Is Ablaze" employs Baudelaire's phantasmagoric imagery to portray the Chinese city as a nest of oppression and misery, the counterpart of the healthy, vital countryside under Communist control. The conclusion of "City" evokes "far, far off" Yan'an, where under Communist leadership the people arise to resist the Japanese. The aura of the countryside as the milieu of healthy, natural humanity recalls the early English romantic poets.

Symbolic details evocative of Baudelaire persist in "Our History Is Rushing Forward," even as He Qifang condemns the French poet's erotic subject matter. In the first section of this poem he narrates the tragedy of his aunt, an epitome of the sufferings of women in imperial Chinese society. The poem is written in simple diction without ornate poetic devices, addressed to an audience of unsophisticated girls. The damning portrait of sexual depravation in his aunt's bourgeois husband displays a concern for innocence and moral integrity that He Qifang associated with the Communist movement, an integrity that he believed to be an antidote to the sexual profligacy of those decadent cities he had left behind.

During the late forties, He Qifang intermittently served as Mao's chief of propaganda and as editor of *New China Daily*. Unlike most writers in this collection, He Qifang kept publishing during the Mao era. He wrote poetry in support of the Communist land-reform movement and verse celebrating the founding of the People's Republic of China. His 1954 poem "Reply" was criticized because it was "demoralizing"; i.e. it lacked enthusiasm for the Party's current policy. From then on, the poetry he wrote was in support of political campaigns like the Great Leap Forward. He turned to literary theory, becoming an authoritative advocate of the revolutionary line in public debates on the arts. After suffering persecution during the early stages of the Cultural Revolution, he began to write in its support, producing such lines as, "Don't let the countryside be lured onto the capitalist road!" When the Cultural Revolution sputtered out and the Gang of Four had fallen, He Qifang reversed course again and wrote equally prosaic poems denouncing them. This undeniably great poet's support of the Cultural Revolution represents an embarrassment to the contemporary Communist literary establishment, who refer to "the He Qifang phenomenon" in speaking of writers who published in support of the Gang of Four's draconian policies. The political vacillations of his later writing are a controversial aspect of the lifelong process of metamorphosis that marked He Qifang's poetic career.

The author's legacy has benefitted from translation into English by Bonnie McDougall. Her collection *Paths in Dreams*, an anthology of his poems and prose pieces written up to the year 1942, conveys the development of his early style and thought. McDougall's introduction situates He Qifang's early career within the context of the political and social upheavals of his age.

To a Friend at the End of the Year

When dry yellow pine-cones fall
And the wings of birds whirr past, flying low,
You halt your solitary steps in the woods;
The water grows cold, the fish hide,
Your lonely fishing-line floats on the pond,
And the white mist of winter blocks your window.

Long secluded in your illness,
Do you still recall your old home in the north?
In the shadows on the wall
And the cane chair in the corner
My worries often found a refuge.
In those days I had worries often,
And you provided a comforting silence.
Twitching its gray legs, a lizard often clung
To the cold, tattered window-gauze.
Outside in the courtyard
The dull, lonely beat of the woodpecker
Tapped, tapped through dense branches of the scholar tree.
You asked me if I liked the sound.
If you were to ask me now I'd certainly say I like it.

A train of camels shed their fur in the west wind;
They lift their feet
And tread softly.
Already the street wears a white coat of frost.

1931

Autumn

The shudder of falling timber shakes down
The morning dew that drapes the secluded glade.
Lay down the sickle, fragrant with rice stalks,
Cram shoulder-baskets with plump melons and hedgerow fruits!
Autumn is perching on the peasant's hut.

Cast round, round nets over the chill mist on the river
To catch shadows of cypress leaves, blue as bream!
White frost coats the reed canopy of the boat
That rocks with the dip of oars rowing homeward.
Autumn sports on the fisherman's deck.

At a cricket's chirp the meadow grows wider.
Boulders rise in the drying creek, its waters cooler, clearer.
Where is the lilt of the herd-boy's bamboo flute
That stirred the warm scent of summer night?
Autumn is dreaming in the shepherd girl's eyes.

1931

Beneath the Moon

This night must be a dream – all silver
Like a white dove spreading its wings as it bathes,
Like a white lotus-petal falling into its shadow on the water,
Like the autumnal sound of the leaves of the parasol tree
Fluttering down on the roof-tiles like shards of stained glass.
But, O charming eyebrows, are there such waves of moonlight where
 you live?
If there are, I am afraid they must be frozen into exquisite cold.
Can a dream free as a boat running before the wind
Sail into a frozen night?

1931

Cypress Grove

The sun is shining on the broad leaves of the castor oil tree,
The two-mile bees have built their hive in the temple of the village god,
And here am I, running around with my shadow
In an enormous circle back to where I started,
Realizing that time has quietly stood still.
Where are the tiny hands
That reached in the grass for the chirp of the cricket?
Where are my childhood playmates' happy cries
That rose straight to the tree-top blue sky?
This vast kingdom of childhood beneath my feet –
Soiled now with the mud of strangers –
Seems pathetically tiny.

The desert traveler prizes the far-off oasis.
The boatman broods over distant whitecaps.
I used to think that I had found paradise and hidden it
In a secret corner of my memory.
But now I know an adult's loneliness
And treasure more than ever mazy paths through dreams.

1933

A Prophecy

Finally it has come – the heart-throbbing day!
I hear your footsteps slowly coming closer
Like a sigh in the night, and I know them
Better than the night wind's secret whisper to the leaves.
Tell me, in your silver bell of a voice, O tell me –
Are you not the young god in the prophecy?

Surely you have come from the fragrant, luxuriant South.
Tell me of its moonlight, of its sunshine.
Tell me of its breeze that blows spring blossoms into bloom,
How its swallows are madly in love with the green willows.
I close my eyes to fall asleep hearing your dreamlike song.
I seem to remember a balmy fragrance – and seem to forget.

Stop, stop your headlong course, and enter.
Sit down upon this pallet covered in tiger skins.
I will kindle the leaves I heap up every autumn.
Listen to a song I made up, sung in a low, low voice,
Its sound now calming the flames, now fanning them
As they narrate the life of the leaves that they devour.

Do not press on. Endless forests lie ahead.
Striped beasts stalk among the ancient trees,
And snakelike vines, half alive, lie intertwined
Where no star can penetrate the clustered leaves.
Dismayed by the lonely echo of your footsteps,
You'll dare to tread no further.

Must you go on? Then wait, I'll go with you.
My feet know all the safest paths,
And I will sing my eternal song of weary oblivion,
Giving you my tender hand.
And if the night's dense dark separates us
Your eyes can stay fixed on mine.

But you do not listen to my impassioned song.
For all my trembling, your feet do not pause.
Like a solemn breeze passing through the night,
They vanish, your proud footsteps vanish!
Is this what was prophesied? Wordlessly do you come,
And wordlessly go, young god?

1933–35

Night Scene (i)

The night sounds of the city have receded
Like tides withdrawing down the sands.
Beneath each ash-gray roof
Souls are peacefully asleep.

A last old horsecart rumbles by.

Outside the palace gate, a labourer
Is resting, his pillow a cold stone slab.
At midnight he wakes up his companion with a kick:
He has heard weeping,
Now near, now distant,
Behind the massive gate of the abandoned palace,
From the tower whose roof is shrouded in roosting crows.
Still more strange is the reply:
Once at dusk his work-mate saw
One of the stone lions shedding tears.

Far off the softly sighing night wind
Rustles the withered grass, rooted atop the fortress wall.

1933–35

The Clouds

"I love the clouds, the fleeting clouds ..."
The clouds I saw were Baudelaire's,
The melancholy wanderer craning his neck
To gaze up at the sky.

I walked into the countryside.
Honest peasants had lost their land,
A few tools were all they owned.
By day they roamed the fields searching out odd jobs.
By night their bed was dry earth under a bridge.

I went to the great seaside metropolis.
Rows of foreign villas
Lined its asphalt roads in winter
Like whores on a street corner
Waiting for summer revelry,
Brazen and crude as their fat-bellied businessmen.

Now I make this off-hand remark:
I prefer a thatched roof.
I do not love the clouds, the moon,
I don't care for the stars.

Published 1945

Our History Is Rushing Forward (i)

Dear sisters,
Young sisters,
Our history is rushing forward,
Look how fast!

You study Marx and Lenin,
You study Party history.
Soon you will all be party cadres,
But you are so much like little girls!
Before you go to sleep at night
You take turns telling stories
And always come to an ancient one.

You would like me to tell a story too.
All right, I will tell an ancient story,
The story of my aunt.

My aunt was an Ophelia.
She went mad.
Ophelia, the mad girl who loved Hamlet
Climbed into a willow on the river bank,
Its silver leaves reflected on the water,
And fell in.
My aunt used to linger behind our ancient family home,
Singing a mad woman's song
Whose meaning only she could understand,
Swinging on the squeaking gate.

Inside the back gate was the room where we ate.
The wall crawled with mosquitoes.
I used to like to swat them
With the palm of my little hand.
Outside were a bamboo grove, an open sewer, and a well.
The grapevine bore tiny grapes.
The green plum tree bore sour plums.
My aunt was a quiet, peaceable person

With the sort of mild, placid smile
That good-natured people have.
My grandfather married her
To the son of a merchant in town
Because his family had wealth
And owned many shops.

When her husband came to our house in the country
In shiny silk clothes,
Smoking a cigarette
And humming a vulgar song from town,
Everything about him
Clashed with our ancient home.

Soon after they married my aunt went mad,
And with hands bound
She was borne back to our family
Shut inside a sedan-chair.
I did not understand what had happened.
All the grownups would say
Was that her mother-in-law was his stepmother.

And so I had a madwoman for an aunt.

After she was cured
She was borne back to her husband's home.
When I went to town to see her
She was a quiet, peaceable person again
With a mild, placid smile.

Years passed and she bore no children.
Her husband married a prostitute.

Finally she died young
Of a strange disease.

My mother said it was a deadly ulcer
That rotted through her whole body,

An incurable festering.
My mother would not speak its name,
But only heave a helpless, tragic sigh.

Only when I moved to the city
And began reading in the library
Did I discover
In a foreign book by Dr Robinson,
Sexual Knowledge,
The name of the impure disease
That infected my pure aunt.

1940

North China Is Ablaze (iv): Cities

Ah, Metropolis, you monster!
You black spider
Spinning your web everywhere,
Sucking your victims' blood,
Gorging your belly with crowds of starving people.

Wartime boom. Roller coaster boom.
Concrete bank buildings rise into the clouds.
Refugee motor cars from Shanghai, from Nanjing,
Rush, flaunting their power just as before,
Down the steep streets of mountain-city Chongqing.[3]

People. People pulling people. People carrying people.
Still more people hurrying through the streets.
Who knows what thoughts whirl through their heads?
Who laughs, elated with triumph?
Who gasps, scurrying day and night just to keep alive?

3 The cars are those of wealthy refugees who have fled inland to Chongqing from Nanjing and Shanghai after these two cities were captured by the Japanese in the autumn of 1937.

Gloomy nights in gloomy hotels.
Through the presiding clack of mahjong tiles
Sounds the summons, "Waiter, waiter!"
And the cries of peddlers, "Melon seeds! Cigarettes!"
A waiter comes to a bachelor's room to ask, "Sir,
Want a girl? Clean. Thirty dollars for the night."
I breathe the stench of a garbage dump
While people crawl about in the refuse searching for food.

Evening paper! Evening paper! Report of the fall of Wuhan![4]
The news makes me tremble. Men and women, young and old,
Crowd the sidewalk for the papers so that no one can squeeze past:
Red flashes in the black of night,
The crack of wooden houses blown apart,
The roar of stone houses exploding …
Meanwhile life goes on here as usual,
Morning till dusk, evening till dawn.

How sick I am of it all!
Of all the cities I have lived in!
My memory of them is a perfect circle
And my present is its center, equally distant from every point in my past.

Beijing. I lived there for years and never learned to like it,
Their polite form for "You," their peculiar word for "Bye."
Kneeling to an official you meet in the lane.
Phone calls dragging on with greetings for all your relatives.
The famous Three Lakes Park,
The Eight Great Lanes red light district,
The New Year's Fair,
The newly sprung-up dance halls and the billiard saloons with
  their hostesses.
Nobody finds it strange that such things exist,
While I felt like the whole city was collapsing, crumbling to the ground,
Its inhabitants about to be buried alive
And I among them, no different from the rest.

4 After occupying Shanghai and Nanjing, the Japanese moved further up the Yangzi River to capture Wuhan in early 1938.

A professor who didn't know
Until he went to lecture to the countryside
That the common people do not eat white steamed buns
But millet gruel.
How meaningless my days were!
Days of grotesque dreams –
I stood on a platform, the whole city at my feet.
A streetcar rushed through the streets shooting sparks.
I said, "Something is bound to happen."
But I lost hope. "Nothing is happening."
Suddenly a whirlwind arose and blew me awake –
Ah, cannon fire! From North Gardens, South Gardens, the thunder
of cannons.[5]
Roar then, roar! Only you can shake this dead city!

Tianjin. The stinking Qiangzi River, the infamous Sanbuguan Market.
When you ride through there on a rickshaw, they said, keep hold of
your hat
Or somebody will snatch it off your head.
Black smoke from factory chimneys blots out the sky.
Factory girls flow through the streets at dusk like fragments of a sunken
ship.
Japanese toughs piss against the gate of the city council.
Half-dead heroin addicts present a petition for an "East Hebei
Autonomous Region."[6]
I want to drive away these gray memories
Like a swarm of flies –
Every night I sat in a rattan chair under an electric bulb
Listening to an intellectual just like me sighing,
"Another five years as junior staff,
Just five more years, and we'll be destroyed altogether."

5 A reference to the Marco Polo Bridge incident on 7 July 1937, the start of Japan's invasion of central and south China.

6 The East Hebei Autonomous Region was a puppet state created by the Japanese in 1935 in the eastern portion of Hebei province, east of Beijing. As the poem describes the scene, Japanese authorities have suborned Chinese heroin-addicts to stage a demonstration in order to create the appearance that the Chinese population "demands" that the local Chinese administration secede from the Chinese government's control, to create a Japanese-controlled "autonomous" puppet state.

A bachelor colleague, like he's offering me a drink,
Asks, "What's the matter with you,
Why don't you find yourself a lover?"

How it all disgusts me!
All the cities I have ever lived in!
My motherland, where is your energy?
How will you resist the enemy and preserve yourself?
Who are your loyal children?
Speak!
Why don't you speak up?
Who clutches your throat?

Long and long I have been unable to sleep,
Like one lying in jail yearning for light and air,
Like one lying in a hospital, weary of moans and sobs.
I am like one in a pitching ship crossing remote seas,
My stomach churning, my eyes searching the horizon.
Hurry, bring me to harbour!
Hurry, set my feet on solid ground!

But from far, far off
I hear an earth-shaking sound,
Chaotic and harmonious,
So ancient yet so young.
My motherland is rousing herself.
It is our soldiers attacking the enemy.
Countless men and women waken, arise,
And thrust history forward.

1942

Dai Wangshu
(1905–50)

One of the foremost avant-garde symbolist poets, Dai was born in the garden city of Hangzhou. The atmosphere of this delicately beautiful southern city with its meandering alleys permeates his masterpiece, "Rainy Lane." After attending local schools Dai enrolled in 1922 in Shanghai University, which was founded by Communists and offered courses in Marxist thought. One of Dai's teachers was Mao Dun, later to become a famous Communist novelist. In 1924 he attended the Catholic Zhendan University, also in Shanghai, where he began a lifelong study of French literature. He joined the Communist Youth Movement and was arrested for taking part in their propaganda work. But although he was sympathetic to the Communist cause, associated with Communist intellectuals, and became a cadre in the Communist government, Dai was never to join the Party. Throughout his career Communist critics attacked his work for its lack of social commitment.

In 1927 he traveled to Beijing where he met Shen Congwen, Feng Xuefeng, and Ding Ling. That same year *Short Story Monthly* published six of his poems, including "Rainy Lane," which was immediately hailed as a milestone in the New Poetry. His first collection, *My Memory*, was published in 1929.

In 1930 he became one of the founding members of the Chinese Leftist Writers Association. He translated Communist literature from the Soviet Union, France, and Spain. In 1932 he went to study in France. When he ran out of money in Paris he applied for support from the Franco-Chinese University Association in Lyon, which provided room and board for Chinese students. He earned money translating French and Italian fiction for Chinese publishers. In France Dai continued to correspond with Chinese Communist writers but his own position was to maintain artistic autonomy rather than submit to Party norms. In Lyon Dai attended no classes but read intensively, deepening his familiarity with Baudelaire, Verlaine, and nineteenth-century French symbolism. His translations include works by

Baudelaire and Supervielle. His second volume of poetry, *Wangshu's Leaves*, was published in 1933. Leftist writers attacked its verse as decadent.

Dai studied Spanish and visited Spain. When he came back to Lyon he was denounced by Guomindang sympathizers among the Chinese students for having allegedly collaborated with Spanish Communists. The Association cut off his stipend and sent him back to China on a fourth-class boat ticket.

In 1936–37 he joined Feng Zhi and Bian Zhilin to edit *New Poetry*. When the Japanese occupied Shanghai, Dai moved to the British colony of Hong Kong. Here he briefly edited a poetry magazine together with Ai Qing, and worked as an editor for *Xingdao Daily*. At Mao Dun's request he helped to found an English-language periodical to publish anti-Japanese resistance literature. In December 1941 the Japanese occupied Hong Kong. With other Chinese intellectuals, Dai was arrested. His experiences in Japanese prison were to become the basis of such poems as "To Endure as a Witness," a first-person narrative of the deprivation and torture of Chinese prisoners in Japanese prisons. Conditions in jail aggravated his asthma. By the time a friend negotiated his release, his health was permanently affected.

After his release Dai translated and wrote for *Hong Kong Island Monthly*, published under the control of the Japanese authorities. After the Japanese surrender, the Chinese National Literary Committee denounced Dai as a collaborator for undertaking this work. Now living in Shanghai, he was constrained to publish a confession of his "collaborationist activities." Meanwhile, a sympathetic Communist publisher, Hang Yuehe, helped Dai publish his third volume of poetry, *Years of Disaster*, which contains poems on patriotic themes. His asthma reached the stage where he found it difficult to climb a flight of stairs. In 1948 one of his superiors reported him to the Guomindang officials for taking part in a teachers' strike, and the authorities ordered his arrest. Dai fled back to Hong Kong.

When the Communists captured Beijing in 1949, Dai resolved to travel there. "If I am to die," he wrote, "let it be with a bit of glory." He attended the first meeting of the National Cultural Committee and was assigned work in the French section of the government news bureau. As his health deteriorated Dai began treatment with ephedrine, which he self-administered by injection. He died of an apparently accidental overdose of the drug on 28 February 1950.

Dai's verse exhibits an amalgam of classical Chinese and modern Western poetry. Some of his early works like "Thoughts of a Wayfarer" treat classical subjects in a classical tone but with modern versification. Michelle Yeh notes Dai's conviction that the essence of poetry is sentiment. In "Rainy Lane" the hazy, languid atmosphere, the heavy scent of lilac, the narrator's melancholy longing, and the elegant description of a delicate young woman are all reminiscent of the mood and subject of classical poetry, but also of the languorous verse of nineteenth-century symbolist Paul Verlaine. Yeh notes the poem's circular structure. The poem ends as it begins, with the narrator lingering in the lane, hoping to meet the same girl. She proposes that the poem's nebulous quality implies that the girl's appearance happens only in the narrator's fancy, so that what the poem renders is the activity of the poetic imagination.

The study and translation of French poetry had a profound influence on Dai's verse. The influence of symbolism appears in Dai's juxtaposed images, synaesthesia, and tortuous narrative development. Early poems like "My Memory" show the influence of Baudelaire and French symbolism in their introspective focus on the narrator. Such verse drew the criticism of Marxist writers for its lack of social engagement. Dai's depiction of dreamlike images of imaginary people shows the influence of the neo-symbolist poet Jammes.

Dai abandoned rhyme after translating Jammes and de Gourmont. Particularly pronounced in Dai's work is the influence of Verlaine, from whom he adopted the free-verse form, in contrast to the patterned stanzas of the Crescent Moon Society poets. The mark of Verlaine on his work goes beyond form. The weary, submissive figure of Verlaine's narrator reappears in many of Dai's poems. The narrator of "Rainy Lane" passively awaits an imaginary girl who never appears. The forsaken narrator of "Homesick for the Sky" longs to return to the sky, there to fall asleep as if "upon my mother's breast." In poems like "Soon Old Age Arrives," the narrator's self-regard verges on the effete self-pity that characterizes Verlaine's late verse: a young man already lamenting the onset of old age.

A number of Dai's poems also show the influence of Buddhism. In some, the listlessness of the narrator merges into an empty-minded state akin to Zen meditation. At the close of "Come Here to Me," the narrator awaits the girl who has left him "in the shade of the Bo tree, musing ..." The Bo tree is the tree under which the Buddha is said to have attained enlightenment. In "Impromptu: At the Tomb of Xiao Hong," the mourning narrator lingers through the night by the grave until it seems to him that the dead one is listening to the waves of the sea: life, death, and nature merge into one. This quiet fusion of the natural setting into an all-encompassing mystical unity is reminiscent of the work of the Tang Dynasty poet Wang Wei, himself influenced by Buddhism.

Already during the thirties Dai was moving from the lush diction and languorous phrasing of "Rainy Lane" towards a more terse style. The catalyst that completed this transformation was his imprisonment. The poems he wrote after his release feature a narrator no longer introspective but socially committed, a voice that speaks in hard-hitting, concrete, colloquial language. In "To Endure as a Witness (ii)" the narrator is drawn, as in earlier poems, by death: "It is peaceful to occupy six feet of yellow earth." But now he rejects death's allure in order to "endure" and bear witness to Japanese crimes against his fellow Chinese prisoners. The poem ends on a tone of courageous resolve new in Dai's work: "Never will I surrender." Dai's masterpiece of this socially conscious phase is "With My Injured Hand." The poem's narrator gropes lovingly over the landscape of China as a lover touches the body of his beloved; he feels her wounds until at last his fingers reach the "one distant corner [that] is still whole / Warm and vigorous." Writing under Guomindang censorship, the author is not able to identify the "distant corner" as Yan'an, the region under the Communist control far away in the northwest.

The forms and themes to be found in Dai's verse are many: from classical to avant-garde, from sophisticated to colloquial, from introspective to political. A poem like "A Fly in Autumn" exploits the techniques of French surrealism to render the sense impressions of a dying housefly. In his own time Dai was criticized by loyal Communists as a poet who disregarded the national crisis, ignoring the tribulations of the masses. Today he appears as a remarkably versatile artist who could shift with apparent ease from one poetic mode to another as he finished one poem and began the next.

Rainy Lane

Beneath my oilpaper umbrella
I linger in a long,
Deserted lane,
Hoping to meet
A girl whose melancholy
Is the colour of lilacs.

She brings
The tint of lilacs,
The scent of lilacs,
The sorrow of lilacs
In the rain, lingering,
Disconsolate.

She pauses in this deserted, rainy lane
Beneath her oilpaper umbrella,
Like my own. Like me,
Silently she walks,
Indifferent, desolate.

Quietly she approaches
Nearer and looks up –
Her glance like a sigh,
Fleeting by
As in a dream,
Graceful and sad as in a dream.

Vaguely, as in a dream, she passes by,
Like a sprig of lilac
The girl fleeting past
Silently, further and further
To the dilapidated wall
At the end of this rainy lane.

In the rain's lament
Her colour dissolves,
Her fragrance fades
And scatters, even
Her glance like a sigh,
Her melancholy like lilacs
Beneath an oilpaper umbrella.

I linger alone in the long,
Deserted, lonely lane,
Longing to meet

A girl whose melancholy
Is the colour of lilacs.

1925

Homesick for the Sky

Homesick for the sky, homesick for the sky,
Everyone, perhaps,
With melancholy face
And grieving heart,
Taciturn,
A cigarette between his lips,
Is preoccupied with this nostalgia.

And I? Homesick for the sky? Ah!
I myself, perhaps, am such a one …
Am I? I long to return
To the sky, a sky as blue as this,
Where I could live and die –
Where, like a child, laughing and sobbing,
I could lie upon my mother's breast.

Am I? Yes, I am one homesick
For the sky, a sky as blue as this,
Where I could slumber in peace
With no aches throbbing through my head, no sleepless nights.

This vexation in my heart –
My heart, O how it longs to be mine again,
But someone has tossed it out
Like an old shoe.

1928

My Memory

My memory is true to me,
As faithful as my closest friend.

It waits for me on a swirl of smoke,
On a brush painting lilies,
On a box for cosmetics, old and cracked.
It lingers on the wood-berries on a dilapidated wall,
On a half-empty bottle of wine,
On a torn manuscript of poems from days gone by,
On the petals of pressed flowers,
On a lantern, dim and lonely, on still waters,
On things with souls and on things with none.
It exists throughout the world, even as I do.

It is faint of heart, and it fears the commotion of people,
But in my moments of solitude it pays me an intimate visit.
Its voice is humble, low,
But it seems to go on forever –
Multitudinous, trifling, annoying – and it will not shut up,
Repeating ancient saws and twice-told tales,
Melodious in tone, but always singing the same song,
Sometimes in the enticing voice of a tender girl,
Weary, mingling tears with sighs.

Its visits are unpredictable;
They come at any time, in any place,
Even when I am in bed, in that dim haze before sleep:
You might say that this is rude,
But we are old friends.

It irks me, always refusing to quit
Unless I am disconsolate and tearful, or sound asleep.
But I can never despise it;
It is faithful.

c. 1928

Soon Old Age Arrives

I'm afraid that I've begun to age, but slowly, slowly,
In step with listless, silent time
Whose every instant
Is burdened with immeasurable sadness.

At dusk in the chill of my armchair
My blurred eyes behold
Vague images float past:
Soft, charming smile, delicate hand,
Eyes blazing with fire,
Or tears lustrous as pearls.

No, I won't be able to recall with clarity
That hushed, low voice at my ear, saying,
"Your lips, place them where they fit best."
Was it Yingzi, that girl, like her name, a cherry blossom?
Was it Ru Lidan, her weary, languid glance
Drifting down to the satin slippers she shed?
All these I won't be able to recall,
Because I will be senile.

I fear these moments of recollection will fade and vanish
One by one, like flowers,
Leaving only the withered, drooping twig.

1931

A Fly in Autumn

Leaves of red,
Leaves of yellow,
Leaves of gray –
Afternoon beyond the window!

With its numberless eyes
A feeble fly gazes, bewildered –
Such a stifling afternoon!
It can't help scratching its head, scratching its belly.

Leaves, leaves, leaves,
The numberless leaves sigh down.

The window is a sheet of ice,
The sun just an orange blur.
Take a walk around, a little inspection tour!
Its feet grow wobbly.

Red, yellow, earthen gray,
The dizzying shapes of a kaleidoscope!

A distant, ancient sound –
The great temple bell? Wind from the ends of the earth?
The fly feels numb,
Its wings so heavy.

Fluttering to earth, fluttering skyward, swirling leaves,
Red, yellow, earth-coloured, gray, a tangled whirlwind.

Its numberless eyes blur, dim.
Something weighs on its silken wings,
Its body, light as a leaf, is borne aloft.
Can it be on the wings of some monstrous bird?

1932

Come Here to Me

Come here to me, if you still exist,
All naked, your silken hair spread over your shoulders,
And I will tell you something only we two can understand.

I will tell you why the rose has golden petals,
Why you have gentle, fragrant dreams,
And why the mallow stretches its head to spy at our window.

All that others do not know, we understand,
Save for the trembling of my hand and the racing of your heart.
Do not fear my eyes that shine with an unfamiliar light.
Come to me, you will find a cozy bed in my arms.

But you no longer exist!
Yet your memory sets me trembling,
And every evening at dusk I await you in vain
In the shade of the bo tree, musing, smoking.

1933

Thoughts of a Wayfarer

When the cattails bloom in my native town
The traveler passes through, his shoes caked in the mud of his journey –
Mud that clings to his heels and to his heart –
And he wonders when a loving hand will brush them clean.

An April of perilous cliffside paths and meals by starlight,
Of scrambling through mountains and hurrying over rivers
When only the cricket's song allays the silence,
Singing of home, the wayfarer's longing.

1933

Village Girl

The village girl walks quietly
With her moss-covered wooden pail.
Its water splashes her bare feet.
Her mind lingers back at the spring beneath the willow.

Quietly she saunters homeward
Beneath the shade of the ancient trees,
Remembers the boy who kissed her at the spring,
Purses her lips and smiles.

She nears the family's wooden shack,
Scatters a flock of pecking sparrows without noticing them,
Dawdles into the kitchen
And in a reverie sets her pail beside the hay.

She helps her mother fix dinner.
Her father returns from the fields, sits on the doorstep
And smokes. Still musing, she feeds the pig
And shoos the chicks into the coop.

At dusk, when dinner is over,
Her father palavers on about this year's harvest.
When he mentions finding her a husband,
She timidly lowers her head.

Her mother grumbles about how lazy she is,
Dawdling at the spring,
But the absent-minded girl hears nothing,
Thinking – that bold young man was a little rough.

Published 1933

White Butterfly

What wisdom can you give me,
Tiny, tiny white butterfly,
Flipping blank white pages open,
Flipping blank white pages closed?

Open the pages –
Loneliness;
Close the pages –
Loneliness.

1940

With My Injured Hand

With my wounded palm I palpate the body of my country.
Here is a corner, nothing but cold ashes;
In that corner, muck and the blood of wounds.
Here a lake has covered my home town
Where flowers once formed a barricade, blooming in clusters on
 the dyke,
And willow branches gave off a mysterious fragrance when they broke;
I touch the flowering water-plants in their liquid beds.
Mountain peaks, white with snow, chill my fingers to the bone.
The rice paddies of the Lower Yangzi, where once the newly sprouted
 shoots
Were so delicate, now bring forth only fleabane and wormwood.
South of the Five Mountains the lychees are abandoned, withered.
At the shore of the southern sea I dip my injured hand into the bitter
 waters.
My invisible palm sweeps over all our mountains and our endless rivers.
Blood and ashes have left my palm cold and stained.
Of all the land only one distant corner is still whole,
Warm and vigorous. Only there spring comes.
Over that place I lightly pass my hand
As if stroking a lover's hair, as an infant strokes the breast.

I gather all my strength into my hand,
And press my palm there deeply, with all my love and hope,
Because only there come sun and spring,
Dispelling darkness, returning life;
Because only there we do not live like cattle
Or die like ants – only there in eternal China.

1942

Inscribed on a Prison Cell Wall

If I am to perish here,
Friends, do not grieve.
I will survive forever
In your hearts.

One of us died here in this jail
Under Japanese Occupation.
Remember forever
The hatred in his heart.

When this place is freed and you return,
Reclaim his broken body from this earth
And with a cry of victory
Raise his soul on high.

Then place his bones on a mountain peak
Open to sunlight and the cleansing wind.
In the darkness of his fetid cell
This was his one good dream.

1942

To Endure as a Witness (ii)

You have fled, leaving me here to endure,[7]
To gaze after ghosts that wander the bloody filth on the cobblestones,
To gaze on hungry eyes that stare from iron cages,
On chests thrust bravely toward glittering blades,
On humiliation distorting every face
That burns with grief and indignation.

You have left me here to test
The depths of degradation, the boundaries of agony,
To be a witness, to be your eyes and ears,
Above all to be your hearts, to be tempered by suffering
Like a patch of earth trampled by iron hooves,
Like a drop of blood which you have shed and left here,
Enduring without tears, without words,
Where life and death are crushed together, so close, so close –
Though parted by crowds of tall years –
Still traveling companions, brothers in anguish.

There are graves only two steps away. I know
It is peaceful to occupy six feet of yellow earth
Covered by six feet of green grass,
But there is no great difference between death and life
Here in the moldy dark of this cramped, stifling cage,
This nest for lice with its pail for slops,
Watching pale beriberi creep up one's legs to one's belly,
Becoming a judo dummy, a target for sword practice,
Drinking water through both nose and mouth, pumped back out by feet
  stamping on the belly;
Kneeling on nails with bricks to prop the ankles high in back,
Hearing the whip dance on skin and bones,
Swaying from the roof beam doing the airplane.[8]

7 The poem addresses refugees who have managed to flee Japanese-held territory.
8 The airplane is a form of torture in which the elbows are tied together behind the back and the body is hung by the rope that binds them.

How many have never returned from here,
While the living still wait?

Let me endure,
Awaiting the day when you return to me.
I have survived as your ears and your eyes,
Survived as your heart. Never will I surrender.

1944

Impromptu: At the Tomb of Xiao Hong[9]

Six hours I walked this lonely path
To lay camellias at your grave.
The night seems endless as I wait
While you lie listening to the babbling wave.

1944

9 The poet and novelist Xiao Hong (1911–42) died in Hong Kong, where the author was living. Her grave lies near the sea.

Bian Zhilin
(1910–2000)

Poet, critic, and translator, Bian was the son of a middle-class family in Suzhou, China's garden city. The traditional Chinese garden, which combines classical architecture with carefully arranged plants and flowers, is the setting for poems like "Untitled No. 1," "Untitled No. 4," and "Disjointed Lines."

Bian attended secondary school in Shanghai where he encountered the New Poetry of Bing Xin, Guo Moruo, Xu Zhimo, and Wen Yiduo. Here began his lifelong interest in Shakespeare. In 1929 he entered Beijing University, where he studied under Wen Yiduo and Xu Zhimo and became acquainted with the work of T.S. Eliot, whose "Tradition and the Individual Talent" he translated into Chinese. In 1936 he would publish a book of translations of French and Anglo-American poetry. Bian's verse displays a blurring of the boundary between symbolists like Yeats and Valéry on the one hand and the formalism of Wen and Xu on the other. His poems are among the most complex of the New Poetry.

Bian graduated from Beijing University in 1933, the same year that the Crescent Moon Press published his first collection, *Leaves of Three Autumns*. He went to Japan in 1935. *The Han Garden*, a collection of poems by Bian and his classmates He Qifang and Li Guangtian, was published in 1936. When in 1937 Japan's occupying army pushed southward Bian returned from Japan, settling in Chengdu, a city distant from the invading forces.

Sharply criticized by leftists for the lack of social commitment in his symbolist verse, Bian replied that commitment to art did not connote abandonment of society. In 1938 he followed fellow poet He Qifang to Mao's base in Yan'an. This marks the close of the most significant period of Bian's poetic career. Like other writers he was assigned to gather material while living with front-line units fighting the Japanese. Here he produced fiction, reportage journalism, and "people's poetry," propaganda literature to stir the masses to resist the invaders.

After two years at Yan'an, Bian left Communist-occupied territory for Kunming. Here he joined the staff of Southwest United University, which had gathered prominent professors from universities situated in Japanese-held territory. In 1947 he received a British Council grant to study at Cambridge, where he completed a novel about the war against the Japanese. When news reached England of the Communist victory, he returned to China. Discovering that the new regime called for fiction about soldiers and peasants, he burned the manuscript of his novel because it only dealt with the experiences of intellectuals. He then took a post in the European languages department of Beijing University.

In 1950 he produced a series of poems as part of the government's propaganda campaign to support North Korea in its war against America. A year later, however, his "Tiananmen Quartet" roused an attack from official critics for its "formalism" – a term for "decadent" Western influence. From then on Bian rarely wrote poetry. He joined the Communist Party in 1956, and stopped writing verse altogether after 1958, the year of the Anti-Rightist Campaign. Instead Bian became a scholar of Western literature, producing translations of Shakespeare, Brecht, Mallarmé, Gide, Verlaine, Baudelaire, and Valéry. He is especially noted for his translations of Shakespeare's four great tragedies.

While still in university Bian had begun writing New Poetry under the tutelage of Xu Zhimo, his English professor. Xu's Crescent Moon Press published Bian's first volume. Some of his early poems, like "A Demon's Serenade" and "Cast to the Earth," are in the "dried bean curd" meter, the prosody advocated by Xu's Crescent Moon Society and by Wen Yiduo. These two poems have both strict stanza-structure and patterned rhyme schemes. Bian would omit "A Demon's Serenade" from later collections of his poetry, perhaps out of uneasiness about its subject, necrophilia.

Bian soon abandoned the personal, romantic mode of Xu and Wen. But he retained their meter and their formal stanza-structure, though he began to vary the number of syllables from line to line. Bian gradually turned away for the use of patterned rhyme; "Train Station" is an exception. (We do not attempt to reproduce Bian's rhymes in our translation of his poems.)

Michelle Yeh notes that classical Chinese poetry's use of metaphors from nature expresses a relationship between the world around us and the human spirit. But in modernist poetry, Yeh notes, metaphor emphasizes the subjectivity of the poet; the poet spontaneously selects images with reference to nothing beyond himself. Whereas metaphor in classical poetry emphasizes connection between the poet and the cosmos, metaphor in the New Poetry joins opposites, emphasizing disjunction. Such a disjunction, says Yeh, structures Bian's verse as a series of images in tension with one another, reverberating in the unconscious. This process appears in "Train Station," a poem whose erratic flow of disjointed images evokes the irrational logic of dreams.

Yeh finds in Bian's verse a synergy between centuries-old Chinese tradition and modernist poetics from the West. His poetry is an amalgam of Buddhism, Daoism, and the verse of writers like Yeats, Rilke, and Valéry. Yeh argues that his familiarity with ancient Chinese schools of thought predisposed him to adopt the modernist style. His mature work echoes contemporary European surrealism (as in "Train Station") as well as the Chinese sages (as in "Untitled No. 5"). The latter poem is an improvisation on an ancient saying, "What is empty is useful," elaborating in modern idiom the deliberate irrationality of this Daoist maxim. Yeh points out further influences of Daoism: the conclusion of "Let the Current Take It," in which the narrator refrains from an assessment of the photograph's meaning, echoes the Daoist rejection of definitive judgments. The shifting points of view of "Disjointed Lines" evoke the Daoist master Zhuangzi's emphasis on the arbitrary nature of every human perspective.

The use of dream and water symbolism in Bian's poems, says Yeh, is a modernist adaptation of ancient doctrines of the fluidity of human experience. In "Untitled No. 4" the flowers in the mirror and the moon in the water are traditional Buddhist images of the transience of human desires. Yeh notes that love in this poem is a matter of give and take. But, Yeh adds, what is exchanged is evanescent, an echo of the Buddhist doctrine of the illusory nature of all experience. She sees a similar theme in "Let the Current Take It," where the girl's abandoned photograph is an image of the ephemeral quality of human affection. Yeh concludes that the Daoist and Buddhist influences on Bian account for his narrator's emotional and intellectual detachment from his subject. In the modernist context, such detachment reflects the influence of Eliot and Pound, who spoke of the poet as a mere catalyst, having no part in the poem's actual content. Bian's use of dramatic monologue distances his narrator from his subject, objectifies the content of the poem and makes it less personal, more typical. His notion that the author can create a work to typify meaning derives from Chinese tradition. Simultaneously, it reflects the modernist belief in the finished poem as a world unto itself, disconnected from the poet who created it.

Like the writings of both the Daoist master Zhuangzi and the modern surrealists, Bian's poems are structured on a yoking together of opposites. We find such a juxtaposition of contraries in the love song to a corpse in "A Demon's Serenade," and in the surrealist interplay of the dreamer's bed and a railroad station in "Train Station." Bian conceives of poetry as founded on empirical experience, says Yeh, but surpassing concrete experience to create something more profound. His poems develop a tension between feeling and thought. This tension is all the greater for the brief, compressed form of the poems, which carefully shape the symbolic imagery to connote a meaning beyond the confines of a tiny scene. This compression is exemplified in "Untitled No. 5," in which a button hole encompasses the universe. Bian's poems seek to imply a deeper reality that lies beyond the misperceptions of the individual consciousness; for this reason his verse has been called metaphysical poetry.

A Demon's Serenade

One night a demon
Sat by the solitary grave
Of a girl
Who once had been disdainful
Because of her beauty,
So lovely, so enticing.
The demon raised his raspy voice,
Strummed his mandolin,
And sang –

"Arise, my love, surrender!
I give you for your mirror
A treasure from a stagnant pond,
This shard of black ice."

"Behold! You now
Are in the season of your bloom:
I love your waxen face,
I love your leaden mouth!"

"Or, if you wish, I'll apply your makeup

With this vial of white snow.
And for rouge – simple,
Here is a vial of red blood."

"Still bashful? Here is a veil,
The soft web of a spider;
And here, a soft cushion,
The bloated carcass of a wolf."

"Let us sit and watch the moon
Sicken in the western sky.
Do not grieve although she dies,
We still have the will o' the wisp."

"Do you love close embraces?
Soft, yielding kisses?
I have serpent arms,
And silkworm lips."

"Come quick, my love, surrender!
The shattered bell peals.
Let us dance together.
We'll make the owl hoot!"

1931

Cast to the Earth

I see you, child,
Alone there on the hillside,
Singing as you walk along,
Bored with everything,
Haphazardly pick up a pebble
And fling it in the gully.

Who knows whether someone,

Child, just for fun,
Once picked you up
With neither love nor hatred,
And flung you like a small stone
Into this dusty world?

1931

Let the Current Take It

With the autumn leaves
The street cleaner sweeps away
The photograph of a girl.

Is it the rain, or is it tears
That blur her cheek?
Who knows? But it reminds one
Of the anxious look on a face one can't recall
Glimpsed in a clouded mirror hanging in an old house.

And inscribed on the back of the photograph:
"Don't lose this ever.
Look at it with tenderness, to deepen our affection."

Like the ancient Tartar girl's love letter,
Lost in drifting sands on the shore of the Puchang Sea,
Discovered by a European traveler
And exhibited in London to the wonderment of blue eyes.[10]

How many fates lie beyond our knowing?
Some people will fret. Others will say:
"Better thus. Let the current take it."

1933

10 The penultimate stanza is based on a true incident.

A Friend and Cigarettes

Like a smoke?
Have another cigarette.
I still remember
You once said
That White and Gold Dragons
Had a mild,
Subtle flavour,
And I asked
If their taste was like a memory.
I felt truly ashamed
When you said just now
That in less than three years
I have aged at least six.
I still haven't learned to smoke
Any more than I've learned the flute,
Though I still love to hear it
Beyond the courtyard wall,
Sobbing at midnight,
Now close, now distant,
Daunting my ambition
Like a lofty mountain
Disheartens a traveler.
Like the sound of a flute
Are these spirals
Of indolent,
Delicate blue smoke.
Have a cigarette?
Please, take another.
I don't like coffee,
But I drink green tea.
I'll have another cup.
The setting sun
Falls through the window,
Tinting the smoke the colour of a dream.
Don't you wish
We could still be a couple of kids,
Sitting on someone's

Doorstep
Watching a white heron
Bathed in the reflected glow of sunset on the water?
Want a smoke?
Have another cigarette.
Thank you
For bringing me
A whiff of the kitchen smoke
From our old home town
Under southern skies.

1933

Disjointed Lines

You stand in a pavilion gazing on the scenery,
Someone on a balcony gazes down on you.

The bright moon embellishes your window,
You embellish someone else's dream.

1935

Untitled No. 1

Three days ago a small stream in the mountains
Swept past the slender shadow of your smile – then vanished.
This morning you met it again; you rubbed your eyes and saw
All round the house the vast currents of springtime.

A hundred turns, a thousand whirls, and not one word for you.
Water feels sorrow, has griefs of its own; it will keep you company.
Where is your boat? Boat? Just go downstairs.
Beyond South Village the almond trees have all bloomed in a
single night!

1937

Untitled No. 4

Brought from across the river, mud for a swallow nest on your roof,
Carried across the courtyard, water for your cup,
Shipped from over the sea, jewels for your breast:
I am researching the history of trade.

Last night I expended a sigh;
This morning I got two small blossoms of smiles.
I pay flowers in the mirror, receive the moon in the water:
I'm keeping a running account for you.

1937

Untitled No. 5

On my stroll I am thankful
That a buttonhole has a use;
Since it is empty[11]
It can hold a small flower.

In that small flower, I see the light at once –
The world is empty
Because it has a use:
It is where you promenade.

1937

Train Station

Pull it out! Pull! From deep inside my dream –
Another night train coming. That's reality.
On the river bank the sighs of the Ancients ebb and flow

11 The poem plays on an ancient saying, "What does not exist is useful." The poet refers to this maxim in a footnote.

While I am here like an ad on the station billboard.
Listen, children, excited bees are buzzing against the window;
A panicky butterfly is impaled on the station wall –
All to adorn, to adorn my present reality.
My brass-wire bed is plucked; it rings,
Calling me to dream myself into a little earthquake.
These heartbeats, these heartbeats –
How could their pulsing come from a train?
Why would I want to be a train station for dreams?

1937

The First Lamp

To grind the grain in their gullets, birds swallow gravel.
Animals are afraid of fire. Men nurture it, and civilization follows.
Blessed are those who wake at dawn and sleep with the sun,
But I praise the first lamp that lights up humanity.

1937

Lin Geng
(1910–2006)

An anomaly among the New Poets, Lin Geng was both a writer of modern *baihua* verse and a scholar of classical poetry. He was born in Beijing. His father, a calligrapher and classical poet who had studied in Japan as a young man, was a literary figure of the late Qing empire, a professor of Chinese and Indian philosophy.

Lin enrolled in the physics department of Qinghua University. After two years he transferred to the Chinese department to follow his first love, poetry. After graduation he remained at Qinghua, working as an editor of New Poetry magazines under Zhu Ziqing. In 1933 he published his first volume of New Poetry, *Night*. In 1934 he began to teach Chinese literary history at the Beijing Democratic Institute. He was to go on teaching this subject for the next three decades, publishing historical articles on classical poetry even as he went on writing the new *baihua* verse.

When the Japanese swept south in 1937, he fled Beijing for Xiamen University on the coast of Fujian Province. When the Japanese captured Xiamen he had to flee inland with his students and colleagues. In 1947 he returned to Beijing to teach at Yanjing University. He went on to publish numerous studies of classical poetry. In 1954 the first volume of his voluminous *History of Chinese Literature* appeared. Late in life he turned to writing poems in a strict-stanza form. He ended his years as a highly respected scholar of classical Chinese literature at Beijing University.

Lin's poetry goes hand in hand with his scholarship. Although he writes in free verse, Lin achieves a quasi-classical tone. He omits personal pronouns and punctuation just as in classical Chinese poetry. Michelle Yeh notes that his abbreviated lines rely on implication while omitting connectives and explanations, achieving a compression reminiscent of classical verse. As in traditional poetry, the range of his subjects is narrow: spring, night, a dragonfly. Like many ancient poets, Lin prefers allusion. While others were writing graphically about war against the Japanese, Lin's reference to it, in the poem "May," is a mere hint: "Now that we've grown used to hearing rifle fire / A long life seems ridiculous." The restraint of these lines recalls the classical masters.

Lin's poems present a series of disconnected images, making the reader fill in the connection between one image and the next. This technique is reminiscent of the demands that T.S. Eliot places upon his reader; at the same time, it evokes the style of classical Chinese poets like Li He. In the poem "Night," for example, what is the connection between the mysterious rider and primitive man's fire? The reader is left to ponder the question. Lin's mysterious aura echoes the Daoist commonplace called in Chinese *xuwupiaomiao*, the floating island of paradise drifting on the misty sea, the locus of truth and joy that can never be clearly visualized. The highest reality must by its nature remain inexpressible. It is just this sort of ultimate reality that Lin hints at in the dragonfly on the dusky road in "Mist at Twilight." The reason the dragonfly represents this "inexplicable hope" is as ephemeral as the dragonfly itself, as it "flits into the underworld of darkening grass."

Lin's experimental verse, while not famous, is significant. The flexible rhythm of his free verse is akin to the metrics of other New Poets. But the way he treats his themes is different. Hu Shi said that the tone of classical poetry should be abolished from the New Poetry. Lin took a different tack. His free verse deliberately echoes the classical masters, especially *The Songs of the South*, the Tang poet Wang Wei, and the Song poet Bai Juyi. Imitating classical verse in new verse, Lin was a lonely experimenter at the start of the New Poetry.

May

If we were to see the springtime only once
How unwillingly would we part from it.
Sometimes – we can't tell why –
We want to snatch a butterfly in flight –
A creature with only one life.

The wind-blown reeds whistle, wake town and mountain
To signal the arriving May.
Isn't this beautiful? Spring dusk
Offers youth to one whom youth has disappointed.

Happiness is a time like this
When I wake, youthful, and the heavens are clear as water,
Just like your eyes.
You say I'm thinner now? My heart
Softly falls out of reach of heaven.
Now that we've grown used to hearing rifle fire
A long life seems ridiculous.
Is it not so?
May – the cuckoo cries, a deer calls from the wild.

1933

Mist at Twilight

Often I hear the footsteps of a child running toward me;
Then they halt suddenly in an instant of loneliness.
Spring is a dark pool
Where all, living or dead, are reflected upside down.

Through the cold, misty twilight
On this road under an alley of green trees,
Is there no inexplicable hope aloft?
Yes, a black dragonfly
Flits into the underworld of darkening grass.

1933

Night

Night walks into the district of solitude –
So tears flow like wine.

The blaze of primitive man
That rages deep inside the forest –
Is it whispering now?

Beyond the wall – frantic, irregular hoofbeats,
Off into the distance –
Fleet is the steed!
Singing, I bless both horse and rider.

1933

Li Guangtian
(1906–68)

Li was born in a peasant village in Shandong province. Before he was a year old his parents gave him to his maternal uncle, who was not so poor as they were, to raise as his own son. In 1923 Li entered teachers college in the provincial capital, Ji'nan, where Zang Kejia was his classmate. In 1928 he was briefly imprisoned for his part in agitation against the local authorities on behalf of peasants.

After teaching primary school, he enrolled in the English department of Beijing University in 1931. Here he made the acquaintance of fellow students Bian Zhilin and He Qifang and began to publish poetry. In 1934 the three friends put together a collection of their poetry which they entitled *The Han Garden*, eventually published in 1936.

Li fled the Japanese occupation of Beijing in 1937, settling in 1941 in Kunming, where he served on the faculty of Southwest United University. Here, after the defeat of the Japanese, he joined Wen Yiduo in political activity against the Guomindang. In 1946, after Wen was assassinated by Guomindang agents, Li fled to Tianjin where he continued literary attacks against the Guomindang until he became a wanted man.

When the Communists took power in 1949 Li was appointed to their executive committee of writers and artists. In 1952 he was transferred back to Kunming and appointed president of Yunnan University. Like many writers, Li had stopped writing after 1949, but he resumed in the period of the Hundred Flowers campaign of 1957–58; some of his new work criticized the ruthlessness of rural party cadres. In 1959, during the Anti-Rightist Campaign, he was attacked as an anti-revolutionary and dismissed from his post.

Rehabilitated in 1962, Li was again denounced in 1964 by party colleagues at Yunnan University. When the Cultural Revolution broke out in 1966, big character posters appeared around the campus denouncing him. He was imprisoned in solitary confinement for seventeen months. On the evening of 11 November 1968, Red Guards took him from a cell for "interrogation." Early next morning a peasant discovered his body floating in a pond. An official autopsy indicated that he had been beaten about the head and strangled.

Li's most important poems are those he published in *The Han Garden*. They show the influence of European romanticism. His favourite theme is nostalgia for the home and childhood that one recalls in memories. His best work balances symbolism with realism: the central image in "Crossing the Bridge" is both an ordinary physical bridge in the eye of adult experience and a bridge to paradise in the eye of youthful imagination. At the close of the poem, the narrator and his companion cross the boundary between the concrete present and the numinous past, stepping into paradise across a bridge.

Window

Is that your face of nine years ago
Passing by chance outside my window?
My green gauze curtains blanch to white,
But nine years gone are nine years still.

Is this your reproachful sigh of nine years past
Borne to me with falling leaves on the autumn breeze?
Your old rebuke, buried in the earth,
Has sprouted today as self-reproach, pure green grass.

You were a migratory bird
Alighted by chance in my autumn garden
(I myself have become an autumn garden)
Then carelessly continuing afar

To some distant, unknowable horizon.
Are you searching perhaps for a new spring garden?
Alone, I gaze in silence through my white gauze curtains,
Brooding on a tiny cloud in the vast blue sky.

1933

Crossing the Bridge

Do you remember? The two of us were children, barefoot,
Playing on the grassy river-bank after the rain,
Kicking, scattering the dew in pearls.
Listening to our singing, the clouds paused in the sky.

"Glow, rainbow, glow!" you sang to the sky.
As you gazed up, you laughed and the song caught in your throat.
"The rainbow is like a bridge, isn't it," you said,
"So long and curved, a single arch across the sky."

"Yes," I replied, "it's a sky bridge
To heaven, the one and only road.
When we grow up I'll take you there,
We'll cross that glowing bridge together."

Thirty years, and we pass this way again.
No clouds, no rainbow. An autumn field.
"Isn't the bridge across the river like a rainbow?"
I don't reply, but take your hand and lead you across the bridge.

1934

Ji Xian
(1913–2013)

Lu Yu, who wrote under the pen name Ji Xian, was born in Hebei province in 1913. His father, a Guomindang general known as "Tiger Lu," fought Mao's guerillas. It is not surprising that such a general's son was one of a small minority of poets loyal to the Guomindang. The author grew up in the garden city of Yangzhou and in Shanghai. He began writing verse when he was sixteen. In his youth he travelled extensively around China before studying painting at Suzhou School of Fine Art, graduating in 1933. He then continued art studies at prestigious Waseda University in Tokyo. As Japanese troops began their sweep southward through China, he returned to his mother country. In 1936 he joined Dai Wangshu in editing Shanghai's monthly *New Poetry*. Both poets were influenced by the French symbolists Baudelaire and Rimbaud. As the Japanese advanced still further the author fled, first to Hong Kong, then westward to Guizhou province and finally to Kunming, where he associated with Wen Yiduo. Returning to Shanghai after the defeat of the Japanese, Ji Xian resumed his connection with Dai Wangshu.

In November 1948 the author fled approaching Communist forces by moving with other Guomindang supporters to Taiwan, where he worked as a high school teacher of Chinese literature. Here he played the role of an elder statesman of modern poetry, influencing a wide number of younger Taiwanese poets. His program for radical Westernization of Chinese poetry involved free verse, intellectualism, and the rejection of classical poetics, especially lyricism. In 1953 he began the *Modern Poetry Quarterly* which published a broad spectrum of modernist verse. In 1956 he founded the Modernist School and issued a manifesto announcing that the group was devoted to "pure poetry" and to "patriotism, anti-communism, freedom and democracy." The document declares that the group will "select and express the spiritual elements of all new poetic schools since Baudelaire." Ji Xian was himself a translator of modern French poetry. In poems like "To Maybe Man" he echoes Baudelaire's fascination with the grotesque and the bizarre.

Ji Xian's manifesto proclaimed that modernist Chinese poetry derives from "horizontal transplantation," (importing Western models) not "vertical inheritance" (following traditional Chinese models). In other words, modern Chinese poetry ought to be the heir not of the Chinese tradition but of the European. The manifesto proclaims that "We regard poetry as the exploration of a new continent, pioneering in a virgin island the expression of a new content, the creation of a new form ... [and] the invention of new techniques." His experimentation appears as early as 1936 in "To Maybe Man," an address by the narrator to his poetic alter-ego in which he prophesies that in some surrealistic future the two will define their own reality in a blank, meaningless universe. The poem can be read as a prophecy of the future role of modernist poetry. Twenty years later in "Incompletion: One" he again splits his authorial persona, this time into the green and the rotting, the high-octane and the languid – i.e. the energetic and the melancholy. In both works the theme is how the poet produces the poem.

Ji Xian rejected ornate poetic language, metrical prosody, and rhyme. Instead he called for clear diction following the natural rhythms of everyday speech. A poem, he said, should be structured on logic and the flow of cognition, not the excessive sentimentalism he saw in classical Chinese verse. In place of sentiment, Ji Xian advocated intellectual content. One of his favourite themes is astronomy, as in "The Star-Snatcher" and "The Lost Telescope." The latter poem, for example, contrasts the changeless pattern of the celestial constellations with the precarious state of human affairs, prone to upheavals like the Chinese Civil War. This does not mean that the poet banishes feeling from his writing. The understated anguish of the expatriate narrator of "The Lost Telescope" makes this clear. But what generates the poem's emotion is the intellectual development of the theme.

A Christian like his mother before him, Ji Xian opposed Marxism. He did not associate himself with any political party; rather, he voices his anti-Communism in his verse. The Communists demanded poetry to stir the masses to revolution and to struggle against the Japanese. Ji Xian's "Autumn on the River" withdraws from social and political upheaval into the peace of a natural scene reminiscent of the classical poets of bygone centuries: the poem could serve as the poetic inscription that often forms part of a classical Chinese painting. The Communists saw China's crisis in terms of class conflict, but Ji Xian's "Burning City" described the conflagration of warfare and revolution as a psychological phenomenon, happening within the "soul." The Communist agenda called for the subordination of the individual to the collective. "The Star-Snatcher" celebrates an individualist's striving after personal glory.

Ji Xian is a versatile poet. He can write a poem reminiscent of the classical style like "Autumn on the River." He can make a tree the symbol of his homesickness in "A Locust Leaf," an image which any reader can readily understand. But more often his poem develops some arcane symbol meant to express the author's subjective inner world. The symbol's arbitrary nature is the theme of "Pipesmoking Psychoanalysis," where each image transforms itself randomly into the next, unrelated to the one before it. Each image bears within itself the seeds of its own negation: the shapes figured in pipesmoke lead to "the annihilation of an army of dreams," the dissolution of every pseudo-meaningful symbol. In "To Maybe Man" and in "Incompletion: One" the author celebrates this method. Every time the poet-narrator of "Incompletion: One" builds a symbol, it dissolves and he must begin all over again to compose a new system of meaning, a new poem: every climb ends in a fall, every fall begins a new climb. The poem's ephemeral meaning is inscribed on a blank cosmos, the "tundra" in the closing stanza of "To Maybe Man." Ji Xian's playful sense of humour bears witness that he is no nihilist. But his notion of how a poem conveys its meaning shows the influence of European existentialism, with its idea that humans must generate meaning within themselves in the face of a meaningless universe. Michelle Yeh observes that like the French symbolists, Ji Xian conceives of poetry as the creation of a world that exists for its own sake, communicating to the reader nothing beyond itself. In his critical writings, Yeh notes, Ji Xian goes so far as to claim that the real world is the internal world of the imagination, and that the external world of the senses is illusory. He differs from other modernists in his conviction that the poet's inner world partakes of reality, albeit a subjective one.

The author is sometimes likened to the great classical poet Li Bai; both are reputed to have relied on wine for poetic inspiration. Like Li Bai's poetry, Ji Xian's is marked by striking imagery, implying the immense powers of the poet. "The Star-Snatcher" reaches up to grasp the stars – with eventual success. According to Michelle Yeh the stars in this poem symbolize the poet's aesthetic ideal, incomprehensible and even offensive to the vulgar world. The image of stars as the poet's refuge, his true home, recurs in other poems such as "Bird Variations" and "The Lost Telescope." He strives to reach this ideal and merges with it. But this union is only momentary, as the last lines of "Incompletion: One" dramatize, and the poet must seek it anew as he begins his next poem.

Half jokingly, Ji Xian claimed that a poet needs to be crazy. His imagery often displays the surrealism that marks the verse of Li Jinfa. In "Burning City" a conflagration rages in human souls, passing like a virus from one person to another by a mere look. The two poets share an individualist perspective: events are primarily psychological and spiritual, not sociological as they are for Communists. Amid the dead earnestness of Chinese poets of the thirties and forties, Ji Xian is a rare poet who offers his reader humour, as when his ichthyological specimens go for a swim in "To Maybe Man." It is hardly surprising that Ji Xian, like Li Jinfa, fled Mao, who demanded that poets cleave to the Party line. In "A Locust Leaf" Ji Xian laments his exile status, a poet barred by his enemies from returning to the homeland for which he longs. In 1976 the author moved to California, where he lived until the age of one hundred.

An enthusiastic polemicist, Ji Xian instigated public debates with rivals, including his friend Qin Zihao. Many of Ji Xian's poems reflect the controversy that he courted: his narrator is often embroiled with adversaries. In his later years his modernism was criticized not only by other poets but by representatives of the Taiwanese public at large, who objected to its irrelevance to the ordinary reader. Earlier in his career, between 1937 and 1949, the years of war and revolution, few other Chinese poets felt free to meditate on questions of metaphysics and the nature of poetry. Socially committed leftist poets denounced art for art's sake, feeling compelled to write about their country's invasion and the plight of the peasants. In the mid-thirties, symbolists like He Qifang and Bian Zhilin turned their back on the aestheticism of their youth to write poems stirring the masses to rebel against the Guomindang and to fight the Japanese. Meanwhile, in "To Maybe Man," Ji Xian was proclaiming the power of the artist to create a world according to his own inner vision. The brash egotism of a poem like "The Star-Snatcher" seems innocuous enough today, but when the poem appeared in 1943, in the midst of a life and death struggle against the Japanese, poets who created imaginative worlds were attacked as irresponsible, even treacherous – as the star-snatcher is attacked. The enemies who vilify the star-snatcher and hunt down the narrator of "Bird Variations" might well represent the leftist critics of Ji Xian's day.

Ironically, the revolutionary poets who attacked the star-snatcher were subjected to Mao's stifling literary regulations on the mainland, able to publish little more than slogans in verse, while Ji Xian went on writing modernist poetry on the island of Taiwan, reaffirming his role as the heir of the experimental verse of the twenties and early thirties. Still more ironically, it was Ji Xian's kind of poetry that influenced the new generation of mainland poets who arose in the 1980s under Deng Xiaoping. Today the socially committed poets of Mao's era appear stodgy and outdated to a younger generation of mainland writers. Ji Xian's modernism represents, one might argue, the authentic current of the new mainland verse. On Taiwan he is called the high priest of modern poetry.

To Maybe Man

Swelling, swelling,
Exploding, exploding
In an incomprehensible whirl

Use your intuition,
Your instinct,
Comprehend it,
Oh Maybe Man
And give me the answer
Precisely
Jotted on your scratchpad:
The unknown X of life

Whereupon we shall say good-bye
Don't sob, and no nostalgia

When the day comes when there is no magic
And no God
All heavenly spheres have gone flat
And ichthyological specimens begin to swim
Maybe Man
We'll have a happy reunion
On the perilous edge of a planet shaped like a clock

Oh Maybe Man
Will you still remember then how to play the mandolin?

I don't know
Maybe my throat has gone hoarse already
From crooning our old waltz

But when we are intimately joined in a single body
We will race fast as a horse
Sketching with our shadow
16 futuristic boundaries
Upon the boundless tundra

1936

Burning City

Peering through the window of your soul
Into its profound depths,
I see a city in flames – no fire brigade,
But heaving tides of naked madmen.

In this endless surge I catch the sound
Of my own name reverberating,
The names of loved ones, the names of enemies,
The names of the countless living and dead.

But when I softly respond,
"Ai! Here I am!"
In that instant I too am transformed –
A horrifying city in flames.

1937

Autumn on the River

Swaying toward the horizon, a hundred acres of marsh
Clad in pale gold.

The incessant waves of the river
Crest above the heads of reeds onshore.

An insect chorus sings,
Ancient natives of the marshes.

After the wind dies down
Eel-boats return through the brown waves.

1939

The Star-Snatcher

The youth who snatched at a star
Plummeted.

The deep blue sky mocked him,
The broad earth mocked him.
Reporters
Thought up the most insulting adjectives
To blacken his name
And mock him.

A millennium later
A museum arises
To exhibit
A statue of the youth who snatched a star:

He holds up Sirius in his left hand
And Vega in his right.
Around his waist he wears
Nothing less than the three-star-studded belt of Orion the Hunter,
Who once tried to shoot him with an arrow.

1942

The Lost Telescope

Overhead once again – the seven stars of the Great Bear
Where could my old telescope be now?
That's the North Star
There's the glorious Milky Way
Those three, Orion's belt that I know so well
That bright blur – the Great Andromeda Nebula, maddening!
Ah, the starry sky! Solemn, glittering, mysterious
Up there is timeless structure, regular motion, eternal order
Can what is lost be regained?
There's no upheaval in the stars of a summer night

1944

Bird Variations

No sooner do I assume
A pose of flight
Than this world bursts into an uproar
Countless hunters
Countless shotguns
Aim
Fire
Through the bullet holes in the sky
Flashes the light of the stars

1947

A Locust Leaf

The world's most beautiful foliage,
Most rare, precious,
Most tear-wrenching, heartbreaking:
A delicate golden tan leaf of the locust tree.
Where along the Yangzi River,

In what city, what garden, did I pick it up
And stick it in a book of ancient poems?

Years later here it is, perfectly preserved.
Light as a cicada wing, a locust leaf that fluttered to earth.
On closer look – clinging to it are specks of my native soil.
Homeland – ah! What year, what month, what day
Will I finally be permitted to return to your breast
To savour the most joyful season in the world,
Fragrant with the drifting scent of locust blossoms?

1949

Pipesmoking Psychoanalysis

Slowly, imperceptibly rising from the bowl of my pipe
Is a mushroom-shaped cloud
A snake
A life buoy
The body of a naked woman:
She dances, she sings,
She is singing of the overflow of a dried-up river
And the annihilation of an army of dreams.

1953

Gold Gate Sorghum

A full bottle of
Gold Gate sorghum liquor stands on the sandy beach
Of my tiny island desk, watching over
The dark blue sea of the midnight window

Its shadow cast by the moon of the lamp
A staunch, faithful sentinel.

1955

The Death of Aphrodite

Stuff the Greek goddess Aphrodite into a slaughterhouse meat-saw
        And slice her up,
Dice the attributes
Of The Beautiful
Into specimens,
Then –
        One little bottle,
        Another little bottle –
All with labels, classified for exhibit to public applause
For the edification of the common people
At the Museum of Ancient Artifacts.

This is the twentieth century. This is ours.

1957

Incompletion: One[12]

They are fond of speed these greens
Being flammable by nature they are all melancholy
Those decayed leaves, having lost octane, dislike haste
Melancholy they are not at all

12 The *I Jing* (*The Book of Changes*) is a Chinese text used for divination. Since ancient times it has been interpreted as a system of cosmology and philosophy. It emphasizes the dynamic balance of opposites, the evolution of events as a process, and the acceptance of the inevitability of change. The poem replicates in a modernist form the cryptic, elliptical syntax of this classic text. The sixty-four hexagrams of the *I Jing* have been shown to represent a mathematical sequence. The poem echoes this notion in its mention of "geometric progression." Shao Yong, the eleventh-century scholar who found a mathematical progression in the hexagrams, arranged them in a circle. In the next to last line the author calls the "progression" of his climbing and falling "a circle."

The sixty-fourth and last hexagram of the *I Jing* is named "not yet fording" (the river). Its meaning has been interpreted as "not yet completed" or "incompletion." At the end of the poem the narrator is caught up in a cyclic action of climbing and falling. His ascent is only a temporary stage in an endless up and down. This sixty-fourth hexagram consists of two trigrams, one above representing fire, one below representing water. The upper trigram's

So I regularly perform a climbing act
Playing a whole note marked hold, sailor-style
On a most unmusical flute
As I mount a skyladder to transcend

Each and every green or decaying leaf
All that is flammable by nature, having lost octane
Whether melancholy or not, loving speed or not
So in a word I have started again (ah! audience
No matter whether you sigh or walk out before the end
Shout out loud, statistically keep quiet or applaud vigorously –
There is no public order here to maintain and observe)

But I progress geometrically in a circle
Climbing up then falling; a geometric progression becoming a circle,
  falling down then
Climbing ...

1959

reference to fire resonates with the poem's mention of the flammable and of octane, a combustible fuel. The trigram below, of water, may have suggested the narrator's likening himself to a sailor.

Incompletion is the last hexagram of the *I Jing*. It suggests that effort never reaches a final conclusion. Just as a hidden melancholy is present at the heart of restless speed-loving energy, just as fully grown green leaves contain the principle of rotting that will dissolve them, so too no end is ever really complete but is the beginning of something else. The author in the poem seeks to ascend a ladder into the sky. His "climbing act" is his composition of a poem. Each time he climbs, he falls down again. He never completes his climb to "transcend." With this interpretation of the last of the hexagrams, the endless circle of change represented by all sixty-four is ready to spin onward, ever varying, ever staying the same. The poet's effort to achieve transcendence is never finished. The transcendence he achieves in the completion of one poem is fleeting, and he must begin his climb all over again as he starts the next poem.

Qin Zihao
(1911–63)

Qin Zhi, who wrote under the pen name of Qin Zihao, was a member of the Miao ethnic minority. Born in Sichuan province, he graduated from college there, then in 1932 went to Beijing where he studied French at the Sino-French University. Here he encountered Western poetry and began publishing verse. From 1935 to 1937 he studied economics and law at prestigious Chuo University in Tokyo. Returning to China, he worked as a journalist for the Guomindang military. In Chongqing during the war years, he advocated modern poetry when others were emphasizing a simpler poetic style to galvanize the common people to resist the Japanese occupation. Qin received his discharge from the forces in 1943.

On business in Taiwan in 1945, he found himself unable to return to the mainland because of the outbreak of the civil war. He remained on Taiwan, cut off from his wife and child, for the rest of his life. He worked at the Provincial Food Bureau and as an editor at the *Taibei Evening Post*. Qin edited a number of poetry journals and taught poetry at the Correspondence School of Literature and Art. A prolific writer, he produced translations of nineteenth- and twentieth-century French literature, as well as literary criticism, including the volume *The Anatomy of Poetry*. Qin's translations of modern French poetry include works by Lamartine, Hugo, Verhaeren, Apollinaire, and Cocteau.

With Ji Xian, Qin was one of the most influential figures in the development of poetry in Taiwan. He was a founding member of the Blue Star Poetry Society, which became the largest such body in Taiwan. Its members opposed the all-out Westernization of Chinese poetry advocated by Ji Xian's Modernist School, upholding the importance in modern poetry of lyricism in the tradition of classical verse.

Although he opposed Ji Xian's call for the total Westernization of Chinese poetry, Qin's verse also displayed the influence of the French symbolists that Ji Xian admired. His early verse displays the lush natural images of a Verlaine or a Mallarmé. In later works like "Hair" Qin introduced images from the arts, such as his reference there to Wagner's *Flying Dutchman*.

Qin's symbols, like the sunflower in "Sunflower," function without any transcendent significance like those of Ji Xian. Qin's sunflower stands for the poet and the sun for the female source of his inspiration. The poet's approaching death becomes a theme of Qin's later poems. The last line of "Sunflower" foreshadows the author's demise, and the way the dying sunflower sheds its seeds upon the earth to sprout in future poems foretells the seminal influence of his poetry after his death. Qin's influence on subsequent generations of Taiwanese poets has been rivaled only by that of Ji Xian. He succumbed to liver cancer in 1963.

Desert Wind

The desert wind ages a young heart
I chase my dream beneath the sun

Its shadow dissolves on the horizon
Hope is buried at the border of the wasteland

On the edge of the desert no bird sings
Nothing is left but pale, silent dusk

At midnight, locked in a madhouse
I paint the honey-sweetness of life

1934

Inkfish

Who knows where
You secretly sucked up a bellyful of ink?
Now you spew it all out,
An author infatuated with himself,
Covering everything
With words that even you don't understand.

1952

Sunflower

You are the sun
I am the sunflower.
Day after day I seek you.
I greet you on the red carpet of sky
I gaze at you from the garden when the dew has vanished
I see you off with the evening breeze
Your dazzling orb
Illuminates my golden yellow petals
I wear a poet's laurel crown
My breast is pregnant with seeds of poetry,
A deathless love
Forming your living body.
My leaves are clouds of green
My petals are rays of light.
I have become a sun on earth.
When you depart from me
At first
I bow my head in meditation,
Then, wan and sallow, long to die.
When autumn comes
My golden petals
Fall like wisps of hair.
In memory of you
As if to spill my heart's blood
I split open my breast.
One by one
I scatter immortal seeds
To an earth awaiting regeneration.

1955

Hair

In this secluded room the evening dark turns thick as your hair
Shadows are sculpted on the wall
Mountain spirits and sea-nymphs
Hide in your tresses
Your smile is pregnant with the moment of bliss

Sprites that dance to the Muses' harp on Parnassus
Naiads sporting in the ancient Aegean
Now lurk in the secret recesses of your hair
Holding their breath
While my breath wafts through your tresses like a breeze
I listen to your heart, a tremor deep in the earth

I can see my fractured shadow on the wall
The melancholy figure of the Flying Dutchman
Wandering through the twentieth century
He will burn his ship
And buried in the tranquility of your hair
With those playful sprites
Listen to your heartbeat foretell his happy death

1962

PART FOUR

“Peasants and Soldiers” Poetry

Introduction

MICHEL HOCKX

Poetry written by or for peasants and soldiers does not feature prominently in the histories and anthologies of modern poetry in most Western countries. This is not because there have been fewer wars in the West, or fewer peasants, but because modern poetry is by and large not seen as a type of writing that might engender mass appeal. Things have been different in modern China. There are two reasons for this. First, there is a powerful traditional Chinese discourse about poetry's socio-political efficacy, going back all the way to Confucius' supposed compilation of the *Book of Odes* on the basis of folk songs in order to remonstrate against the government. Secondly, the ambition to bring literature to the masses for purposes of propaganda and stimulation of patriotic feeling has been part of the socialist-realist aesthetic in China from the mid-1930s onwards. When the War Against Japan broke out in 1937, patriotic poetry came to be considered even more important.

While non-political writing continued to be the main trend in the occupied parts of China, with the Shanghai scene seeing a craze for comedies and the Beijing scene featuring many formalist poets, writers in the rest of China urged the populace to unite in resistance against the invaders. A national union of anti-Japanese writers was joined by writers from the left, right, and center of the pre-War political spectrum. Writers' groups traveled to the front to observe conditions first-hand and write about them. And poets, especially, turned towards more easily intelligible and, crucially, recitable verse. Inspired by Mayakovsky, Tian Jian even invented a kind of "street corner" poetry featuring short, slogan-like, easily memorized lines meant to be shouted out in public. The following lines, from "One Rifle, One Zhang Yi" may serve as a good example of this style:

Oh, the blizzard!

Rifle fire from snowdrifts,

Resounding,
Resounding.

Hot blooded
Like the struggle,
Your red, stuffy nose
Stops sniffling –
Fierce,
Breathtaking!

The colder the weather,
The fiercer the battle,
O, the fiercer the battle!

As John Crespi has shown, live performance of this war poetry tended still to be limited to small gatherings in lecture halls with poets standing on stage, rather than actual agitation on actual street corners.[1] Nevertheless, the importance of this trend in terms of the self-perception of poets and their "social value" should not be underestimated.

Some poets who initially favoured more autonomous styles of writing made the switch to "peasants and soldiers" poetry shortly before or during the war, in some cases with considerable effect. Ai Qing, who started out as a symbolist, produced his best work after he decided to devote his imagistic skills to the portrayal of bleak, wartime scenery, as in the famous "The North." The poem starts out with familiar scenes of decay and dilapidation, which might appear in any symbolist poem:

Dilapidated walls, abandoned graves – all
Shrouded in earth-coloured melancholy.
A solitary traveler
Walks bent over,
Covering his face with his hand,
Gasping in the sandstorm.
Step by step
He struggles forward.
A few donkeys,

1 John Crespi, *Voices in Revolution: Poetry and the Auditory Imagination in Modern China.*

> Beasts with sad eyes
> And drooping ears
> Stoop beneath the burdens
> Of this agonized land.
> Wearily they tread
> With listless steps
> The Northland's
> Long, lonely road.

Yet as the poem continues, it becomes clear that it contains a declaration of love and concern for the poet's northern homeland, now occupied by the Japanese, and it ends on an emotionally charged note, merging the imagery with an expression of the common fate of the nation and the "race" that is at war:

> They left this land to us.
> Its vast barrenness
> Has given us a sparse language
> And a broad outlook
> That will never perish.
> I cherish this ancient land,
> That has nurtured the longest-suffering race in the world
> Whom I love.

Compared to post-1949 socialist-realist poetry written according to Mao Zedong's literary policy, work like this, although obviously ideological, appears more spontaneous and genuine in its expression of collective aspiration.[2] Even during the war, however, the emphasis on the "correctness" of such expressions was strong, and critics gave very little breathing space to poets in the non-occupied areas who wished to continue writing and publishing non-political work. An exception was the wartime literary scene in Kunming, Yunnan province, where the various universities from the occupied territories had established a temporary joint campus known as "Southwest United University," and where autonomous writing continued to flourish, as we shall see in the next section.

2 Mao's policy was formulated in the 1942 "Talks at the Yan'an Forum on Literature and Art." It was applied initially only to the Communists' Yan'an base area, but became state policy after 1949.

Yin Fu
(1909–31)

Unknown during his brief lifetime, Yin Fu became a celebrated poet in Mao's China twenty years after his execution by the Guomindang. Yin Fu ("Ardent Man") was the most common pen-name of Xu Baiting. He was born in Xiangshan county, Zhejiang province. At the age of seventeen his family sent him to finish high school in Shanghai where he became involved with the Communists, who in 1926 still formed a wing of the Guomindang party. When Chiang Kai-shek liquidated the Shanghai Communists in April 1927 Yin Fu was arrested, but released through the intervention of his elder brother, a Guomindang air-force commander loyal to Chiang Kai-shek.

Using a false high-school diploma, Yin then enrolled at Tongji University in Shanghai to study German. Arrested for Communist activity again in 1928, he was once more released on the recognizance of his brother, who sent him back to his hometown and had him shut up in a local temple. The author escaped and returned to Shanghai, reestablished contact with the Communist underground, and began work with their youth league. His poems appeared in small Party newspapers and journals.

Following a third arrest and release in 1929, he joined the League of Left Wing Writers and met Lu Xun, the chief figure of the literary left, to whom he gave a manuscript of his early writing. Yin Fu was arrested a fourth time when security forces raided a secret Communist meeting on 17 January 1931. Chiang Kai-shek ordered twenty-three of the captives shot. Yin Fu was executed on the grounds of Longhua Military Headquarters on 2 February 1931. The dead were buried in an unmarked grave.

Yin Fu wrote when the Communist movement was at low ebb, driven into hiding in the cities of China or surviving in remote areas. The author wrote his poems living underground. "Metropolis at Dusk" describes Shanghai of the early thirties: leisured capitalists riding in their limousines past factory girls leaving work. Falling night represents capitalist hegemony. Hope for the revolution lies in the distant dawn.

The work of Yin Fu belongs to the first, romantic phase of communist art. It records the dramatic conflicts in the poet's heart, his despair, his hope for the future revolution. This phase would soon be supplanted by the socialist "realism" of the late thirties and forties.

Shot at the age of twenty-two, Yin Fu died without ever publishing a book of poems. At the time of his last arrest the authorities confiscated manuscripts of his poetry, a story, and his translations of Soviet literature. These have disappeared. His surviving work comes from manuscripts he left in the hands of Lu Xun. In the early fifties, after the Communist victory, his poetry was rediscovered and honoured in the official canon as the writing of a "revolutionary martyr."

Metropolis at Dusk

A shroud of smoke settles on Shanghai streets
That ring with the laughter of homebound factory girls.
A constant stream of traffic rushes past.
Dusk deepens, electric lights switch on.

Limousines purr, mock the workers' laughter,
Acrid exhaust inflames their lungs.
The rich are returning from the racetrack;
Foreign chatter spills from their passing windows.

Gray roadside houses tremble,
Structures sag toward collapse, while past them flow
Motorcars and factory girls – opposed, continuous currents –
The decadence of a city, emphatic in the dusk.

The gentlemen need thoroughbreds to rouse them from ennui
But the work-worn girls have energy to laugh.
Well, let the masters enjoy another night.
We'll see who wins the dawn.

1929

Feng Xuefeng
(1903–76)

Born in a peasant village in the mountains of Zhejiang province, Feng was to become a poet, essayist, critic, literary theorist, and translator. After studying in local schools, he enrolled at age seventeen in Jinhua No. 7 Normal Institute. Expelled in 1921 for taking part in student demonstrations, he went to study in Zhejiang First Normal College in Hangzhou, the provincial capital. Here he joined his teacher, Liu Dabai, in composing short vernacular verse and took part in a poetry society whose moderator was Zhu Ziqing. Among his other teachers were the New Poets Ye Shaojun and Liu Yanling. In 1925 he went to Beijing to audit classes at Beijing University, supporting himself as a proofreader and private tutor. He also went briefly to study in Japan. After the Guomindang liquidated the Communists in Shanghai on 12 April 1927, he joined the Communist Party. As a result of a poem he wrote in memory of those who were executed, he became a wanted man in Beijing. He fled to Shanghai, where he became a close literary associate of the foremost leftist literary figure of the times, Lu Xun. Feng also served as secretary of various Communist writers' groups and translated Russian revolutionary authors like Plekhanov, Lunacharsky, and Maxim Gorky

In 1933 he traveled to the sole remaining Communist base in rural Jiangxi province, where he served as assistant head of a Communist Party college and became acquainted with Mao Zedong, one of the leaders. In October 1934, Chiang Kai-shek's Guomindang forces surrounded the Communists. Another Communist commander, Fang Zhimin, led a successful diversionary action to enable the main force, including Mao, to escape. Fang Zhimin was captured and executed. His last stand took place on Soul Mountain, which gives its name to Feng Xuefeng's poem in commemoration of Fang and his men.

Feng himself was one of those who escaped the encirclement. With Mao he took part in the six-thousand-mile Long March from Jiangxi to Yan'an, an epic event in Communist mythology. In 1936 Mao sent Feng as a secret envoy to Shanghai. It was Feng who first passed the news of the

Long March to Western journalists. He arranged for the visit to Yan'an of American correspondent Edgar Snow, whose subsequent book, *Red Star over China*, first made Mao known in the West.

Arrested by the Guomindang in 1941, Feng spent two years in a rural prison camp at Shangrao, within sight of Soul Mountain, where Fang Zhimin made his last stand. Here he had the first opportunity in over fifteen years to devote himself to poetry. The poems he wrote in this prison camp were published in 1943, and republished in Shanghai in 1946 under the title *The Song of Soul Mountain*. After the defeat of the Japanese, when the civil war began, Feng returned to Shanghai to work in the Communist underground. After the Communist takeover he was named vice-chairman of the Chinese Writers Association and served in prominent editorial posts in Beijing.

Feng's poetic output was not large. He only wrote poetry for some three years. His work falls into two periods. His early poems were written between 1922 and 1923. His later revolutionary poems were written in the Guomindang prison camp from 1941 to 1943. Influenced by the short poems of Rabindranath Tagore, the early poems are fresh in language, languid in feeling. They show the influence of Japanese haiku: understated emotion expressed in imagery from nature, like the narrator's mourning in "Qingming Festival" for his sister, whose death is recalled to him by the sight of a willow branch.

Feng maintained that every change in form and content of literature was bound up with a change in the life of society. Accordingly, after he joined the Communist movement, he moved from the short, emotive nature poems of his youth to the revolutionary verse of *The Song of Soul Mountain*. Feng renders this historic peak into a symbol of the revolutionary impulse that motivated his generation. This poem written in a Guomindang prison camp has a style and content practically unique in Chinese socialist literature. Cut off from the Party's literary authorities, Feng was free to develop his own voice to express his personal feelings about the spirit of the revolutionaries who were his compatriots and fellow prisoners. *The Song of Soul Mountain* is about revolutionary soldiers, but the mystical aura with which Feng endows Soul Mountain is poles apart from the socialist realism of Ai Qing and Zang Kejia's soldier poems.

In light of the quasi-mystical expectations expressed in *The Song of Soul Mountain*, Feng's fate was bitterly ironic. As editor of *Literary and Arts Daily* in the early fifties, Feng criticized the government's censorship policies for lowering literary standards. Demoted, he spoke out again during the Hundred Flowers Campaign of 1956. In 1958 he was denounced as an enemy of the party and sent to a rural labour camp. During the Cultural Revolution he was subjected to public attack at mass "struggle sessions." He died in 1976 without being readmitted to party membership.

Qingming Festival[3]

Qingming Festival:
Silently I walk out into the street.
Under a willow branch hung above a door
I see the shadow of my little sister, bean flowers in her hair.

1922

Songs of Spring (ii)

Sun in the east, rain in the west.
Alarmed, the partridge cries.

Gazing at your house in morning fog beneath the mountain,
I pluck a willow branch, clasping a handful of the willow's tears.[4]

c. 1923

A Poem from the Mountain

As a bird departs from the mountain
I place a petal in its beak
To tell the maiden who dwells at the mouth of the valley
The flowers of the mountain are in bloom.

1923

3 Qingming: literally "clear and bright," the period in the solar calendar – generally around the 5th of April – when the Chinese pay respects to the dead.
4 Symbolic of spring, the willow is associated with the awakening of erotic desire.

The Song of Soul Mountain[5]

In the distance stands Soul Mountain:
A chain of rugged crags,
Its summit, the jagged spine of some gigantic beast,
Its foothills standing guard like an iron castle rampart.
It looms against the blue wall of cryptic heaven
Beyond a river rushing through open fields.
The people of this place whispered,
"A holy place, Soul Mountain.
The great battlefield!
There long ago pioneers
Gathered armies
And raised the bloody banner
Of universal justice.
Soul Mountain, eternal sign of victory!
Constant battle, endless resistance!
Soul Mountain gathers the spirit of all the earth.
Its aura reaches a thousand miles.
The whole year round it radiates a beauty that urges men's hearts,
And morning to evening we breathe that beauty!"

In the distance rises Soul Mountain,
Awesome height,
Massive and august,
A chain of peaks stretching to the horizon,
Wreathed in dreamlike clouds,

5 Soul Mountain (*Lingshan*) is located in Jiangxi Province. After the failure of the 1927 Communist revolt in Jiangxi's provincial capital, Nanchang, routed Communist troops under such leaders as Mao Zedong and Fang Zhimin withdrew to remote areas of the province. Fang Zhimin and his guerrillas made Soul Mountain their base, spread out, and eventually controlled parts of four provinces, until the Guomindang's anti-communist campaign of 1934–35 slaughtered his men and captured Fang, who was later executed. Some of his men made their last stand on Soul Mountain. "And so," the author says in a note, "all sorts of legends grew about Soul Mountain. The mountain and the name of Fang Zhimin came to be worshipped by the people. During the war against Japan, the Guomindang's third military zone concentration camp was set up south of here." The author wrote the poem in 1941–42 while imprisoned in this camp. "Day and night, we could raise our heads and gaze on Soul Mountain. Among my fellow prisoners were local men who had fought in Fang Zhimin's peasant army."

Itself entrancing as a cloud.
The people pointed: "There on Soul Mountain
In our own time guerrilla chiefs rallied an army once again,
Raised the banner of justice, written in blood,
And unfurled it over the broad Southeast.
That mountain is tragic ground.
They retreated to that mountain
And there they made their last stand,
Shed the last of their blood.
That mountain of calamity is a shrine of holy relics,
Spirit-ground for all who follow in their footsteps!"
Soul Mountain, glorious, image of the unconquered!

In the distance looms Soul Mountain,
Eerie!
From contemplating this mountain I see that the tragedies of history
  are inevitable!
From this mountain I learn why we rush unflinching toward those
  tragedies,
That we are born to fulfill the ideals of the universe,
And hence I understand the beauty of all mountains and rivers.
From this mountain I have fathomed the souls of the men of our
  generation,
Whirled by indomitable human energy,
Thirsting – as if for blood – for the mysterious beauty of that force.

In the distance we can see Soul Mountain,
Mesmerizing!
At dawn alluring and delicate as the mist;
At twilight, blue – lone and sublime against the setting sun.
Glittering beneath a clear sky, it appears empty, vacant,
But at night, far off in the foggy moonlight, ten thousand warriors
  are galloping!
Indomitable mountain,
Towering image of the heroic spirits of this generation,
A memorial of grief, a sacred shrine,
A portent and a call!

1941–42, published 1947

Tian Jian
(1916–85)

Tian Jian was a poet whose work embodies, more than any other writer in this collection, Mao's prescription for the role of the arts in the Communist state. Tian Jian is the pen name of Tong Tianjian. The pen name means "in the fields," intended to evoke the life of peasants, who were both the author's theme and the audience for whom he wrote.

Tian Jian was born in Wuwei, Anhui province. In his local village school he studied the Chinese classics, but also the New Poetry of the revolutionary poet Guo Moruo. In 1933 he enrolled in the foreign language department of Guanghua University, Shanghai. Here he became associated with Communist intellectuals. In 1935 he published his first book of verse; it was followed in 1936 by two more volumes, including the long poem *The Story of a Chinese Peasant Village*. His writing was suppressed by the Guomindang authorities for its revolutionary content and he was briefly arrested. To avoid another arrest, Tian Jian fled to Japan, where he encountered the revolutionary poetry of Mayakovsky. When the Japanese armies moved southward through China in 1937, he returned in the company of Guo Moruo. At the invitation of leftist novelist Mao Dun he came to Wuhan, then China's capital, to join other writers in support of the resistance. Here he published his popular collection of poems, *For the Fighters*, written in a declamatory style. Radio readings popularized his work. In 1938 he finished his most famous work, the long poem *She Too Will Kill*. In September 1938 he joined a group led by novelist Ding Ling to travel to Mao's revolutionary base in Yan'an. He was then twenty-two years old. His greatest writing lay behind him.

In Yan'an he helped begin the street-poetry movement, using public reading of poetry as propaganda. His experiences at the front are the source of poems like "One Rifle, One Zhang Yi." After the Communist victory over the Guomindang in 1949 he helped found the Literary Research Committee, which later became the Chinese Writers Association. He wrote in support of China's involvement in the Korean War and served as a literary ambassador to Communist Bloc countries. In 1958 he went to the countryside to encourage the writing of revolutionary folk songs to publicize the Great Leap Forward. He stopped writing at the start of the Cultural Revolution in 1966, resuming only after Mao's death ten years later. Tian Jian died of bone cancer in 1985.

"I want my poetry to become a weapon," he wrote, "a weapon of the revolution." In his early twenties, Tian Jian developed the distinctive style which became his trademark: short lines (sometimes no more than a single syllable), drumbeat rhythm, plain diction, peasant characters, military scenes, and stirring drama urging readers to collective action. His poems are composed for public reading to audiences of common people. "She Too Will Kill" (1938) portrays the peasant mother, raped by the Japanese soldiers who murdered her infant son, as a personification of all China. The poem narrates her transformation from victim to resistance fighter.

Kai-yu Hsu notes Tian Jian's belief that the truest, most intense human feelings can be captured in the pauses and halts of speech. In "She Too Will Kill" the deliberately broken syntax and emphatic rhythm render the psychic turmoil of a protagonist traumatized by war. Wen Yiduo saw in Tian Jian a poet who addressed the common people, and praised him as the "Drummer for our Times": "Here there are no 'implications,' no 'lingering harmonies' ... Every sentence is simple, unadorned, genuine straightforward language, concise and solid ... drumbeats ... striking ... into your heart." "She Too Will Kill" dramatizes how the cruelty of war plunges the mother into a despair that drives her to self-awareness, then to revenge against the Japanese. Tian Jian depicts this archetypal mother's experience of Japanese atrocity to motivate readers to take up armed resistance at a time when Mao's nemesis, Chiang Kai-shek, allegedly refused to engage the invaders in all-out war.

Tian Jian is the Communist Party's mythmaker. His simple diction and use of folk-song devices rendered his verse comprehensible to common people. His poems often build to a climax in a revolutionary slogan like the last line of "Song of the Hill Country" – "Everything under heaven will be ours!" MacDougall and Louie point out that "She Too Will Kill" represents Tian Jian's adaptation of the futurist revolutionary poetics of Mayakovsky. The poem concludes with a proclamation of the immortality not of the individual, but of the collective masses. "*We* do not die."

In his talks on literature and art at the Yan'an forum in 1942, Mao said that art should be written for the common people to understand; it should draw its inspiration from peasants and soldiers, and serve party policy.

Tian Jian's works of the late thirties and early forties were a prototype for that agenda. His writing already embodies the distinctive plot-structure of Maoist literature: common people are roused to action under Communist leadership and overcome their oppressors.

Song of the Hill Country

The sun, our torch, scatters light
Over this hill country
Where we are picking cotton.

Picking cotton,
Our bellies hurt from hunger,
Our backs ache,
We don't get home till late at night.

When cotton is picked in this hill country,
We carry it home. Someone takes it away
And we swallow our bitterness –
How many times have we played pack-beasts for nothing!

Have no fear!
Let the wind blow
And the rain pour.
When the storm is over,
Everything under heaven will be ours!

1935

from *She Too Will Kill*

1

Who
Killed
My son?

Who
Killed
My son?

She sobs,
Laughs,
Howls.

Riflemen
Pushed in the door,
They pawed me,
Hit me with rifle butts,
Blocked my way with bayonets.
A gang of them
Beat me,
Shoved me down and held me.

Alone
She came running,
Haggard,
Hair disheveled,
Face swollen,
Her narrow nose
Pointed to heaven.
Gnawing bloody lips,
In the salt-and-wine Shanxi dialect
She roars out
Through narrow teeth:
No!
Get your hands off me!

Opens
Her white blouse,
Unwinds
A bloody halter.
With bent fingers she can't straighten,
Strokes bloody nipples.
Her primitive, untrammeled cry

Pierces the dark,
Boundless as the wilderness,
Shining through
This May night
In the northern wilds.

The villagers
Dig up
Their buried muskets,
Clean them
To a bright shine,
Pour in powder,
Then
Slaughter all their sheep,
Pour all their wine.
Eat up!
Drink up!
The bandits are coming!

They pack their flour
Into cotton sacks,
Pack their children
Into bamboo baskets,
And lift them on shoulder poles,
Ready to flee.
But what about her?
Where will she flee?
Ah, woman,
Where are you going?

Out of my way!
She walks out into the fields,
And with a bloody hand
Points into the wilderness.
She wants to kill a man!
She,
Who has never killed
An ant!

When a neighbour cruelly beat
A dog
Or a horse,
She would run up
And cry out in protest:
Put down your whip!
If a child
Had been abandoned on the road,
Hungry,
Sobbing,
She would take it in her arms,
Lick away its tears,
And raise its shriveled mouth
To her breast,
Comfort it
With a smile
And give it suck.

Now
The Japanese
Have burned her son
And raped her.

2

Her heart is on fire
As she thinks of her village.
Her eyes flame,
Remembering:
Gunmen!
So many of them!
Wearing hobnail boots,
They jabber in Japanese,
Draw gleaming pistols
From their leather belts,

Spray volleys of gunfire
Amid blazing piles of corpses.

She watches
Her mud walls,
Her door
Collapse.
She watches
Flames swallow
Her red kerchief,
Her embroidered shoes,
Her bucket
(The one she carried every morning to the well),
Her stove
(Where she baked wheat cakes every noon),
Her donkey
(That she rode every evening through the gritty wind),
The jacket
That she sewed from embroidered silk
For her son,
The cradle
She lashed together from strips of wood –
Her son's cradle,
The cotton,
The herbs,
The wheat,
The noodles,
The red dates –
Burned!
She watches
Her son
Shrink from the flames,
His tiny head
Turning,
His hand
Waving.
The fire
Swallows him.

They say
She reached in the window
Of her blazing house
And snatched a sword,
Then rushed up the hill,
Sat in a trance
Beside the monastery graveyard
And put the sword
To her throat,
But suddenly laughed
And threw it down:
Why die like this – useless?

Now, howling,
She brandishes the sword feverishly
Before her naked belly.
Across her hot breast
She wipes it madly
With her bloodied hand,
Praying to it.
It bewitches her,
Calls to her:
I command you,
Live on!

She has no fear of death,
She who understands shame,
Who understands vengeance.
She cries wildly to the villagers,
Her voice coursing along the sword's blade:
What are you afraid of?
Stand up!
Are you deaf!
Are you blind?
Follow me!
Follow my sword!
Japanese devils,
Do you want to kill me?

Do you think I can't kill too?
Here I am!

3

The May
Night
Is a great crucible,
A flesh-consuming fire.
In the dark
The villagers
Advance
To the fight.
Blood fans
The flames.
The peals of a bell
Clang,
Clang,
Burst the air
Like shards of iron.
Horses' nostrils snort,
Their manes flutter,
Their chests heave like bellows,
Their mouths spew foam like snow.
The peasants raise
Broad faces.
Callused, scarred hands
Jerk tight
The reins.
Like madmen
In uproar
They lash their whips:
Crack! Crack!

As if from a nightmare
The enemy wakes

To behold
Doom.
As if bombarded,
One frantically lashes
His horse's neck,
Cursing.
Another sings out:
Aiyeee!
An evil star is on us!
Death!

They seem to hear
A strange voice
Pierce
The May night
And fill the wilds.

4

Woman!
The peasants call:
Come join our band!
Go before us
To light the road!

From deep sockets
Her eyes
Peer ahead fiercely.
Sleeves rolled back,
She grasps the torch,
She lifts the sword.
The wilderness night
And the wilderness road
Receive her.

She sobs,
She laughs,
She howls
In a chant as mighty as the Yellow River:
This sacred flame
Can never die.
For my village,
For my son,
I too will kill!

Her voice,
Her sword, blood, madness, sobs, laughter
Shine through
The night
On China's forests, rivers and mountains.

5 Epilogue

Do not call her mad.
It is not she
Who is mad!

Do not say
She is dead.
As long as there are enemies to kill,
China's sword does not die!
We do not die!

1938

One Rifle, One Zhang Yi

"The colder the weather,
The fiercer the battle."
– Soldier Zhang Yi[6]

Oh, the blizzard!

Rifle fire from snowdrifts,
Resounding,
Resounding.

Hot blooded
Like the struggle,
Your red, stuffy nose
Stops sniffling –
Fierce,
Breathtaking!

The colder the weather,
The fiercer the battle,
O, the fiercer the battle!

It's our number one
Sharpshooter,
Zhang Yi,
A real Hebei man.

He's turned his cotton-padded jacket
White lining out,
Our Zhang Yi,
Manning the front line.

6 Zhang is a common family name. The given name "Yi" means justice.

Zhang Yi
Chants
"I'm from Hebei, Jinchaji,
I'm from Hebei, Jinchaji,"
With his finger on the trigger.

The enemy
Storm up –
Only ten meters away –
No problem.
But O, the blizzard!

Bullets, like snowflakes,
Fill the mountain,
Fill the valley.

Zhang Yi's company
Crouches
Low to the earth,
Firing.

The captain commands
Our center to withdraw
While our flanks fan out
To surround the enemy.

As the center
Pulls back,
Zhang Yi grabs his rifle
And rolls into a snowbank.

Look!
He covers himself with snow
And lets the enemy
Charge over him.

One rifle,
One Zhang Yi –
Brilliant,
Brilliant!

Once more from the snowdrift
Rifle fire,
Resounding,
Resounding!

1939

Zang Kejia
(1905–2004)

Zang was born of well-to-do parents in Zhucheng county, Shandong province. His father took part in Sun Yat-sen's revolution that overthrew the imperial Qing government in 1911. After study in private schools, Zang entered Shandong First Normal Institute in the provincial capital, Jinan, in 1923. When the local warlord suppressed the May Fourth culture movement in the institute, Zang set out with classmates to Wuhan, where he enrolled in the Central Military and Political Institute and joined the Guomindang's Communist faction. But in April 1927, Chiang Kai-shek instituted a purge of the Communists from Guomindang ranks. A brief civil war ensued between the Communist wing of the Guomindang and forces loyal to Chiang. Zang served as an assistant squad leader under the command of pro-Communist generals. After their defeat, Chiang began a roundup of Communists. Zang fled back to his home town. Guomindang authorities there sought to arrest him, so he fled to northeast China. His poem "An Arrest" relates the experiences of a man on the run.

Zang subsequently returned to Shandong under a changed name. In 1929 he enrolled in Qingdao University, where he majored in Chinese language and literature. From 1930 to 1934 he studied with Wen Yiduo. From Wen he learned the notion that a poem's effect springs from its inner dynamism. Zang was also influenced by Wen's preference for plain diction. His early poems, written under Wen's tutelage, display an intricate craftsmanship. Zang eventually would turn to free verse, but in a number of poems he does adopt Wen's formal metrical system, among them "The International Cemetery," "The Old Horse," and "The Rickshaw Puller." In other poems, like "The Execution Ground," he employs a verse structure of irregular line-length.

Like Wen, Zang was a populist. But unlike Wen, Zang was also a Communist. In a 1934 essay he denounced Wen, along with Xu Zhimo and Dai Wangshu, for their preoccupation with aestheticism. Zang's poem "Stagnant Water" is a reply to Wen's poem of the same title. In Wen's poem the stagnant water is often taken to stand for China's corrupt society, especially its rotten political culture during the warlord era. In Zang's poem, the common people dive into the stagnant water, bringing it alive – the participation of the masses brings vitality to China's rotten politics. Many of Zang's finest poems, like "Refugees from Famine," are steady-minded descriptions of the poor and downtrodden.

When Zang graduated in 1934 he had already published two volumes of poetry. In 1938 he joined Communist troops fighting the Japanese, working with a cultural unit, sometimes going behind enemy lines to gather news. He was to continue this work for the next four years. In 1942 he moved to Chongqing where with Ai Qing, Wang Yaping, and others he published works in support of the war effort.

After the defeat of Japan he went to Shanghai where he helped produce *Poetry Creation*, one of two journals publishing writers who would later be called the Nine Leaves poets. In 1949 he fled to Hong Kong to escape arrest by Guomindang authorities. After the Communists completed their takeover he moved to Beijing, where he worked as an editor of the *New Journal*. Zang edited the only anthology of the New Poetry to appear under Mao, published in 1956. During the Cultural Revolution he stopped writing. His silence continued until the late eighties.

A prolific writer, Zang produced a total of twenty-one volumes of poetry, thirteen of them between 1936 and 1945. He is often paired with Ai Qing as an action-oriented, politically committed, revolutionary poet. Both were strenuously opposed to the obscurantism of Li Jinfa and of Dai Wangshu's early poems. He also avoided foreign-sounding words and the themes of love dear to writers like Xu Zhimo.

Ai Qing characterized Zang as a realist. "There is no sentimentality in his poems. [They] are grounded in the soil of China." Novelist and fellow Communist Mao Dun praised Zang, saying that he "does not beautify reality, does not flee reality." In his earliest poems, Zang develops an intimate personal quality. The inner life of common people comes alive in poems like "The Rickshaw Puller" and "Workmen Resting at Noon." "Refugees from Famine" portrays Chinese peasants driven from place to place by the same famines that have afflicted them for centuries.

Wen Yiduo praised the seriousness of Zang's poetry – "This is not some mixed-up game – this is life!" Zang's greatest poems, like Wen's, are meditations on human existence. Sometimes Zang depicts a worker's state of mind symbolically, as in "The Top" and "The Old Horse." The latter portrays in the figure of a worn-out draught horse the long-suffering Chinese peasant, ever ready to slog on. Zhou Liangpei argues that "The Old Horse" is not a depressing poem, in spite of the dark shapeless shadow of the whip before the horse's eyes, because it presents an image of eternal endurance.

In his early poetry Zang's imagery often raises questions which the poem leaves unanswered, or answers only by implication. At the end of "The Execution Ground," for example, the spirits of the executed cry out, "Twenty more years!" What does this mean? The phrase "Twenty more years!" was a condemned man's cry of bravado from the cart that carried him to his death. It was his affirmation of his inevitable reincarnation back into the world: "Twenty more years and I will appear reincarnated among you!" In other words, "You can't really kill me!" But in Zang's poem, the cry could be a revolutionary prophecy: "Twenty more years and our cause will triumph!" In "A Grave" why does the dead peasant's spirit long for a heart-to-heart talk with some passer-by on the road? What does he wish to say? The author does not tell us.

Beginning in the late thirties Zang abandoned this calculated ambiguity. He turned from the theme of the steadfast individual who bravely faces a grim reality in favour of explicit political themes which the Communist Party prescribed. In this he was anticipating Mao's call in his "Talks on Literature and Art at the Yan'an Forum" in 1942 for the subordination of art to party policy. As a result of his loyalty to the cause he served, Zang is a somewhat problematic figure today. After Mao came to power, Zang insisted that a poet who wrote about the peasants had to enter into the spirit of the rural collectivization. He followed his party's call to glorify its social revolution in his verse. During the Anti-Rightist Campaign of 1957, Zang joined in the Party's attack on writers who failed to support Mao's line. During the Cultural Revolution Zang wrote in praise of the May Seventh cadre schools, where intellectuals were sent for "reform through physical labour" among the peasants. In the Deng era, Zang's support of these work camps for the educated was an embarrassment for his admirers. For the iconoclastic younger generation, it was disgusting. Zang, for his part, attacked the apolitical, ambiguous works of the "obscure" poets who came to prominence in the 1980s. Zang's troubled image among Chinese intellectuals today is a measure of the gap that separates the new generation of writers from their revolutionary elders, whom Zang glorified in his poetry.

The Old Horse

He always lets them overload the cart,
And anyway, what can he do about it?
The weight of the shafts digs into his back,
And his heavy head sags.

Who knows what command is coming next?
He gulps down the pain.
The shape of the whip floats before his eyes.
He lifts his head and stares at the road ahead.

1932

The Rickshaw Puller

A howling gale lashes the treetops;
Rain drips faster from the tip of his nose.
The murky lamp on his rickshaw
Cannot pierce the surrounding shadows.

His heart is a riddle.
He pays no attention to such a storm
But stares ahead like a drenched bird.
What does he await in the depths of the night?

1932

Workmen Resting at Noon

All they can think of is rest.
They set aside their work,
Lay everything down
And fall sound asleep,
Their bed, the broad earth,
The quilt that covers them, the sun,

A strip of shade the pillow for their heads.
One's hand rests across his friend's chest.
On a sweaty arm
A drop hangs gracefully from a hair,
Glistening in generous comfort.
Under the sun, skin the colour of iron
Blossoms white.
Their rough snores mark the rhythm
Of their even breathing.
Let the steel wings of sleep cover their hearts,
Let not the lightest dream draw near them
Till they have slept though this exhausting noon
And climbed back to their feet and shaken themselves,
A new strength coursing through their bodies.

1932

Refugees from Famine

The sun sinks behind the birds' nests,
But twilight has not yet melted into the wings of the crow.
A drifting mist leads a crowd of people
Down a strange road into this old town.
Their slow shapes cluster beside the road like piles of grain,
Swathed in shadow, face after silent face,
Silent, desolate, dreary.
Their odd, dusty clothing
Tells the story of a long journey.
Smoke spirals from a cook-fire, drawing expectant glances.
In their hearts rise memories of home:
"Twilight is lingering over our ancient trees,
Slowly spreads over our deserted houses.
The cold, dark forest devours the village we've left behind."
An iron weariness crushes their vision of the past,
An even fiercer hunger snaps their minds back to this alien town.
Before the crowd, like a god in a dream,
A tall figure in gray appears, the rifle flashing in his hands.

His voice resounds, tremendous in their ears:
"Food is short. We can't take strangers here."
"Ai! Wherever we go, famine!"
A burst of sighs. The dark has grown more vast.
Step by step, the crowd trudges down the broad street,
And tramps out of this village.
The adults' hearts quaver at the children's sobs.
An iron gate clangs behind them.
Dark creeps over the walls of the town.

1932

The International Cemetery

Perhaps, alive, they scorned to know each other.
Now, fallen, they lie side by side,
Strangers no more and harbouring no resentment.
Flowers sprout from one grave to bloom above the next.

A discoloured headstone
Once announced his glories.
Now he has no power to rise and remonstrate
Against the moss that veils his name.

Some are just a handful of earth,
A lowliness that causes them no grief now.
Buried deep, they hide their simple lot,
Maintaining an eternal ease.

Above, the spring birds' song
Cannot tease out one more smile from them.
Beneath the autumn moon the insects' gloomy cry
Can prompt them to no further tears.

They too once lived in this world,
Were enemies, were friends.
Now mud stops every mouth.
If they have anything to say, it's sealed inside their hearts.

International Cemetery, Qingdao
5 December 1932

A Goddess[7]

On feet so light they are a gift from heaven
She circulates among acquaintances,
A delicate fragrance wafting from her robe
Where flowers upon moss blossom with love.
(Never has she said that she is weary.)

With clever conversation, she knows how
To prompt merry repartee from guests,
And, even better, with a flicker of her eyes
Knows how to bathe their hearts in honey.
(Never has she once poured out her own.)

Wines of every hue and savour
Bring fresh flowers to bloom upon her face.
Her body's scent intoxicates more than wine,
A madness like the fire of her youth.
(Never has she stopped to see how fast spring flies.)

Song is what best becomes her throat;
Hearts echo to her singing, note after note:
Songs joyful or tragic, she can sing them all,
Just tell her your desire.
(Her own song she has never sung.)

7 The poem describes a sing-song girl, a young woman who has been trained to entertain male clients in "sing-song houses" with singing, dancing, and personal companionship.

Alone, she waits in the solitude of night;
Her lamp lights up her own four silent walls,
And all her crowding memories shine at once.
With a long sigh, she closes both her eyes.
(The universe embraces her alone.)

1933

The Top

Like a top beneath the whip that sets it whirling,
At the peak of night
I am lashed by anguish
Round and round this windy, dew-drenched courtyard.

Vagabonds in the deep dead of night –
The bright moon above
And I on earth below:
Two eyes of the universe, never closing.

1935

The Execution Ground

Before it, a gloomy curtain
Of decrepit willows planted in a row
In which hangs the setting sun.
Behind it, the city wall hides it from the road.

Lines of graves pierce tangled yellowed grass
Like hairpins thickly bunched,
Headstones press together like brothers
With arms around each other.

Neither at Qingming[8] nor at Zhongyuan[9]
Is there paper money on these tombs.
No one visits here to meditate on the past.
At dawn and dusk crows sweep the murky sky.

Night falls cold on the willows by the canal;
Fireflies attract swarms of moaning ghosts
Full of defiance unquenched by death
Who cry, "Twenty years and we shall come again!"[10]

Linqing, Shandong Province
1937

Home Leave

Older brother is home on leave.
The whole family
Unloads anxiety from their hearts.
Since he walked out the door
There's been no letter.
He himself
Is the first news they've had
For years.
His mouth
Is a small river
Gushing.
Mother sits at her spinning wheel
As if she's in a dream.

8 See above p. 244, note 3. Part of the holiday ritual to honour the dead involves burning paper money at the grave for the use of the deceased in the other world.
9 The fifteenth day of the seventh lunar month; another day when money was burned on graves.
10 "In twenty years I shall be just such another stout young fellow" was a defiant phrase shouted by young criminals on their way to execution, alluding to the reincarnation of the soul. The poem was written when Qingdao was under Japanese occupation. The executed dead could be understood as members of the Communist resistance and their cry as prophesying the continuation of the struggle against the occupiers.

Just back from the fields, little brother leans forward,
His hoe resting across his lap.
Everyone watches attentively
As though they were listening to a stranger
Reading them a "letter home."
His little son shuttles back and forth,
Squeezing in among the grownups.
Happily, timidly,
He reaches out a curious hand
To stroke Daddy's revolver.
When no one is watching
His wife,
Her face aflame,
Steals shy, furtive glances up and down his body.

1942

A Grave

A life of toil
Bent his body.
On the burial plot he once cleared
There is another mound of yellow earth.
His grave, like his life,
Is humble, poor.
On it sway a few stalks of plain, pale grass,
Rolling in the bosom of the west wind.
When he was alive
He worked these fields.
Now dead, he watches over this plot of ground
For his sons and theirs and theirs.
As twilight comes on
He wants to rend the earth and leap out
To stop a passerby
For a talk, heart to heart.

1942

Stagnant Water[11]

A pool of greenish water
Festers with slime.
The sun's heat
Raises tiny pustules
On its skin.
Men
Water their cattle here.
Women line its banks
Washing clothes.
White geese
Paddle over its surface.
Children
Dive
And float up again.
This pool of stagnant water
Rings with laughter,
Gleams with light.

1942

An Arrest

A brutal fist
Hammers the door,
Shaking the stars
Down from the sky.
Dogs bark madly
Rousing this mountain village.

A moment's deathly silence –
Then more pounding, louder,
No longer with hands,
The hammering is massive.

11 The poem replies to Wen Yiduo's poem of the same title (p. 115). Like Wen's, the poem is a socio-political metaphor, the ditch of stagnant water representing China.

Delaying, delaying –
The door
At last scrapes,
Creaks open.
Chaotic footsteps
Rush inside.

Now –
Ransacking.
Then the sound of rope.
Feeble resistance,
Like a sparrow's
Clutched in a huge hand.

More confused footsteps
Resound in the courtyard.
Threatening torches flash
Past my paper window.
An old woman's shrill wail rises –
Like a stone thrown into the dark sea,
Its ripples
Receding further and further,
Till they grow faint.

April 1945

Ai Qing
(1910–96)

Ai Qing (literally "Mugwort Green") is the pen name of Jiang Haicheng, born in Jinhua, Zhejiang province, the son of a landlord. His first major poem, "Dayanhe," recounts the unusual circumstances of his upbringing. A fortuneteller told his mother and father that their son was destined to "put down his parents." This prediction that he would violate Confucian filial duty led his father to send the baby to be reared by a local peasant woman named Dayehe. The child was taught to call his father and mother "Uncle and Auntie." In "Dayanhe," Ai Qing calls himself his nursemaid's son, and declares his solidarity with common folk like the nursemaid who brought him up in her home.

Ai Qing was sent to the local village school, not tutored at home like a landlord's son. He left China in 1929 to study art in Paris, where he supported himself by painting porcelains after his family cut off his financial support. He became a devotee of the French impressionist school of painting. His reading of Baudelaire, Rimbaud, and especially Apollinaire developed his interest in symbolist poetry. Michelle Yeh notes Ai Qing's conviction that the poet comprehends reality in terms of images. The strength of his verse lies in the images he employs. An equally great influence on Ai Qing's work was the verse of Mayakovsky and Whitman, "poets of the people." When he returned to Shanghai in 1932 he was arrested for political subversion and jailed for three years. Unable to paint in prison, he turned to poetry and began his first book of verse. It appeared one year after his release, in 1936, under the title *Dayanhe*. Although it appeared merely as a pamphlet, it immediately established its author's reputation.

When the Japanese swept south through Shanghai and Nanjing in 1937 he joined with Zang Kejia, Zou Difan, Tian Jian, and others to form the July Poets group. Their objective was to write simple, direct poems to stir the masses to resist the invaders. In 1938 Ai Qing moved to northwest China. This area, the cradle of Chinese civilization, was then (and still is today) the poorest, most backward part of the country. Ai Qing evokes this anomaly in "The North" and "The Wilds." He taught at Linfen Revolutionary University before moving south to Guilin where he served as a newspaper editor. In "The Street" he describes the chaos of life in this city under Japanese attack.

In 1941 Zhou Enlai helped him to travel, disguised as a Guomindang official, to Mao's base at Yan'an. He taught at the Lu Xun Arts Institute and was elected a representative to the local people's congress. He attended the 1942 Yan'an Forum for Literature and the Arts, where Mao called for art's subjection to political policy. This marked an end to the period of Ai Qing's greatest writing. He was forced to write a self-criticism after the conclusion of the forum, and abandoned the style that characterizes his greatest work.

After 1949 he became a vice-editor of *People's Literature*. Ai Qing was denounced during the Anti-Rightist Campaign of 1958 for failing to celebrate the new Marxist society. In 1959 he was sent to Xinjiang in the far northwest. Jailed and paraded through the streets during the Cultural Revolution, and attacked in public "struggle sessions," he was put to work cleaning toilets. In 1975, blind in one eye, he was permitted to return to Beijing as vice-president of the Chinese Writers' Association.

In all, Ai Qing published fifteen volumes of poetry, as well as translations of the French poetry of Emile Verhaeren. His work shows the influence of a variety of Western poets. Like both Whitman and the French impressionists, Ai Qing disregards the strictures of versification and stanza-form. Like Whitman, Ai Qing sacrifices conciseness of expression in favour of colloquialism. Whitman's style appears in Ai Qing's long catalogues of realistic description, and in the loose, rambling sentence-structure of some of his verse. As McDougall and Louie point out, the author avoids the prosiness that burdens some free verse by varied line-lengths, dramatic repetition, and striking colour imagery. Whitman's influence also is evident in the prominent role that the narrator assumes. Like Whitman's, Ai Qing's poems are often semi-autobiographical, like "Dayanhe" and "A Young Man's Journey"; like Whitman's his verse has an extempore feel to it, appearing to follow the narrator's spontaneous memories and observations. The narrator seems to be conveying to the reader just what he hears and sees.

But Ai Qing goes beyond mere realism. Rather, his poems are structured on a series of sensual images that typify the inner life of the common people whom he chooses as his subjects. For example, the hallucinatory quality of "Diaphanous Night" captures the kaleidoscopic whirl of drunken men's revelry. In "The Street," a rapidly shifting series of images conveys the social dislocation caused by the Japanese invasion. But unlike the French symbolists and their Chinese imitator Li Jinfa, Ai Qing presents symbols that are unambiguous. He makes clear what they mean. The fog that threatens to swallow the ragged peasant in "The Wilds" is an objective correlative for the peasant's befogged political consciousness. The last line of "Burdens" assigns an explicit meaning to the scene of carnage left by the Japanese bombing raid: "These are blood debts."

Though some of his stylistic devices may derive from Europe and America, Ai Qing transforms them into verse that is quintessentially Chinese. Like Tian Jian – but with Western sophistication – he writes about ordinary people. The gamblers of "Gambling Men" are China's poor. They are politically illiterate. They have no solidarity, no plan to throw off their crushing poverty, but only strive to beat each other out, to win each other's money in a futile resort to blind luck.

The concluding image of "The Street" – the girl dressed in a soldier's uniform – conveys commitment to the war against Japan, but without resort to any slogan. Significantly, the girl's uniform is green, the Communist uniform's colour, not grey, the colour of the Guomindang's. The poem's conclusion exemplifies the Communist policy of all-out resistance to the Japanese occupation. The propagandistic point of the poem is clear, if unstated: "Join the Communist army!"

More and more in the late thirties Ai Qing sought to write for the ordinary reader, anticipating Mao's prescription at the Yan'an forum. As his career went on, his work began to reflect a tension between populist realism and Mao's call for support of party policy. Sometimes, then, Ai Qing fell short of realism, as in his portrait of the main character in "He Dies the Second Time," which idealizes the life of the soldier, deemphasizing the blood and agony of war. Parts of this long poem are plain propaganda, written to encourage enlistment. Gunned down by the Japanese, the poem's soldier hero dies with "tears of joy" in his eyes.

It was Ai Qing's commitment to poetry about common people, intended for an audience of common people, that led him to criticize the obscure young poets of the early eighties for their vague, "misty" symbols. Ironically, this symbolism is not unlike that of the French symbolists whom Ai Qing himself admired and imitated in the early phase of his own career.

Diaphanous Night

1

Diaphanous night:
Coarse laughter rises from a path through the field.
An uproar of carousing men
Moves toward the slumbering town
Where sudden barking of dogs
Shakes the stars scattered across the sky.

Through the town's
Sleeping streets
And its slumbering square, they rush
Into the wide-awake wine shop.

A commotion of wine, lanterns, flushed drunken faces
And rowdy laughter:
"Let's go to the slaughterhouse
And drink beef soup!"

2

They head for the edge of town,
And through a gaping door into the glare
And the stench of blood, piles of meat, the hot sour stink
Of freshly stripped cowhides
And the clamour of men.

The oil lamp shines like a brush fire
On a dozen mud-stained faces
Of men from the grasslands.

This is our amusement hall.
All the faces are familiar.
We snatch up

Steaming beef-bones
And with open mouths we chew, we chew.

"Wine, wine, wine!
We want a drink!"
Like a brush fire, the oil lamp shines
On cows' blood, on the butcher's blood-stained arms,
On his forehead,
Spattered with drops of blood.
Like a brush fire, the oil lamp shines
On our muscles, afire with pain
And the strength of our anger and hate.

Like a brush fire, the oil lamp shines
On all the night's sleepless –
The drunkards,
The prodigals,
Roving bandits,
Cattle-thieves –
They come from every direction.

"Wine, wine, wine!
We want a drink!"

3

"Let's go while the stars
Are still bright and twinkling."
Coarse laughter rises from the path through a field.
The gang of carousers leaves
The slumbering town, making for
The slumbering grasslands,
Taking their uproar
Into the night, the clear diaphanous
Night.

1932

Dayanhe

Dayanhe was my wet nurse.
The name she went by was the name of the village where she was born.[12]
She was a child bride,
Dayanhe, my wet nurse.

I was a landlord's son;
And a child who sucked Dayanhe's milk,
Dayanhe's son.
By raising me, Dayanhe fed her family,
And I too was fed on your milk,
Dayanhe, my wet nurse.

Dayanhe, today I watched the falling snow and thought of you,
Of your grass-covered grave under the weight of snowfall,
The withered tile-grass on the eaves of your abandoned house,
Your mortgaged ten-square-meter garden plot,
The stone seat covered with moss in front of your door.
Today I saw the falling snow and thought of you, Dayanhe.

With your thick palm you held me to your breast and caressed me.
After you built the fire in the stove,
After you brushed the charcoal ash from your apron,
After you tasted the rice and to make sure it was done,
After you put the bowl of black-bean sauce on the black table,
After you mended your son's clothes, torn by hillside thorns,
After you bandaged your youngest son's hand, cut with a firewood cleaver,
After you crushed one by one the fleas in your husband's and sons' town clothes,
After you collected the day's first egg,
With your thick palm, you held me to your breast and caressed me.

I was a landlord's son.
After I had sucked Dayanhe's breasts dry

12 Dayanhe: literally "Big Weir River."

The father and mother who bore me took me back into their home.
I thought, Dayanhe, why are you crying?

I was a stranger in the house of the father and mother who bore me!
I touched the red-lacquered furniture carved with flowers,
I touched the ornate gold design on my parents' bed,
I stared uncomprehending at the inscription on the eaves, "The happy
ties that bind,"
I fingered my new silk clothes with their mother-of-pearl buttons,
I saw my mother holding at her breast a little sister I didn't know,
I sat on a lacquered *kang*[13] warmed by the brazier of flaming coals
inside it,
I ate white rice milled three times over.
But I was so nervous and bashful! Because I –
I was a newcomer in the house of the father and mother who bore me.

To live
After she had given me the last of her milk,
Dayanhe began to labour with those hands that cradled me.
She smiled, washing our clothes,
She smiled, carrying baskets of vegetables to wash in the frozen pond
outside the village,
She smiled, slicing parsnips still covered in bits of ice,
She smiled, scooping up in her hand the mash she fed the pigs,
She smiled, fanning the flames of the stove beneath the stewing meat,
She smiled, carrying baskets of soybeans and wheat on her back
to dry in the sun of the village square.
Dayanhe, to live
After she had given the last of her milk,
Laboured with the hands that had cradled me.

Dayanhe deeply loved the boy she had nursed.
At New Year's she was busy slicing winter-rice candy for him,
For him, who often stole back to her house at the end of the village,
For him, who would walk to her side and call her "Ma."

13 The *kang* is the traditional bed of north China, a hollow rectangular structure made of brick. One builds a fire inside it and sleeps on top.

Dayanhe stuck on the wall beside her stove his bright-coloured painting of the wargod Guan Yu.
Dayanhe bragged to her neighbours, praising her nursling.
Dayanhe once dreamed a dream that she could never tell anyone –
She was celebrating her nursling's wedding
In the splendidly decorated main hall,
And the charming bride called her "Mama."
Dayanhe loved her nursling dearly.

Dayanhe died without awakening from her dream,
And when she died, the child she had nursed was not by her side.
When she died, her husband who had beaten and cursed her wept,
Every one of her five sons wept, griefstricken.
When she died, she feebly called her nursling's name.
Dayanhe is dead,
And when she died, the child she nursed was not by her side.

Dayanhe departed holding back tears.
With forty-odd years of insults from the world,
The countless sufferings of a serf,
A four-*yuan* coffin and a few bunches of straw,
With a few feet of earth for her grave,
With a handful of ashes of burnt paper-money,[14]
Dayanhe departed, holding back tears.
Dayanhe does not know
That her drunkard husband is dead,
That her oldest son became a bandit,
That her second son died amid cannon fire,
That her third, fourth, and fifth sons
Live to the sound of masters' and landlords' curses,
And that I am writing this curse on an unjust world.
When I returned to my native land after a long time wandering,
And in the mountains or fields
I came upon my brothers, they were far dearer to me than they had been six or seven years earlier.
This, this, silently sleeping Dayanhe,
You do not know.

14 See above p. 269, note 8.

Dayanhe, today your nursling is in prison,
Writing this eulogy in praise of you,
Dedicated to your spirit, a purple shade under yellow earth,
Dedicated to your arms that reached out to embrace me,
Dedicated to your lips that kissed me,
Dedicated to your earth-dark face, warm and gentle,
Dedicated to your breasts that nurtured me,
Dedicated to your sons, my brothers,
Dedicated to all of them on earth,
The wet nurses like my Dayanhe and their sons,
Dedicated to Dayanhe, who loved me as she loved her own sons.

Dayanhe,
I am your son
Who grew by sucking your milk.
I revere you.

On a snowy morning, January 14, 1933

Old Man

The light falls on his profile,
On half of his ragged uniform,
On three brass buttons in the half-darkness.
Three pale yellow lamps gleam,
Their oil almost dry.
On his copper face, an ancient shine.
The cracked skin of his gnarled hands
Curls like frail roots, tentacles
That clutch the convulsing tail of a small life –
A loach that has slipped into the mud.
He rocks his old bronze forehead
Splattering seeds of saliva with his curses.
The tint of hunger
Dyes his words.

1933

Beggars

In the North
Beggars wander the banks of the Yellow River,
Roaming up and down the railroad tracks.

In the North
Beggars sound out their suffering
In poignant, sickening voices,
Moaning that they have fled from famine, floods,
War.

Hunger makes the elderly forget kindness,
And the young learn hate.

In the North
Beggars stare at you
With dogged eyes,
Watching you eat
And pick your teeth with your fingernail.

In the North
Beggars with soil-black hands outstretched,
Ask for pennies
From anybody,
Even from a soldier with nothing in his pocket.

1938

The North[15]

One day
A poet of the Ke'erqin grasslands
Said to me,
"The North is sorrowful."

Yes,
The North is full of sorrow.
The desert wind
From beyond the Great Wall
Sweeps all green from the life of the North
And with it the brilliance of the sun,
Shrouded in an impenetrable, dusty yellow,
A gritty haze
That never dissolves.
The wailing that rushes from the horizon
Terrifies
As madly it devours the earth.
The bleak wilderness
Freezes in December's icy wind.
Villages, hills, riverbanks,
Dilapidated walls, abandoned graves – all
Shrouded in earth-coloured melancholy.
A solitary traveler
Walks bent over,
Covering his face with his hand,
Gasping in the sandstorm.
Step by step
He struggles forward.
A few donkeys,
        Beasts with sad eyes
        And drooping ears

15 Although the poem is titled "The North," references to the Yellow River and to the desolate landscape make it clear that the poem is set in what is now called "the Northwest," the upper Yellow River basin, the cradle of ancient Chinese civilization. Today, as in 1938, it is the poorest region of China. The previous poem, "Beggars," is set in the same region.

Stoop beneath the burdens
Of this agonized land.
Wearily they tread
With listless steps
The Northland's
Long, lonely road.

The streams have long ago run dry;
Wheel ruts crisscross the riverbed.
How the North and its people
Thirst for the flowing springs of life!
Shriveled forests
And squat houses,
Thinly scattered,
Lie in gloom
Under the ashen canopy of sky,
Its sun invisible.
The huge flocks of geese,
Distressed, tumultuous,
Beat black wings,
Crying their restless sorrow,
And flee this desolate land,
Flying
To the South, where lush vegetation shuts out the sky.

The North is full of sorrow.
The three-thousand-mile Yellow River
Rages in muddy billows,
Sweeping disaster
Over the vast landscape.
Ages of wind and frost
Have engraved
Poverty and hunger on its face.
And I,
A traveler from the South,
Love this doleful North.
The sandy wind that cuts my face,
The cold that pierces me to the bone

Cannot drive me to curse it.
This bleak, endless waste
Moves me to reverence.
I see our ancestors
Tending herds of sheep,
Blowing Tartar flutes of reed,
Engulfed in twilight on this vast desert.
This spongy yellow earth
Holds the bones of our forefathers.
Here they first began to till the soil.
Here they struggled
Against the blows of Nature,
Guarding the earth,
Undaunted.
They left this land to us.
Its vast barrenness
Has given us a sparse language
And a broad outlook
That will never perish.
I cherish this ancient land,
That has nurtured the longest-suffering race in the world
Whom I love.

1938

The Street

Once I lived on this street.
My neighbours were refugees from flames of war:
Pregnant women, sick men, old grandfathers coughing and choking,
And grandmothers cradling small children in their arms.

Every day was another madhouse –
Innumerable people shipped to this small city in crowded trucks,
Its streets swarming with refugees, wounded soldiers, and children
forced from school.
Medleys of local accents swirled past my ears.

Then the street changed. Each day war brought greater prosperity.
Stalls with all kinds of goods lined both sides of the street.
Bean curd shops turned into restaurants, variety stores into hotels.
The house across from me became a hospital.

One day, black-winged formations covered the sky
And roar after roar convulsed the tiny city.
The enemy dropped deadly fire that destroyed this street.
Half the city was demolished.

Imagine it! Roofs torn off houses,
Parts of walls connected to nothing,
Wells choked with gravel, shattered roof-tiles,
Rafters burned to charcoal.

Grief-stricken, the people scattered and vanished,
(And who cared where they had gone?)
But I caught sight of someone,
A young girl who used to live in my courtyard.

Walking past me on a different street,
She said hello so cheerfully.
Her hair was now cut short and she wore leggings;
She wore the army uniform of grass-green.

Guilin, 1939

He Dies the Second Time

1 A Stretcher

By the time he wakes
He is already lying on a stretcher.
He knows he is still alive.
Two of his buddies are carrying him.
Neither says a word.

The air is thick with cold.
Low clouds blow overhead.
The chill wind shakes the treetops.
Hurriedly they
Carry his stretcher
Through the winter forest.

After flaming pain
His heart is still now.
After the horror
The field of battle has returned to quiet.

But the blood
Still seeps through the bandage on his arm
And continues dripping, drop after drop,
Onto the frozen roads of the motherland.

That evening
A regiment ten times more impressive than his own
Passes his stretcher in the opposite direction.
The feet of ten thousand men
Wipe from the road the red-purple traces of his blood.

2 The Hospital

Where are our rifles
And our blood-soaked uniforms?
Other comrades have put on our steel helmets.
Now we wear cotton-padded jackets embroidered with red crosses.
We lie here and lie here
Looking at countless bodies
Chewed by metal, gnawed by poison gas.
Each one greets and bids farewell to countless days that pass
Like an endless procession of black coffins
Under the dark eye of fear,
Here where no one's suffering

Is less brave than another's.
To oppose the enemy's attack
Every one has faced cruel gunfire
With the only life he has.
Each one has spilled his blood
On the place he was defending.
But today we lie here and we lie here.
People say this is our glory.
We want none of that!
We lie here, cherishing our memories of the battlefield
More dearly than memories of the villages where we grew up.
We would still rejoice
To charge through the flames of war
But now today we are
Trussed up like animals,
Groaning on these iron beds
In agony. How long
Must we wait?

3 A Hand

Each day at the fixed hour
A nurse arrives in uniform and white cap.
Without a word she unwinds
The gauze bandage from a wounded man,
Gently pulls off the cotton wad soaked in medication,
And washes away the stinking, bloody pus.
Her slender fingers are so nimble!
We could never have such a wife!
Nor such a sister –
Washing away the blood and the pus, rebinding the wound
So deftly, and all of it done with those ten fingers.
On one of those fingers a radiant glint of gold
Flashes over our wounds
And flashes into a certain place in our hearts.
She walks off, still without a word.

When she has walked away, he looks at his own hand:
A hand that once held a hoe, once hefted a rifle,
A hand worn rough and clumsy with hard work,
Now lying limp on his chest,
The hand at the end of his wounded arm.
Looking at his hand, then looking at her hand,
He thinks and frets,
Frets and thinks again.
What fate is it that has brought together
Two hands so different?

4 Healing

Time has passed in a void.
He walks out of the hospital
Like a convict released from prison.
He has taken off the cumbersome cotton-padded clothes
And put on a uniform of grey cloth,
Still embroidered with a red cross.
Freedom, sunlight – the world has come to spring.
The crowds of people in the street
Make him feel a stranger, and yet belonging.
The sun illuminates the street.
Startled awake from a long, deep sleep,
Life leaps in its radiance.
People hurry past.
He is the only one still weary.
No one notices him,
A wounded soldier. Today his wound
Is healed. He is happy,
But he is sobered by the understanding
That he is a soldier.
When a soldier's wound is healed he must return to battle –
This he thinks as he walks along.
His steps seem so unnatural;

His pallid face is painful to see.
None of the passers-by
Notices his suffering.
Only the sun stretching down its gleaming fingers
From the top of the telephone pole
Soothes his sorrowful, jaundiced face,
A face with a wan smile in its pain.

5 Military Bearing

Embroidered with a red cross, an unbuttoned grey shirt
Lies draped across his shoulders, its two sleeves hanging down.
The country boy walks along a straight, broad avenue through the
twilit city.
The thoroughfare intoxicates his senses.
A hubbub swirls all around him: noisy throngs of people,
Car horns and police whistles
Press him, stimulate and push him
Along the smooth sidewalk
Beneath dazzling electric lights,
Over slippery, tarred streets,
Past processions of late-model automobiles,
In front of elegantly dressed women.
He looks so ragged!
Yet suddenly he feels he should lengthen his stride
Because he wears a robe of glory.
He feels it is only right
To walk through the world with this proud bearing,
That only a man like him should
Walk this way through the world.

But even now as he strides along, head high,
His grey army shirt draped over his shoulders,
Feeling that everyone's eyes are watching his steps,
His face, bathed in electric light,
Begins to blush with embarrassment

For fear that people
Have guessed the secret in his heart.
In fact nobody notices him.

6 An Open Field

It is a bright, sunny day.
He walks toward the open fields
As if someone were calling him.

Today, the tread of his feet
On the soft, warm earth of a paddy-dike
Gives him an inexpressible joy.
He takes off his shoes,
Soaks his feet in the shallow water of the irrigation ditch
And playfully splashes his hand in the running water.
For so long every one of his days
Has been uniformed and regimented.
His days to come will be
Uniformed and regimented.
But he must spend today in the fields –
If only for the last time –
Searching for the thing that calls him.
What calls him, he does not know himself.
He sees a rice paddy,
He sees a peasant,
He sees a water buffalo pulling a plow.
O, it's all as usual, so familiar,
The same everywhere:
People call this China.
Trees turn green, grass grows to cover the earth,
These earthen walls, and further off
Those tile-roofed houses with people walking past.
He thinks of what they say – that this is China –
As he walks and walks.
What kind of day is this

That he should feel so silly, so happy?
Happier even than on New Year's Day!
Everything so radiant!
He smiles at the busy peasant.
He does not know why he is smiling,
And the peasant does not notice that he is.

7 A Glance

On a shady tree-lined road that stretches off to the suburbs
He walks in dense blue shadows
To avoid the eye-piercing glare of the sun. In the shade
He sees a horse and carriage roll past jauntily.
In it young men and women are riding,
All of them so neat and fashionable.
From their mouths come gales of laughter,
And a clear-voiced repartee that unsettles him.
He trudges on like a feeble old man.
Slowly he approaches a park.
At the foot of its marble moon-gate
He sees – a crippled soldier.
A pang of unexpected emotion rouses him.
He thinks – maybe this crippled comrade
Was the bravest one of all, maybe
He wanted to be buried on the battlefield.
But now he has to lie here, moaning,
For the rest of his life.
O, who would have the heart to look at this?
Who would not burn with fury to see it?
Let us return to battle,
Let us die happily in battle,
But not return with only one leg
To sob in front of a crowd
And stretch a filthy, scrawny hand
To beg for pitying alms!

8 Changing Uniforms

He takes off the grey uniform shirt embroidered with the red cross
And puts on the khaki uniform he wore months ago.
Where did the blood stains go?
The bullet-hole has been patched too.
Putting it on, he feels excitement in his heart,
Deeper than when he enlisted.
This khaki uniform and that grey uniform embroidered with the red cross
Have some eternal connection.
He and his comrades will be wearing them forever, forever changing them.
That's right, they must forever go on exchanging them, one for the other.
That's how it should be for a soldier until his country's war of liberation has been won.
These two uniforms are the banner
Of his life
As long as the war of liberation lasts,
A banner that must fly fiercely
Over the trampled earth of his motherland.

9 Send-off

Led by constant explosions of firecrackers,
By bugle calls that rouse the whole boulevard,
By the cries of spectators who crowd both sides along the way,
Let's march down the road paved with the hopes of the common people,
From the world of today to the world of tomorrow,
Let's march in step down this road that tomorrow's children will recall with gratitude.
Chests out,
We march between walls of people,
Embraced by their self-assurance and pride.
We march with thoughts on nothing but glory,

We aim at nothing but glory,
We no longer think of anything but a death for glory.

10 Thoughts

Have you understood
What death is?
To survive, to perish?
Plants too and insects
Cast their slough in a metamorphosis of life.
What does all this suggest to you?
Right – to be a soldier
And sacrifice your life to the war –
To die on a riverbank.
To die in the wilderness.
Icy dew will freeze our chests;
Our bodies will rot among clumps of weeds.
Throughout so many ages
Human beings have sacrificed their lives
To enrich the soil,
And used that soil to nourish
Their lives.
Who can escape the cycle of nature?
Well then what is wrong
With our dying in this war?
With our rifles on our backs
As we swing along in one long column,
Is not your heart too
Often troubled by something more powerful than love?
This day, as you set off for the field of battle,
Don't you feel
That you have lived
But that now you should die,
And that your death is for

Future millions
To live more happily than you?
Glory,
Praise –
What good are they
If we do not remember
That we die of our own pure, holy will.
After all, isn't ours the inexorable will
Of the nation?

11 The Charge

Forward! Courage!
Fix bayonets, comrades!
Let us bind our thousand hearts together
Into a single will –
To fight for the liberation of the motherland!
What is there to fear when we know it is glorious to die in battle?
Courage! Forward!
Humiliation and shame
Must come to an end.
We must wrest the fate of our motherland
From the hands of the enemy.
Only this holy struggle
Can bring us freedom and happiness.
Courage! Forward!
This glorious day
Is ours to seize!
Our lives
Can decide the battle
If we are steadfast in attack.
Comrades, fix bayonets!
Courage! Forward!

12 He Falls

It happened too fast
For an instant's thought.
In a lightning-flash of shock and wonder
A burning bullet –
A second time, the last time –
Pierced his body.
The life that he had lived in this world
Fell at last
Like a tree brought down by an enormous axe.
The instant before he closed forever
Those windows through which he had looked out on the world –
His eyes, covered in tears of joy –
He could think of nothing.
His mother was dead,
And he had no intimate memory of any woman:
A simple life!

A soldier
Knows no more.
All he knew was that he must die in the war of liberation.
And when he fell
All he knew was
That where he lay was the earth of the motherland;
People who knew more than he
Had once told him so.

After a while
His comrades searched him out.
It was the last visit they would pay him,
But this time
What they brought was not a stretcher
But a short-handled steel shovel.
Without choosing any special place
On this ground that he had guarded,

Not far from a riverbank
They dug a shallow hole.

After the earth, mixed with spring grass,
Had covered his body,
What he left behind to the world
Was one among numberless, pitiful earthen mounds
Scattered over the wilderness like countless stars.
People have never marked a grave with the name of the dead.
Even if they marked it,
What would be the point?

1939

Autumn Morning

A morning, pleasant and cool,
Just after sunrise
In a pitiful village.

A bird with a white eye-ring
Perches on the black roof-tiles of a squat shack.
Pensively it looks
At gold and purple clouds that fill the upper air.

It is autumn,
Already a year since I came to the South,
But here is no breath of the tropics,
No groves of lofty coconut palms.
In this village an inexpressible gloom has filled my heart.

Yet today as I am about to leave
I am strangely troubled.
Everywhere I go
The villages of China are destitute, filthy, dark,
But always they make me linger.

1939

The Wilds

How thin fog obscures the barren wilds!

The distant prospect is concealed from view.
What lay beneath a clear blue sky in bygone days is hidden:
The pine forest traced the horizon,
And behind the pines, the white chalk cliffs
Sparkled to greet the sunlight.
Now, dimly visible ahead,
A tortuous road, ash-yellow,
Gradually fades into fog.

These plots have been left to grow wild,
A chaos of clods turned by the plough,
Withered weeds,
And scattered,
Rotted stalks of grain.
Amid the expanse of gray-white
Loom the mingled shades of earth –
Yellow
And dull red-ochre, blurring into the colour of charred tea.
Only a few plots of turnips and other vegetables –
Scattered green patches
Cloaked in frost –
Grace
These monotonous, shabby fields.

In an irrigation pond
The water is drying up
After a long drought.
A few ragged earthen dykes
Zigzag through the opaque glow of fog.
The lush emerald
Water plants of bygone days
Have long since rotted, mired at the bottom.
All that remains are
Withered, twisted twigs

Standing dazed
Amid the steam that rises slowly from the water's surface.

Across the foreground stretches a hill,
A road winds up,
Undulating,
Then drops down into sparse woods and vanishes.
Scattered along the ashen yellow road,
Burial mounds
With neglected black headstones
Sink into oblivion.

Everything is like this –
Cold, and lonely.

O winding ashen yellow road!
People tramp and tramp along
In different directions,
Always chasing the same shadow,
Arriving at the same fate.
Up the toilsome, hungry road
What waits is calamity, disease and death.
What wanderer through this wasteland
Has known joy?

Still
I feel an intimacy
With these winter wastes.
In the bone-chilling frost
I walk rough paths
Along banks between neglected paddies
Through the dark brown hills
Until my steps grow heavy, and I feel stricken
Like an old ox dragging home its weariness.

But the mist!
Ashen, murky,
Vast and impenetrable.

The power lines and poles grow dimmer and dimmer,
Stretching in the distance,
Into endless expanse and depth.

You wretched, accepting,
Toil-worn, impoverished wilds!

There is no sound,
As if everything is stifled by the fog,
But over there,
From within a clump of brush
Comes a clamour of sparrows,
Their feathers trembling
In awe of the enormous cold.

Inside a fence of plaited brambles
A few tiny shanties huddle –
All alike –
A jumble of firewood heaped by each wall
And ragged clothes hung from bamboo poles.
Frost-rimed bark covers the hovels' backs.
Their feeble smoke dissolves into the fog.

What squalid days
Must the people spend in these hovels!
In and out they breathe the same air with their animals.
Their beds are like stalls for livestock,
Their tattered blankets
As rigid and black
As dried clay.

Cold and hunger,
Ignorance and superstition
Close their iron grip
On these shacks.

A peasant walks out of the fog
Toting a pair of bamboo baskets that sway from his shoulder pole,

Containing nothing but a few bunches of onions and garlic.
His felt hat is in tatters,
And his face as filthy as his clothing.
He sticks his hands, cracked with cold,
Into his waistband.
His bare feet
Trudge the frost-encrusted road.
Without a word
He slowly
Disappears into the fog
To the soft squeaking of his shoulder pole.

O desolate wilds!
Will you forever suffer
Injustice in silence?

How the thin fog obscures the barren wilds!

Early morning, 3 January 1940

A Pond in Winter

A pond in winter,
Lonely as an old man's heart
Bitter with experience of the world of men.
A pond in winter,
Dry as an old man's eyes,
Their luster dimmed by toil.
A pond in winter,
Untidy as an old man's hair,
Scant and white like grass after a frost.
A pond in winter,
Desolate as an old man full of sorrows,
Twisted by rickets, prostrate under a bleak winter sky.

1940

Burdens

Please make way,
Please step onto the sidewalk.
Let us lift them,
No need to push,
Please move aside.
Let us take them up,
Please don't cry out,
Please mourn in silence,
Let us raise them.

This one is a woman,
Her skull blown open.
Let her sleep well with eyes closed tight.
Let us carry her home
Where her family will make arrangements with sobs and hate.

This is a man from the Service Corps.
See where his gray sleeve is hanging?
That's his armband.
You recognize him, don't you, though his face is covered with dirt and ash?
The bomb shattered his arm that worked so hard.
While shielding you from harm he was murdered.
Please make way, but express your grief.

No need to push, there are more here,
Wounded soldiers, bedridden,
Wounded even worse
When the shameless enemy attacked the hospital.

Everyone please make way.
Let us lift them up.
Please, everybody, stand aside,
Let us through with the stretchers.
And everybody, please remember –
These are blood debts.

1940

Gambling Men

In the shadow of a city wall,
In a dark corner between houses,
Squat crowds of gamblers
Peering to see who won, who lost.

Ragged, fanatic,
They sway, heads clustered together.
Cries of victory, curses of loss
Accompany the clink of bets for the next round.

Women with children in their arms,
Hair disheveled, stand behind them.
The children struggle, sob with hunger,
The women gape, the men win and lose.

The players squat, stand, then squat again,
Crying out, slapping their legs in ecstasies of surprise.
With flushed faces and tensed mouths
They scheme to change fate in a single play.

A winner loses, a loser wins.
Changeless is the filth, the rags, the vacant stares.
Night comes. They scatter,
Returning one by one to somber shacks.

1940

A Young Man's Journey

Like a drifting canoe
Departing from a fragrant desert island,
A passionate, downcast young man
Leaves his tiny village.

I take no pleasure in that village,
As ordinary as a banyan tree
And ignorant as a buffalo,
But that's where I spent my youth.

The stupid villagers laugh at me.
I say nothing and hide my dream in my heart –
I want to know the outside world,
To travel to places I haven't even dreamed of.

They will be better than here;
There people live like gods.
There you don't hear the heartbreaking sound of a rice-mortar,
Or see the repulsive faces of monks and witches.

After Father counted out the silver dollars, five at a time,
He wrapped them in red paper and gave me a lecture,
But all the while my mind was elsewhere,
Thinking of that seaport dazzling in the sun.

What are you chattering about, you cheeky sparrows?
Don't you know I'm leaving?
And you, our trusty, honest family farmhands?
Why are you looking so dejected?

The morning sun shines on the cobblestone road.
In my heart I pity this village of mine.
It's like a decrepit old man,
Standing here between two mountains.

Good-bye, my poverty-stricken village,
My old dog, go home – hurry, hurry!
May the twin peaks bless you and keep you safe,
Until I too am old and return to you again.

1941

On a Chilean Cigarette Package

The Statue of Liberty
On a package of Chilean cigarettes
Is just a black silhouette
Though she holds her torch high.

For a trademark
This wrapper has room for the Goddess of Liberty.[16]
For some loose change you can buy it –
Finish the contents and she's gone up in smoke.

A cigarette pack tossed by the roadside –
I step on it, you spit on it,
But real or only a symbol,
The Statue of Liberty is a pack of cigarettes.

Santiago, Chile, 1954

16 "The Goddess of Liberty" is the common Chinese term for the Statue of Liberty.

Wang Yaping
(1905–83)

Wang Yaping was born in Wei country, Hebei province, the son of a relatively prosperous peasant family. As the local economy deteriorated, their landlord took advantage of Wang's family and reduced them to poverty. This experience of exploitation laid the foundation of Wang's subsequent allegiance to the Communist movement.

At Xingtai Fourth Provincial Normal Institute he encountered the new poetry and read radical writers Lu Xun and Guo Moruo. In 1927 the local warlord closed the institute and Wang returned home. When authorities jailed three of his collaborators on a small magazine, Wang fled to avoid arrest. He began a wandering life, living underground, moving from city to city, still studying poetry. In 1930 he was hired by a railroad company in Tanggu as a primary-school teacher. The next year the Japanese began their incursion into northeast China. Here Wang witnessed crowds of starving refugees choking the railroad stations, fleeing the Japanese army. It was these scenes, he later wrote, that impelled him to set out on the demanding road of art.

He accepted an invitation to go to Beijing to edit a poetry magazine. It was closed after two issues for anti-Japanese content. In 1931 Wang joined a league of leftist Shanghai poets whose ranks included Yin Fu. Then he moved back to Beijing. When another magazine there was closed in 1934, he moved to Japanese-occupied Qingdao, the setting of "Winter in the City." Here he met Zang Kejia and Wang Tongzhao, who encouraged him in his poetry. His first volume, *Winter in the City,* appeared in 1935. Images of winter, cold, and darkness convey the suffering of those who live under the Japanese.

In December of that year he participated in a protest against the Guomindang's failure to oppose the Japanese occupation of northeast China. The Guomindang issued an order for his arrest. Ironically, the one place he could find refuge was Japan, where the imperial regime was welcoming

Asian students in order to teach them Japanese culture. There Wang met leftist writers Guo Moruo and Tian Jian. When the Japanese swept southward through China in 1937 he returned to join the resistance, engaging in cultural work with Communist soldiers who were taking part in the defence of Shanghai. For an audience of illiterate peasant soldiers, "I wrote short songs ... and news report poems. They were crude, they weren't art, but they were useful to encourage the peasants in the resistance."

After the fall of Shanghai he made his way to Chongqing, where he worked with the Communists under Zhou Enlai, editing wartime journals with Guo Moruo and Gao Lan. He officially joined the Communist Party in 1946. After 1949 he studied folk poetry, incorporating its techniques into poems that celebrated Mao's transformation of Chinese society, and wrote the libretto of a revolutionary opera. Still, Wang's writing did not enthusiastically endorse every aspect of Mao's policy and he was arrested in 1955, released, rearrested in 1958, and imprisoned. During the Cultural Revolution he was subjected to public humiliation. Wang was exonerated and reinstated in the party ranks in 1981, two years before his death.

Wang said the impulse behind his poems was anger: anger against the Japanese and against the Guomindang regime that supported the landlord system. He embraced a populist style that abandoned the sublimity of the classical Chinese poetry he had studied in his youth in favour of an extreme realism. This realism can verge on the grotesque, as in "To Pawn an Arm."

The folk tales his grandmother told him left an indelible impression on Wang. The protagonist of "Before the Troops Marched Off" is already preparing for his own death in the upcoming battle by burning paper banknotes that (according to folk custom) would become money for him in the afterlife.

The New Poetry provided Wang with a medium to put common people's speech into a poetic form. His verse features short, clipped lines, with frequent exclamations, similar to the declamatory poetry of Tian Jian. The highly dramatic situations of "To Pawn an Arm" and "Before the Troops Marched Off" were created to reach this audience in clear, colloquial language. His work is a striking example of the New Poetry that is not derived from translations of European poetry but written in colloquial speech for "the masses."

Winter in the City

Before the moon has risen, dark sunset shadows
Weigh on lanes cut by a sharp wind.
Layer upon layer of gray smoke mingled with fog
Engulfs Chinese- and Western-style roofs.

Faded signs hang before shop doors.
A policeman pulls his face down into his leather collar.
A shriveled poster on a bulletin board proclaims:
"We're putting the city government in order and restoring prosperity!"[17]

Heaps of snow melt into slush
Along a chill, desolate avenue.
Dry leaves tremble on the naked branches,
Murmuring, "Here it is, winter in the city."

Qingdao, 1934

To Pawn an Arm[18]

Outside the window an endless drizzle fell.
Orchids wilted.
He flung aside the quilt.
"Where's my arm?" he cried in rage.
In pain he struggled to get up.
The nurse sang him a lullaby,
The story of the white-robed fairy.
His grief-filled eyes
Held back angry tears.
With his left arm he struck the bamboo bed.
Its creaking echoed his demand.
The nurse brought in his amputated arm,

17 When the poem was written, the city of Qingdao had been under Japanese occupation for fifteen years.
18 The poem satirizes the Guomindang army's failure to pay its soldiers.

Dripping antiseptic.
He lifted it with a coughing laugh:
"Baby, you killed so many Jap devils,
Today I'm going to pawn you!"
In his delirium he shoved the nurse aside,
Leaped the hospital fence
Like a prisoner in a jailbreak
And bolted straight in the pawnshop door.
"I'm pawning this arm! Five silver dollars!"
Thump! He flung it on the counter.
The proprietor of the shop cringed speechless
As antiseptic splattered his paper window.
"No pledges accepted today,"
Stuttered the nervous shopowner.
"Bastard! This arm is precious!
Worth ten thousand suits!
A thousand gold bars!
You stupid parasite,
I haven't been paid these three months
While you tradesmen gorge on rich food and wine,
And don't care whether the country lives or dies."
The proprietor lit a cigarette,
Forcing a smile.
In a rage the would-be client grabbed his arm from the counter,
Darted into the bustling street
With a mad laugh
And flung it at a passer-by.
Rain drizzled down from heaven,
So gloomy was the sky.

1937

Before the Troops Marched Off

He too had a wad of bills,
Wrote his name on all of them
And facing the yellow rice plants in the paddy,

The lovely green water, the blue hills,
He burned the paper money at a crossroads.[19]
With iron faces
They watched the paper magically transform to smoke
(It would be their money after they were dead),
Blown east to snuff out the Japanese bastards!
No one expected to come back alive.
With tears in his eyes, the captain exhorted them.
The people cheered and lamented their fate.
The willows stirred regretfully
And crickets played a song of parting.
They marched off and never gazed back.
A path of dust boiled up from the road.
The brims of their caps lowered,
The ranks of steel advanced, advanced,
Defying the rising sun.[20]

1937

19 See above p. 269, note 8. Realizing he may never receive proper burial, the soldier burns money in anticipation of his own death.
20 A symbolic reference to the Japanese flag.

Ding Ling
(1904–86)

Ding Ling was the pen name of Jiang Bingzhi, one of the foremost fiction-writers of early twentieth-century China. When her widowed mother moved to Hunan's provincial capital, Changsha, to enroll in a progressive women's school, she took her four-year-old daughter along. Her mother, who became an educator, became the author's model.

In 1920 she left Hunan province for Shanghai. In 1924 she moved to Beijing where she met the young writer Hu Yepin, who became her common-law husband. In the late twenties she returned with Hu to Shanghai where in 1927 she published her first fiction, the novella "Mengke," based on her own experience trying to become a movie actress. A second fictional work, "Miss Sophie's Diary," raised a furor with its portrayal of a progressive Chinese woman's psychosexual turmoil. Ding Ling continued portraying the psychology of the urban woman in a series of works that brought her wide popularity.

In 1931 the Guomindang arrested her husband Hu and shot him as a revolutionary. Ding Ling joined the Leftist Writers League and undertook editing one of its journals. In 1932 she joined the Communist Party. Her fiction began to move away from subjective personal narration to describe the life of peasants and the proletariat, developing many techniques later associated with the school of socialist realism. Detained by the Guomindang in 1933, she was placed under house arrest. In 1936 she escaped and made her way to Yan'an. A famous figure, Ding Ling was assigned important cultural duties. She organized drama troupes that performed propaganda plays and skits to rouse the local peasants against the Japanese invaders, and edited the literary supplement of *Liberation Daily*. She also served as vice-commander of a Red Army guard unit, wearing the soldier's military belt and revolver which she describes in "Yan'an in July." Her outspoken criticism of the inequality of women at Yan'an prompted a response from Mao in his 1942 "Talks on Literature and Art at the Yan'an Forum."

When the forum was concluded, Ding Ling was compelled to write a self-criticism. Her decade at Yan'an came to a close in 1946, not before she was subjected to further ideological censure. Early in 1949, just before Mao's final victory, she published *The Sun Shines over the Sanggan River*, often cited as a classic example of socialist realism. The novel is based on her experiences in the rural land-reform movement. It describes the reform's complex effects on a rural village, following Mao's prescription by avoiding gender issues.

"Yan'an in July" displays Ding Ling's social realism in verse form. The description of young people bent over the works of Marx and of the debate of common people on the street concerning the upcoming election of party representatives are concrete details that portray the nurture of the new revolutionary society. The poem's ultimate purpose is to rouse its audience to fight the Japanese, in accord with Mao's policy of all-out resistance. At the same time, the structure of the poem harks back to Ding Ling's earlier subjectivity: the entire poem takes place within the consciousness of the female narrator, a full-fledged participant in the new society which affords a place for women on an equal footing with men – the New China as Ding Ling herself boldly envisioned it – a vision which Mao was to reject. The poem's portrayal of life in Mao's base does not flinch from presenting physical challenges like the toil of harvesters and bloodshed in battle, but Ding Ling's Yan'an is free from internal strife. She presents its political system as a participatory democracy, with even the illiterate entitled to vote and everyone eligible to stand for office. Free from the beggars, streetwalkers, opium, and gambling dens that bedevil the rest of China, the society of Yan'an is "paradise." Such enthusiastic proclamation of the Party's policies and unmitigated praise for its achievements would become the norm for literature under Mao from 1942 onward.

But Ding Ling would not always restrain herself from conflict with the highest authorities. Denounced during Mao's Anti-Rightist Campaign of 1957, she saw her writings banned. During the Cultural Revolution she spent five years in jail, then was sent to the countryside for twelve years of manual labour before her eventual rehabilitation in 1978.

from *Yan'an in July*

  Listen! What's that sound?
The distant murmur of the Luo River
Carries a joyful folk song –

This year rains are heavy, the land is rich;
Trucks bring an enormous pile of plowing gear.
Our soldier-brothers urge us to the tilling:
"We hoe, you harrow,
And the land will sprout shiny green.
The scent of the shoots will float all round us.
No taxes! No levies! We've got travel passes.
Every plowman has a field.
This year a bumper crop, don't you waste it!"

A break in the rain, and the sky briefly clears
Over Yan'an's mountains and rivers. Its fields
Of lettuce and cucumber cover the city's outskirts,
Fragrant, sweet.
Jade-bracelet millet, buckwheat and wheat spread over the hills.
From dense coppices
Ruined forts rise toward heaven.
A constant mist of hazy rain
Blankets the mountains and rivers of Yan'an.

People in workers' clothes
Gather briskly from the streets,
Their accents from Wuhan, Xian, Shanghai,
From everywhere,
Arriving for the evening meeting –
We've been here only half a year.
Can't say the buildings are grand,
But the streets are clean,
Lined with scholar trees and mulberry trees,
No beggars, no street girls peddling their smiles,
No opium dens, gambling halls.
Just eight hours work a day,
And help if there's disaster – that's security.
What place is this?
Paradise.

Listen,
The wind stirs the branches,
Birds sing under the eaves.

Time to vote! Ah Huang,
You write Chinese
Like I write Latin.
Zhang Laobo can stand for office,
Li the Bull can be elected too.
Come on –
We can manage our own affairs.

Foggy clouds fly off, kitchen smoke vanishes.
Thousands of students, lively and clever,
All splendid children of the emperor[21]
And resolute
Give a hearty cheer
To close the evening meeting –
"We swear to die rather than be slaves in a conquered nation!"
A gust of wind,
A sheet of rain –
Yet our final song drowns out the downpour –
"Protect our country!
Guard peace throughout the world!"

The courtyard is lonely and still.
Inside the candle flickers uncertainly.
Under its light, readers are silent,
Absorbed in the teachings of Marx and Lenin,
Studying revolutionary theory
And technology of war,
Training for the front,
Not forgetting that over the horizon
China's elders, sons, and daughters
Suffer slaughter and cruel wounds.
These youth will risk their lives, heads falling to earth,
Bones shattered, flesh shredded,
To wrest back our land.

I enter my little room
With its new ceiling

21 I.e. every child in Yan'an is a now as fortunate as children of the emperor used to be.

And the graceful pattern
Of a new window lattice.
I pull off my boots,
Unfasten my military belt,
Hang my uniform on the wall,
Lay my pistol under my pillow,
And feel an instant wave of relaxation.
A thousand pounds slip from my shoulders.
The warm July breeze
Strikes the window with fine cool rain.
Yet my roused heart
Cannot sleep for eagerness.

Strong sons,
Bravely forward! Strike the enemy!
Let artillery roar again at Lugouqiao![22]
Exterminate the thieves!
Our guns, a hundred thousand strong,
Shake all the planet with their power
As we write a new chapter of history.
Our army of steel scares even the Japanese devils,
And will burst their surrounding wall of cannon fire.
Ready your gear, shoulder your packs,
Fix bayonets,
Ten years of struggle lead to this morning!
Fresh flowing blood will enrich
The field of battle,
Free our people!
The signal-cannon sounds,
Charge, charge!

In July's breeze freedom
Blows gently

22 Located in the Beijing suburbs, Lugouqiao (Marco Polo Bridge) was the site of a clash on 7 July 1937 between Chinese soldiers and Japanese troops who had seized a nearby railway station. Already in control of adjacent Northeast China, the Japanese used this incident as a pretext to occupy Beijing and subsequently to invade the rest of China.

Fluttering through Yan'an.
A wind – turbulent –
Surges.
The spirit to kill the enemy awakens
A reek of blood in the breeze
Wafting to Yan'an
From the land of death.

Rage gnaws
My wakeful heart,
Goading me to my feet.
Uniform down from the wall,
Belt drawn tight,
I pull on my boots,
Thrust my pistol in my belt.
I rush from the tiny room.
Rain still drifts through the sky,
Continual, warm,
Lightly caressing my cheeks.
July in Yan'an – so pleasant,
But my eager heart
Blazes
To transform all China into Yan'an.

1937

Zou Difan
(1917–95)

Zou was born in Tianmen, Hebei province. His father was a wood craftsman. In middle school Zou became acquainted with the New Poetry of Bing Xin and the leftist fiction of Mao Dun. After graduation he entered Hubei Normal College in Wuhan. His early verse was in imitation of Zang Kejia. In 1938 the Guomindang authorities suppressed his narrative poem "At Tianmen," which portrayed corruption on the home front in the war against Japan. Two years later another narrative poem on the exploitation of rural craftsmen was also suppressed. Zou joined a committee of the July Poets, working with Zang Kejia and other Communist writers to rouse the public to resist the Japanese occupation. In 1938, with Zang Kejia, Zou joined the Communist Eighth Route Army propaganda team, writing and performing plays to encourage resistance against the Japanese.

In 1939 he transferred to a Guomindang army propaganda unit. Here he boldly wrote plays criticizing the Guomindang's alleged inaction against the Japanese. When these were suppressed, he moved to Chongqing. His plans to travel from there to the Communist base at Yan'an had to be aborted because of the Guomindang surveillance of routes leading there. In fact, Zou never managed to set out for Mao's Yan'an. His 1937 poem, "Trekking North," portrays an imaginary journey there. Its narrator describes the arduous overland trip through the northern landscape where the ancient culture of "our ancestors" was born, a journey bearing the flame of freedom to "450,000,000," the population of all China. The poet avoids direct mention of "Yan'an" to slip the poem past Guomindang censors.

After the Communist victory in 1949 Zou moved to the new capital, Beijing, to serve as an official in the bureau for foreign cultural exchange. His writing in the fifties staunchly supported Mao's policy of collectivization in the countryside and the formation of people's communes. He glorified in verse the disastrous policies of Mao's Great Leap Forward, in which agricultural "modernization" caused famines in which tens of millions died. Zou's support of Mao's policies did not protect him from persecution during the Cultural Revolution. Following a decade of silence, he resumed writing after Mao's death.

Zou writes verse in straightforward, colloquial language. His poetry reflects his rural background. "Trekking North" represents the grueling journey that Communists made to the Mecca of the revolution during the thirties and forties. Zou's realistic description of the bleak, abandoned countryside can also be read as symbolic of the bleak social and political landscape of "unliberated" China, awaiting revolution.

Trekking North

Through forests dripping green
And far-off inkwash mountains,
Along the ochre highway
We trudge toward the vast north.

Now that we have entered
Among its blurred, uncertain shapes
We long still more fervently
For that distant,
Cloud-covered
Ancient city[23] with moss climbing its houses
And pines sprouting from the black ridges of its roofs.

Each day
We plod
Along the blazing, dust-choked roads.
Grit and perspiration clog our ears.
Our sweaty shirts
Cling to our backs.

Sand grinds into our straw sandals,
Wearing through them.
Day after day
The soles of our feet are rubbed rough as whetstones.
Soon our toes

23 Yan'an, Mao's base.

Will have trodden every road of China.
Joyfully free,
We retrace the footsteps of our ancestors.

At night
We fling ourselves down
In a damp room with moldering walls
And sit round the leaping candlelight.
We wash down stale biscuits with unboiled water.
Pulling off our mud-soaked sandals on the grass mat,
We recall our many footsteps:
Back there – a farm windmill has breathed its last.
A copper lock, corroded green, hung from its door,
Its owner long departed,
Leaving only a yellow dog to bark at emptiness.

The candle flame leaps up,
And our hearts blaze, leaping with its light!
Motherland,
Struggling in search of your radiance and your freedom,
Our blazing hearts pursue distant swirls of sand,
Never forsaking our three-thousand-mile route!
The candlelight, now feeble, casts black shadows.
Motherland,
Can our feeble strength join
To kindle the prairies ablaze,
Igniting, one by one, 450,000,000 candles?[24]
The candle flame leaps.
With red pencils
We mark tomorrow's line of march.
Braver and still more resolute,
We trek toward the north of north.

1937

24 The estimated population of China at the time the poem was written.

from *Five Short Poems*

1. Rickshaw

The day will come that brings no night thereafter.
The clear sky will be a canopy for our heads,
The sun will become the wheel,
And a high ideal will pull our rickshaw
As we ride to the climax of time,
The limits of outer space.

1942

Wang Tongzhao
(1897–1957)

Wang was born in Xiangzhou, Shandong Province, the son of a landlord. After studying in the provincial capital, Jinan, he went to Beijing in 1918 to enroll in China University. After graduation he worked in Beijing as a university lecturer and high-school teacher while publishing short stories as well as translations of articles by Lenin. In 1921 he joined Ye Shaojun, Mao Dun, and others to found the Literary Research Association, dedicated to the reform of traditional Chinese literature through the introduction of foreign models. The society had a populist goal, to encourage writing that reflected the life of the people; their preferred style was social realism. The society's membership was to include Bing Xin, Xu Yunuo, and Zhu Ziqing. Wang served for a time as editor of their publication, the *Poetry Monthly*. In 1922 he began his association with Lu Xun. In 1933 he published his novel *Mountain Rain*, which portrays peasants crushed beneath the weight of Chinese landlords and Japanese occupiers. The Guomindang banned the book and the author fled to England. He studied half a year at Cambridge before returning to Shanghai, where he worked for the revolutionary magazine *Literature*.

Wang was an eyewitness of the Japanese invasion of Shanghai in 1937. He spent the rest of the war years in Shanghai under Japanese control, supporting himself as a teacher, writer, and editor. In 1946 he returned to his native province as a professor in the Chinese literature department of Qingdao University. His health was already deteriorating. After years in hospital, he died in 1957.

As a translator Wang was familiar with foreign literature. His knowledge of European prosody appears in his own metric system, a more flexible version of the "dried bean curd" metrics of Wen Yiduo. From the romanticism of his early verse, Wang turned to patriotic, revolutionary themes, using realistic detail to convey political content. Poems like "The Battle Hymn of Shanghai" were written to mobilize the public to resist the Japanese occupation after the fall of the metropolis to the Japanese.

The Battle Hymn of Shanghai, I

Who mourns the destruction of the Enchanted City by the river?
Who laments its nightly Carnival of Lanterns?
Desperate, we struggle for our lives in the enemy's rain of blood,
We implore and struggle and scream to all points of the compass –
Come back, O soul of our country!

Look, a herd of wild beasts is startled by hunters,
Look, the flames of war cover the sky by day,
Look, a naked urchin, lying in the street, grips his wound,
Look, a plummeting white cloud explodes in streams of red!

Open more land! Extend the borders!
And how many young men are sent to their bloody graves on the river bank?
A punitive expedition! Conquest! And all at the whim of soulless generals.
But the enemy too have their widows and orphans, refugees – the common people's sufferings.
Why? To settle bloodstained history's tangled pile of debts.
Now the remote mountains and rivers open the way to enemy horses, trucks, and boats.
Now we are bound in iron chains,
Now can you bear our present shame?

By night sweet music floated on the spring river.
And the moon shone bright on the river of autumn
When a fearful wind arose, heaving a tide of blood to heaven,
Dissolving sweet song and bright moon in the flight of bullets and the swirl of gunsmoke.

The city's millions smile and grit their teeth
To reckon up this era's debt of blood.
We steel our hearts to pay it back! To take revenge!

We root out carefree pleasure from our thoughts.
You and I, all of us, must swallow the bitterness of our times.

Listen, can't you hear it? From north and south of the Yangzi, the neighing of enemy horses!

c. 1938

A Long
(1907–67)

A Long was the folksy nickname which the Guomindang military officer Chen Shoumei used as a *nom de plume*.[25] Chen was born in Hangzhou, Zhejiang province, the son of a struggling merchant family. After briefly serving as an apprentice at a silk farm, he undertook, against his parents' wishes, to support himself by publishing traditional-style poetry. He saved his publication fees for three years to enroll at Shanghai Institute of Science and Industry. In 1932, after witnessing Japanese military activity in their enclave in north Shanghai, he resolved to join the army. In 1934 he entered the Guomindang Military Academy in Nanjing. Observing Guomindang forces oppressing the common people, he secretly turned against the regime, began reading Lu Xun, and started to publish free verse about Guomindang oppression using a series of pen names to conceal his identity.

When the Japanese invaded Shanghai in 1937, he served at the front with the rank of lieutenant. A shell fragment pierced his cheek, knocking out most of his teeth. While recovering in Changsha in south central China, he began his long literary collaboration with poet and critic Hu Feng. He joined Zang Kejia, Ai Qing, Tian Jian, and other leftist writers as a member of the July Poets, dedicated to encouraging armed struggle against Japan. "Old Soldier" is an example of his war-front poetry written to stir readers to resist the invaders. The collection *The Stringless Lute*, which contains "Old Soldier," was first published in Guilin in 1942 under the pen name "Yi Men." The poem's last line unites two images: Japan's imperial symbol, the rising sun, glints on Japanese soldiers' blood, which has dried on the Chinese soldier's sword.

A Long moved in 1939 to Yan'an. Here he trained as an intelligence officer, then returned to Guomindang-held territory and rejoined their army where he acted as a spy, passing information to Zhou Enlai, who was working with the Communist delegation in Chongqing.

25 The "A" in "A Long" is pronounced *Ah*.

While being treated for an eye injury he wrote a novel which was eventually to become the first published in Chinese about the Nanjing Massacre, the most notorious Japanese atrocity of the war. The novel was awarded first prize by the editorial committee of the All-China Literary Resistance Association but remained unpublished for forty years, perhaps because it laid bare a disastrous Chinese defeat at a time when only victories were made public, or because it refuses to demonize the Japanese and is highly critical of Chinese military leadership.

In 1947 A Long received a warning that he had been denounced as a Communist spy. Abandoning his one-year-old son to the care of friends, he began a life of wandering, living under assumed names. Three years later he managed to obtain a position as an instructor with the rank of colonel at the Guomindang Military Academy's postgraduate school, where he continued his espionage on behalf of the Communists until their victory in 1949.

In the late forties A Long developed a theory of the individual creativity that he expected an artist could exercise under the coming Communist regime. After the Communist victory he was appointed chief of publishing for the Tianjin Literary Association. In May of 1955 he was arrested as a leading member of the "Hu Feng clique," Communist writers who were imprisoned as counter-revolutionaries because they published critiques of Mao's transformation of Chinese society. (A Long's refusal to follow the party's rubric can already be seen in his vignette of the battle-tried veteran of "Old Soldier," who is asleep in the saddle – hardly a pose for a propaganda poster.) He was also charged for having spied for the Guomindang against the Communists. He was incarcerated for twelve years in Tianjin prison, where he died of a bone disease in 1967. He was exonerated of all charges in 1980. A Long's literary reputation took flight in 1987 with the posthumous publication of *The Bloody Sacrifice of Nanjing*.

Old Soldier

An old soldier
On a scrawny horse
Rides out of the thin dawn mist.
His silhouette – a blur – reaches the end of a wood,
Then is lost again in fog.
His filthy army cap is pulled down over a deeply lined forehead,
His beard is stiff with frost,
Steam puffs from his nostrils,

His sunken eyes are shut,
His shriveled cheeks sag,
His hands are pulled inside his padded sleeves.
The reins lie slack on his horse's hairless, scabby neck.
Weary, he slumps forward.
His nag's rocking gait carries him who knows where,
Day after day.
Across his back, a sword
With a bit of dust,
A glint of steel,
A streak of frost,
And a smear of blood catching the rising sun.[26]

from "Into the Battle," 1939

26 A reference to the Japanese flag.

Gao Lan

(1909–87)

Gao Lan ("High Blue") was the pen name of Guo Dehao. His father, who died when he was one year old, was a minor officer in the Qing dynasty army in Heilongjiang province, northeast China. His mother came from the Daur minority nationality. Gao Lan grew up in Qiqihar in the home of his uncle. In 1926 he graduated from Qiqihar First Normal Institute and went off to school in Beijing, where in 1928 he enrolled in the Chinese department of Yanjing University, where Bing Xin taught. In 1930 he started work as an editor of the literary section of the daily newspaper *Jingbao*. After the Japanese army invaded northeast China in 1931, he served as a volunteer secretary for the underground fighting the occupiers. From this point on, the bulk of his writing – poetry and reportage – was to encourage resistance against Japan. His output included pieces urging women to join in active struggle against the invaders. After graduating from Yanjing he worked as a middle-school teacher in Tianjin, where he involved himself in the Communist movement.

In 1936 he moved south to teach in Wuhan, then the capital, where he worked with leftist writers under the novelist Mao Dun. When the Japanese occupied Wuhan in 1938 he joined the exodus to Sichuan province, where he taught and wrote propaganda poetry for public readings and radio broadcasts in support of the war effort. He was dismissed from one teaching post when the school authorities learned that he was really the Communist poet known as Gao Lan. Eventually he had to take a low-paying job as secretary in a milk plant. In 1941 his seven-year-old daughter Sufei died of misdiagnosed malaria. A year later, he commemorated her in "Elegy for My Daughter Sufei."

After the Communist takeover he was named professor of Chinese at Shandong University, but in 1957 he was denounced as a rightist. Subject to persecution throughout the Cultural Revolution, he was not rehabilitated until 1979.

Gao Lan wrote in a realistic style employing plain diction. He played an important role in the declamatory poetry movement, writing verse for public reading. Rhyme and rhythm – both of which he employed flexibly – were to make his verse attractive to the listener's ear. Poems of the war, he wrote, "should address the street, and reach poor villages." Poetry should "give expression to the thoughts and feelings of the masses, with a clear revolutionary purpose." It is ironic that his finest poem, the elegy for his daughter for which he is chiefly remembered today, has no revolutionary content at all but instead is filled with what he ordinarily strove to eliminate from his writing: personal sentiment.

Elegy for My Daughter Sufei

Where have you vanished to, my Sufei?
A year ago today
You stood on the terrace singing
"Drive out the Japanese, take revenge!"
Now grass has grown over your grave.

My child, I thank you for the joy you gave me
Through years of poverty.
But will the grief you brought me last forever?
One year!
The spring grass turned yellow, the autumn wind rose,
Snowflakes fell, the swallow has returned,
And still I dread
Walking to your little grave
For fear my weeping
Will trouble your soul's rest.

One year!
Dawn and daylight slip away,
Twilight fades, and night comes again,
But still I cannot lift my pen.
Anguish for you so tears my heart
That I cannot write my grief.
The moment I think of you
Tears blot the page,

Tears wet the brush,
Tears soak my memory
Through the bleak and bitter days.
My child!
All that you left was so tidy, so well arranged:
A sky-blue bookbag,
Your scarlet skirt,
Pictures collected from cigarette packages –
And, O my child! – the green marble that you treasured.
"Sufei," I whisper,
Bending over the box, suddenly weeping.
When I wake it is deep night, the moon in the west.
Sighs of cold wind carry the distant cry
Of the lone watchman – "Three o' clock."

I didn't take care of you, my daughter!
You had malaria,
And I threw away money on doctor after doctor,
Useless man that I am!
What I got for the last of my possessions
Was the price of the white boards
For a coffin to carry you under the ground.
My cursed convictions
Kept me from burning money on your fresh grave
To take with you below.
Your seven years upon this earth
Were toil and squalor,
And you went among the dead with empty hands.

Tell me, child, in that world
Do you still put your fingers in your mouth,
Stare at other people's children eating peanuts,
Still admire the bright clothes of other girls,
And lower your head?

I know your soul will float forever
Through endless night! O, where are you?
Come back, Sufei!

In dreams I search for you.
I know you can't retrace that crooked road,
But my breast could warm your ice-cold body.

Far in the hills the wailing of a bird
Wakens my memory.
Night rain pours down, cold and desolate.
Quietly I put on my robe,
Take the deathly green lantern, and walk out into the storm,
The dark,
The hills,
The fog,
Calling out your nickname, "Little Fish, Little Fish!
Come here, it's your father!
Walk toward the green light!
Don't be afraid!
It's your father, waiting in the storm!"

The tears of the candle turn to ash, the light goes out.
My throat grows hoarse,
I hear the cold frost settle
And the worms turning the earth.
My child, why won't you answer?
The sky-wind is fleeing across the peaks
And a star is twinkling over Cemetery Hill.
Is it your tear, my child?

Child,
Seven years you wandered with me
Across mountains and hills,
And every day ill-clad.
Do you remember winter in that old city?
The snowstorms so frequent in the long nights,
The thin blankets, our family of three,
Our supper only sweet potatoes, and afterwards, weeping.

Yet poverty did not daunt us,
You were so beautiful,

Adorning our distressed home.
Leaves fall, blossoms scatter.
What is left me now?

You loved to write and draw,
So when I laid you in your coffin,
Mad with grief,
I placed a pencil in your right hand,
And in your left a roll of writing paper –
A year ago!
And I have no tidings from you since.

What should I write to you?
This year's passing has been as ten.
Life as a writer reduces me to a beggar.
My back is bent;
My hair grows gray;
The rich grow richer, the poor poorer.
The world is as it was.
My last youth and tenderness
Went under the burial mound with you.

What should I write to you?
Every stroke a tear,
Every sentence a sigh.
Putting down my pen, I sob.
Finished weeping, I take it up again.
For others, spring came late this year;
For others, birds call and flowers bloom.
I have wept for my daughter into the cloud-filled sky
Against the east wind.
Now I burn this poem as a sacrifice to you.

Little Fish, my daughter,
Rest quietly.
The night grows deeper,
The frost colder,
Harsh winds course through the wilderness.

Thunder and lightning will rock the massive peaks,
And I will walk into the storm.
I have nothing left to care for,
My daughter!

If in your coffin you hear a small tapping sound,
It is my last tears falling into the world below.

1942

Liu Jia
(1916–)

Liu Jiayu, a soldier-poet who became a high-ranking army cadre, exemplifies the prominent role that Mao Zedong assigned to literature in the Communist army. The author wrote under the pen name "Liu Jia." He was born in Haicheng, Liaoning Province. In 1935 he entered Northeast University in Beijing to study history and geography. When the Japanese occupied Beijing in 1937, he left to join the Communist Eighth Route Army in the Jinchaji region along the borders of Shanxi, Henan, and Hebei provinces. The next year he began work as an army political cadre, serving as an administrator of literary and artistic productions. In 1940 he began writing one-act plays and musical dramas, comic dialogues, and skits with titles like "The Red Riflemen" to be performed for the soldiers, plays that reflected Mao's guidelines, propaganda pieces in support of party policy, portraying soldiers and peasants and incorporating folk song and folk dance. His poem about the tax collector of General Yan Xishan – a warlord in alliance with the Guomindang – is an example of poetry in service of the party line, an attack on Chiang Kai-shek that describes oppression of the common people allegedly committed by Chiang's warlord allies.

In 1948 Liu was named vice-director of the northern military region's literature and arts bureau. He went on to hold a series of administrative posts. In 1975 he became director of the August 1st Film Studio, and in 1979 vice-director of the army's academy for literature and the arts.

Governor Yan Xishan's Collector of the Grain Tax

Governor[27] Yan Xishan's Collector of the Grain Tax
Comes to the village.
He grabs the village chief:

27 The word in the original is *dujun*, a Guomindang term for military governor, rather old-fashioned by the time the poem was written. The poem is set during the Civil War between the Guomindang and the Communists in northwest China. General Yan was a Guomindang ally.

"In three days I'll collect the levy of wheat.
If one grain is missing
I'll make up the difference with your head!"

When he's finished, he mounts his horse and rides away,
Taking two sheep and a cow behind him
Tied to his saddle.
The people peer out their barely opened doors
Clinging to the doorposts,
Tears in their eyes.

The chief of the village strikes his gong
And the people's hearts freeze.
They rush home,
Ransack the grain bin,
Even scoop rice, dripping wet, from the pot,
And sell their few possessions
To buy grain for Governor Yan Xishan.

Take your choice: the Japanese
Or General Yan –
Six of one or half a dozen of the other.

When the Tax Collector returns,
His horse munches corn in the trough.
He sits in the big house getting drunk.
The people, in rags, crowd outside the village office door,
Watch their grain loaded on the scales,
And feel stones weighing on their hearts.

Someone who'd scampered over the wall
Is roped and pulled back.
Those hiding in haystacks
Or lying sick on their *kangs*[28]
Are dragged out.

28 See above p. 279, note 13.

The Tax Collector raises his whip higher and higher,
He binds the people tighter and tighter.
Wooden chests, cotton quilts, clothes, pots, bowls, pans –
His men tote it all out their owners' doors.

Then from up the street a woman comes running,
Her hair disheveled,
Pushes her way through the crowd
And drops a sack on the ground.
"Here's my grain tax,
Give this to General Yan! If it's not enough,
Take us and give us all to the General!"

The village chief is stunned.
He opens the sack and pours out its contents.
The people shrink back. "Good God!"
Dripping blood, the heads of two children.
The one with pigtails
Is the woman's daughter,
Little Silver, three years old.
With cries of "Murder, murder!"
The crowd recoils.
Falling to the ground, the woman spins round,
"I'm the murderer,
With my own hands I killed them
To pay my tax."

The tax man grins
And coldly prods the village chief,
"Hurry up! Next!"
The crowd stands dumbstruck.
The north wind rises and blows shrilly.

20 November 1945
As heard on the western front

PART FIVE

The Nine Leaves Poets

Introduction

MICHEL HOCKX

The group of poets known as the "Nine Leaves" is interesting not merely for aesthetic but also for historiographical reasons. Officially no such "group" or "school" existed in pre-1949 China, as its name derives from a collection that was not published until 1981. They have been written into literary history retroactively based on their activities, their position, and their aesthetic concerns of the 1980s. The group became known as the Nine Leaves from the title of the 1981 anthology, edited by several of the group's members. In our book we include poems by eight of the group's nine.

Many of the Nine Leaves poets studied at Southwest United University in Kunming during the war. In this relatively peaceful setting, far away from the front, on a campus where many of the leading intellectuals of prewar China were assembled, they shared a love of Western poetry, especially the modernist work of T.S. Eliot, and the treatment of war in the work of W.H. Auden. They were also inspired by the presence on campus of foreign professors of English, most notably I.A. Richards. After the war ended in 1945, and before the Communist takeover of 1949, the poets who later were to become the Nine Leaves were active in academic circles in Beijing and Tianjin. Their names were frequently seen in the pages of literary magazines, especially two published in Shanghai in the late forties, *Poetry Creation* and *New Chinese Poetry*.

While mostly sympathetic to the left, the poets who came to be known as the Nine Leaves were writing in Guomindang-held territory and so were in no way bound to observe Communist Party literary standards like poets who had joined Mao in Yan'an. This helps to explain why among leftist poets writing after 1945, their work stands out for its quality. They were not restricted to versifying Communist Party policy but freely expressed their reactions to the political crisis and wrote about personal subjects as well. Many of their poems reflect the social and political ferment in Shanghai, still under the control of the Guomindang. Hang Yuehe's "Last Performance" gleefully anticipates the downfall of Chiang Kai-shek. Less optimistically, Yuan Kejia's "Thinking about Our Times" expresses the confusion of the non-aligned intellectual caught in a swirl of leftist rhetoric. In "Nanjing" and "Shanghai," Yuan portrays the social and political chaos that preceded Chiang's flight and the arrival of the Communist forces.

After Mao's takeover in 1949, the Nine Leaves poets found no favour with the new literary establishment and were refused publication. Some were persecuted. Both Hang Yuehe and Tang Qi spent time in labour camps. But most of them managed to survive the Cultural Revolution and emerged in the late 1970s as highly respected members of an intellectual, academic, and literary elite representing a bygone era of internationalization and cosmopolitanism. With the 1981 publication of their joint collection they not only produced a testament to their literary camaraderie in the forties, they also gave a signal (no doubt supported by the new Party leadership, which still tightly controlled all publications in those days) that more "obscure" poetry was once again legitimate. Many of them also used their cultural influence and status to provide active support to "obscure poets" such as Bei Dao as they tried to create a niche for their own work.

Most of the writing by the Nine Leaves group is modernist in nature, and much of it has the war as its topic, treating it in a very different way than the "peasants and soldiers poetry" of the preceding section. See for example Mu Dan's 1945 poem, "The Flag":

We are all beneath you as you flutter in the sky.
The wind is your body, the sun your fellow-voyager
As you long to fly beyond mere matter tethered to the earth,

A word that everyone knows, now written on the sky,
Simple, clear, vast, formless,
The roving spirit of ancient heroes, once more alive.

Your slight body sets war aflame,
And when war ends, you alone remain untouched.
We turn to ashes, but glory survives in you.

We are sometimes in confusion, too ready to assume guilt
As capitalists and landlords make you their pretext,
Seizing the peace that belongs to us.

You are everyone's mind, but wiser than all,
Ushering in the dawn, suffering through the night,
Most able to express the joy of freedom,

First to feel the four winds' tempests,
Everyone's orientation. Thanks to you victory is confirmed.
It is you we admire, who belong to the common people.

In terms of expression of patriotic feeling or collective sentiment, this poem is about as far as the Nine Leaves poets were willing to go. More often they capture the war in rich, fragmented imagery that fosters sentiments of intellectual distance and emotional alienation, as in the poem "Isolation" by Chen Jingrong:

Frequently I stop short
As a stray breeze blows past.
Often I lose my way
At the chance peal of a bell.
A cloudless sky
Induces me to muse
On the unfathomable blue-green
Of pines and grass.

About to be launched, a ship stands poised.
An arrow is ready to soar;
The taut bowstring contains its feathered flight.

Terrified by fire alarms,
Vague human forms rush through the tormented night.

Amid the sudden unfamiliarity of daily things
We are isolated from the cosmos.

In terms of critical reception, the most successful of the Nine Leaves poets is undoubtedly Mu Dan, who is nowadays considered to be one of the greatest modern Chinese poets. In terms of continuous impact, however, Zheng Min, who produced much new work in the 1980s and 1990s and was also influential as a critic and scholar of literature, should perhaps count as the greatest of the Nine. Most remarkably, it was Zheng Min who, in the 1990s, having been influenced by recent developments in poststructuralist and postcolonial theory, called for a re-thinking of the "Westernized" values of New Poetry and a return to the resources of the classical tradition, attacking the "translation style" and questioning a style of writing of which her own work was the epitome.

Mu Dan

(1918–77)

Mu Dan was the pen name of Zha Liangzheng, who was born in the coastal city of Tianjin into a family which had included distinguished Qing dynasty scholars. In 1935 he entered Qinghua University, Beijing, where he soon transferred from geology to foreign languages and literature. After the Japanese occupied Beijing he joined many of his professors and classmates in the long trek to Kunming where, at Southwest United University, he studied modern British poetry under William Empson and encountered the poetry of T.S. Eliot and W.H. Auden. After graduation he taught at Southwest United for two years, then joined the Chinese army as an interpreter. He survived his unit's retreat from Burma into India under conditions of extreme hardship; many men in his unit died of starvation and disease.

Mu Dan's first collection of poetry was published in Kunming in 1945. Other volumes appeared in 1947 and 1948. He had left China in 1945 to study English and American literature at the University of Chicago, where he supported himself with a series of menial jobs, including work as a delivery boy. He returned to China in 1952 to teach at Nankai University in Tianjin.

Mu Dan's verse displays elements of formalism. He writes in stanzas, but the number of characters in each line varies. Of his "Eight Poems," numbers 1 and 7 employ near-rhymes in a formal pattern. In other poems the use of rhyme is less systematic. Under the new Communist regime, the writers who would later be known as the Nine Leaves Poets were censured for failing to put politics first. Barred from publishing their own work, they turned to translation. Mu Dan produced translations of Russian and British literature, especially of romantic poets like Pushkin, Byron, Shelley, and Keats.

During the Hundred Flowers Campaign of 1957, when censorship was temporarily relaxed, Mu Dan wrote an article for which he was soon denounced. Branded a counter-revolutionary in 1959, he was dismissed from teaching. During the Cultural Revolution, Red Guards burned his library.

With one side of his head shaved, he was exposed to mockery and attack at public meetings, then sent to the countryside for "re-education" through manual labour. His health deteriorated. In 1972 he was permitted to work again as a librarian in Nankai University library and he returned to writing poetry in 1976. Struck by a bus in 1977, he never fully recovered and died of a heart attack two years later.

The influence of Eliot and Auden appears in Mu Dan's use of concrete imagery to portray metaphysical subjects. To convey nuanced themes, the author preferred a longer line than is usual in Chinese poetry. Not infrequently his language is coloured by Western syntax. Under Mao such poetry as Mu Dan's, conveying complex thought and emotion, was denounced for "modernism." Complexity was risky when it came to political themes. In "Demobilized," Mu Dan's praise of the soldier (a hero figure for leftist poets) is qualified; the soldier's heroic service has contributed to a mistake of humanity – war. This sort of moral subtlety was anathema for a Maoist regime demanding that literature enforce the party line.

Mu Dan was no supporter of the Guomindang either. "The Flag," written in 1945, denounces the "landlords and capitalists" who commandeer the benefits of peace that rightly belong to "the people." This is a political stance that accords well with the Communist agenda. But the sophistication of a poet who wrote that love "is born in the crossing of swords between the sexes, and dies in overintimate, overcasual submission" was not welcome under Mao, who required that poetry be simple and explicit in order to galvanize the masses. Even after Deng Xiaoping's reforms, the complexity of Mu Dan's work troubled older Communist critics. But for the younger generation it has been otherwise. The post-Mao poets of the "obscure" school encountered Mu Dan's translations of Western poets in the "Brown Cover Books" that circulated in secret while they were living in the countryside during the later years of the Cultural Revolution. For them, Mu Dan's willingness to confront metaphysical darkness and psychological complexity made him one of the most influential authors of the first half of the twentieth century.

Spring

Green fire shimmers on the grass
And yearns to embrace you, O flower.
Struggling from the earth, blossoms stretch upward

As warm breezes ruffle them or soothe them.
If you are awake, open your window
On the loveliness of this garden full of desire.

Under a blue sky, the eternal mysteries bewitch
Our twenty-year-old bodies, so restrained,
Just like the songs of birds made out of clay.
You are kindled, curling, curling, with nothing to yield to:
Light, shadow, sound, colour all stripped bare,
Agonized, longing to stretch out, to form new alliances.

1942

from *Eight Poems*

1

You are watching this great conflagration
That I lit for you, but me you cannot see.
Alas, the fire is just the maturity of age,
Yours, mine – and our separateness, the separateness of mountains.

During the natural transformations over the years
I loved a fleeting you.
Though I weep and turn to ash, and turn to ash and burn again,
Girl, it is nothing but God playing some game with himself.

3

That tiny beast of your passing years
With its breath like spring grass
Brings you colour, fragrance and the ripeness of your flesh –
And wants you to act crazy in the warmth of the dark.

I have passed through the marble palace of your Reason,
Cherishing its hidden life.
Our touching of hands is like a seeded field,
Nurturing your stubborn logic, and my shocks of pleasure.

7

Storm, a distant road, deserted night,
Loss, remembrance, time infinitely unveiling,
Fears that all of science can't dispel
Lead me to seek the serenity of your breast.

Ah, in your untrammeled heart
Lovely images appear, then as quickly vanish.
I see your lonely love,
Rising, growing, parallel with mine.

8

There is no closer intimacy;
All that is between us falls into an accidental pattern:
Only the sun that penetrates the profusion of leaves
Divides, shining at once on our two willing hearts.

Come season's end, each will flutter and fall,
But the enormous tree that grants us life is ever-green;
Its cold, heartless mockery of us (and its sobs)
Turn to peace in the unity of its ancient roots.

1945

The Flag

We are all beneath you as you flutter in the sky.
The wind is your body, the sun your fellow-voyager
As you long to fly beyond mere matter tethered to the earth,

A word that everyone knows, now written on the sky,
Simple, clear, vast, formless,
The roving spirit of ancient heroes, once more alive.

Your slight body sets war aflame,
And when war ends, you alone remain untouched.
We turn to ashes, but glory survives in you.

We are sometimes in confusion, too ready to assume guilt
As capitalists and landlords make you their pretext,
Seizing the peace that belongs to us.

You are everyone's mind, but wiser than all,
Ushering in the dawn, suffering through the night,
Most able to express the joy of freedom,

First to feel the four winds' tempests,
Everyone's orientation. Thanks to you victory is confirmed.
It is you we admire, who belong to the common people.

1945

Demobilized

The destroyer of cities is back in the city.
The anonymous soldier is a person again.
War brought you loneliness, but the thought
Of that iron companion gives you joy.

Here it's of no use. What was strange is still strange.
There are no words of fire to sacrifice your life for,

No quick intimacy, no childlike boldness
To shatter this banality.

Here danger begets no illusions.
Accustomed to getting, the people all wait greedily,
But in ignorance, and with no means to live.
The protector of the city is back at his mother's bosom.

Your past was death, and now you long to be reborn.
Reluctantly you left,
But now our victor returns to face defeat.
You who brought peace, perhaps you find it impossible

To return to peace at once. Peace shatters you.
After war's vicissitudes, you cannot bear the sameness of every day.
Companion of martyrs, you came back alive, unprepared
To discover that your bright future concealed a new enemy.

We groped to find words to express
Your great significance, as it suddenly ended.
You have to return to the ordinary, to the void that follows action.
Take off your uniform, hot-blooded dreamer.

Yet, though it's worn, maybe you'd better wear it for now;
It's easier. The past gave you the joy of sacrifice,
But this is daily life. Now you must try to take up
What you left behind, though you're already among us!

Weary brother, you are almost a mystery,
Longing for the youth you spent in famous places.
Since you return from war, a mistake of humanity – yours included –
An honour is yours that you cannot forget.

1945

Du Yunxie
(1918–2002)

Du is the lone poet in this collection who was born outside China. His self-taught father and illiterate mother emigrated to work on a banana plantation in Malaysia. Their son attended a school established by the plantation-workers for their children. At the age of fifteen he returned to Fuzhou, the capital of his parents' native Fujian province, where as a senior middle-school student he began to contribute essays to the literary supplements of local newspapers. In 1938 he entered the agronomy department of Zhejiang University. As the Japanese invasion moved inland from the coast, this department relocated southward to become part of Xiamen University, which had itself relocated inland from the city of Xiamen to Changting, Fujian province. Here Du sat in on the lectures of Lin Geng, who ignited his interest in poetry.

Lin wrote Du a letter of recommendation to enroll in the foreign language department of Southwest United University, located in distant Kunming. The journey to his new university took him several thousand kilometers westward. On the way he passed through Japanese bombardments and also fell ill, having to recuperate in a hospital.

Finally arriving in Kunming, he began his studies. Among the New Poets on the faculty of Southwest United were Wen Yiduo, Zhu Ziqing, Feng Zhi, Bian Zhilin, Li Guangtian, Chen Mengjia, and the novelist and poet Shen Congwen. Among Du's classmates were Zheng Min and Yuan Kejia, who would later be classified with him among the Nine Leaves Poets. Shen Congwen arranged for Du to publish poems in the literary supplement of Hong Kong's daily newspaper, *Dagongbao*.

In 1941 Du secured a job as English interpreter for the Flying Tigers, a squadron of American airmen based in Kunming, fighting in support of the Chinese against Japan. In 1943 he became an English interpreter for Chinese troops stationed in Bihar, India. Here he wrote much of his finest work, including army life poems like "Bivouac" and "A Common Soldier Left Dead by the Side of the Road." Returning to Kunming in 1946, he wrote poems denouncing the Guomindang as responsible for China's post-war economic and social turmoil. In poems like "Language," Du attacks what he sees as the Guomindang's sclerotic conservatism.

From 1947 to 1950 Du took work as a reporter in Singapore. After serving as a literary editor for *Dagongbao* in Hong Kong, he moved to Beijing to take an editorial position with Xinhua Press. During the Cultural Revolution, Du was sent to the countryside for two years. He published only two poems between 1951 and 1979. From 1974 to 1978 he taught in the foreign languages department of Shandong Normal University. After Deng Xiaoping returned to power, Du published several more volumes of poetry as well as translations of Auden and Pound.

Du's poems generally have a loose structure: he writes in stanzas composed of lines of unequal length, with occasional rhyme. But while he is a New Poet, Du frequently deals with traditional themes. His early poem "The Well" develops a central image from ancient Daoist texts: the well is the unobtrusive, ever-present, eternal source of water, the basis of all life. "A Common Soldier Left Dead by the Side of the Road" dramatizes the anguish of a soul whose remains have not been afforded the traditional rites of burial amidst the chaos of war. After his study at Southwest United University, Du's verse began to develop the tension between tranquil classical themes and the disorderly images of modern life. "Moon" contrasts a traditional theme, the beauty of the moon, with the tawdry modern city it shines upon. "Language" denies the possibility of using dignified language amid the turmoil and corruption that characterized the post-war period, with its profiteering and runaway inflation. In the disjunction between his imagery and his themes, Chinese critics have seen in Du an anticipation of the *menglong* school of poetry which came to prominence in the 1980s. Indeed, it was a volume that included Du's poem "Autumn," published in 1979, that ignited the debate over "obscure" verse.

The Well

I am silence. A few blades of grass,
A few blossoms of cloud that drift across a tiny sky –
These are my world, harmonious and complete.

Only when you feel hunger and thirst,
Abandon your warmth, and come to draw water
Can I glimpse your careworn face.

I am resigned to exclusion from warmth,
Content with solitude in the wilds: only in solitude
Can I maintain myself limpid, full.

You draw from my surface only, leaving behind
The cold and lonely depths of my spirit,
Where withered leaves, drifting in from everywhere, decay.

You can ruffle only my surface.
My life comes from the dark depths of the earth,
Where I am one with the boundless universe.

You dirty me with rubbish, abandon me.
I accept it all in silence,
Cleansing your refuse, remaining eternally myself.

Silent, clear, simple, reverent,
Never reclusive, never zealous,
When it drizzles, I utter a wry laugh.

1940

Moon

Age has not lessened your magic,
Dreamy-eyed,
Surveying all the earth tonight
With a love as pure and faithful
As in olden times.

Those who place their faith in science
Dismiss you as just another heavenly body,
Cold and expressionless,
That bewitches millions
By borrowing the power of the sun,

In daytime seeking refuge in the sea,
To emerge, bathed and fresh,
In the company of flashing-eyed stars,
And to wander until dawn,
When, shivering, you hide yourself again.

But their derision has not diminished
The hunger of our love.
Electric light is mere electric light;
Only you rouse floods of feeling,
Transcending every time and vision.

By the river two young lovers
Flutter down like petals on the disheveled grass,
Softly singing a favourite old tune
Of you. The pale, sparkling river
Hauls off garbage as it flows along.

Travelers from afar, like dried leaves
Trapped against the gate at the end of the bridge,
Mouth Li Bai's verse:
"Look up and see the moon, look down and think of home,"
As if it were a stick of chewing gum.

By the road, coolies in rags
Crouch around a dying fire. They say nothing.
The remaining gold of their blaze
Leaps and flashes on their faces,
Lingering there in search of a line of poetry.

Like a floundering refugee ship
I drift, rudderless, along the asphalt road –
Behind me, no family; before me,
Who knows what shoals? I gaze at heaven
And puzzle out the feeling in the bark of a dog.

Tonight is like any other night.
Here we are cramped together on this earth,
As you, silent and gentle, contemplate
These, our waves of strange emotion,
Shy as a granddaughter, kind as a grandmother.

1944

Bivouac

Suddenly this evening I discover
A different beauty in a tree;
For me it unfurls
A pure blue sheet of silken sky.

Amidst a chaos of leaves
Delicate stars jostle one another.
A bare, leaflorn branch sustains
The roundest, fullest golden moon.

A leaf comes fluttering down
Like a distant face.
It strikes the ground with a deadly noise,
And at once I hear the chatter of winds

That arrive from far-off villages
With a simple rustic shyness.
Dogs catch cold, humans rage,
And herds of cattle huddle together, trembling.

Two facetious blackbirds
Mimic people snoring,
Then burst out laughing
And fly off into mountain's hazy moonlight.

So many impassioned little insects
Take me for their audience
And play me all their new tunes,
So lugubrious they break my heart.

Beside my pillow stands my jeep,
My rifle – assembled – and my uniform,
All numb with silence.
I find such frankness rather attractive.

In the depths of night my heart plummets.
These profound regions prove cold.
Pressure mounts, my heart aches,
I long to turn into a cock and crow aloud.

India, 1944

A Common Soldier Left Dead by the Side of the Road

Give me a grave,
A grave like a black-bean-paste bun.
A flat one's okay,
Like a small vegetable plot –
Or like a manure pile.
Any grave is okay, any grave,
Just so long as it's a grave
And I don't have to lie here in the open
Like a heap of cow bones.
I'm scared of dogs.
Ever since I was little I've been scared of dogs,
Scared of their tickle.
My mother knew
I was scared of dogs licking me.
It gave me goose bumps,
My eyes went red, I wanted to bawl.

A dogfight scared me.
The noise was frightening,
Especially when they fought over a bone.
Their white teeth terrified me
When one ripped at the meat
And the other tugged at the bone
And between them blood dripped like tears.
I used to vomit and faint.
I'm scared of this barren field,
A field with nothing but wind and weeds.
Wild animals search here for food.
None of them is afraid of blood.
They grin strangely
When they've drunk it,
And gnaw the bones
With teeth sharper
Than the teeth of dogs.
I'm scared of the black crows too,
Big as roosters.
Their cries from the trees frighten me at night.
Their beaks are cunning and sharp.
I'm afraid, I'm afraid.
The wind has run away,
The fallen leaves have run away,
The dust has run away.
The trees struggle, tossing their heads.
They want to pull up their roots and run away.

O, give me a grave,
Any pit of earth,
Any pit of earth.

Published 1946

The Season's Mournful Face

One after the other, flowing drearily, silently dripping, one after another,
The bubbles spin beneath the eaves, then sink,
A chaos of memories: the dead, the stiff, the moaning,
Those who stretch and gape. Their melancholy eyes
Stare, begging me to sigh
A sigh as cold and grey as this old lead roof.

A chaotic swirl of raindrops spins across the roof
Like winter wind, all needle and thread; they also want
To pierce my bones. The treetops hang their heads
And blink, eyes brimming with tears.
My heart is a pool with endless ripples
That reflects nothing but the mired battlefield.

India
Published 1946

Language

The only language I believe in is simple,
The language of fire. It is strongest.
The sun trusts it to deliver blessings
And rancour. Passion employs it to paint
Scenes of human drama.

I burn with fever. My tense body
Fills with a vocabulary of crackling fire.
Only such words can liberate
Imprisoned feeling
And give expression to life's potency.

I long to burn, to be a conflagration,
A cleansing destruction,
And leave behind a shining memory,

A mound of ashes the colour of steel.
Right now only wild words please me.

When we have subdued our enemies
And smashed their strongholds, we too
Shall be particular about elegance, discuss elaborate courtesy,
Good taste and carefree leisure. But now
I must use the kind of language that is crude.

1948

Tang Shi

(1920–2005)

Tang graduated from the foreign languages and literature department of Zhejiang University in Hangzhou, southwest of Shanghai. In the late 1940s he was active in Shanghai, editing *Shi Chuangzao* (*Poetry Creation*) and *Zhongguo Xinshi* (*New Chinese Poetry*) together with Chen Jingrong and other Nine Leaves poets. In 1981 he helped to prepare the *Nine Leaves Anthology*, which gave the group its name. Like others in the group he gave up poetry for translation after 1949, working on Keats, Shakespeare, Milton, and Rilke.

Along with most of his Nine Leaves companions, Tang Shi wrote against the Guomindang, but in a subtle way. "The Girl Who Steals Ears of Wheat" describes a peasant woman forced to glean wheat from a landlord's field. The last line reminds the reader that she fears the whistle of the watchman. The notion of a landlord ready to arrest a starving mother implies a critique of the Guomindang regime, vilified for its support of the traditional system of land tenure.

After the end of the Cultural Revolution when it became possible to publish poetry again, Tang Shi turned his hand to the sonnet, producing more than a thousand poems in this genre.

The Girl Who Steals Ears of Wheat

The earth is your skin,
The barbed ears of wheat are your hair,
Your hands are parched branches,
Your palms covered in wrinkled bark.

From plot to plot you scurry over crisscross paths
Like a field mouse dodging through the grain.
Reflecting the evening sun, your eyes
Shine with confidence.

Searching the harvested field like a mother hen
You scratch up grain after grain encrusted in mud.
Then putting your ear to the ground, you wait
For the footsteps to pass on the ridge at the end of the field.

Slipping quietly into an uncut field, you pluck some ears
And hide them in your blouse, which covers a joyful heart.
Wind puffs through the towel wrapped round your head,
As if the alert night had lightly blown the watchman's whistle.

1946

Tang Qi
(1920–90)

Born in Suzhou on the lower Yangzi River, Tang spent his teenage years as a refugee from the Japanese occupation on the remote Gansu-Qinghai border. He graduated in history from Northwest United University in 1942, then went to Chongqing, the Guomindang wartime capital. Here he spent the remaining war years, working in close association with He Qifang. In 1947 he moved to Shanghai, where he helped to edit *New Chinese Poetry,* a journal publishing poets who would later come to be known as the Nine Leaves.

Fellow Nine Leaves member Zheng Min described Tang Qi as "a poet who walks with history." Like several others in the group, he sought to transform political and social reality into art. "Fog" deals with the pervasive surveillance of the Guomindang's secret police. "Time and Banner" looks forward to the Communists' ultimate defeat of Chiang Kai-shek and their founding of the People's Republic of China. "The First Light of Dawn" describes Mao's treatment of political prisoners. Both "Fog" and "The First Light of Dawn" present their themes in terms of grotesque images. Tanq Qi employed surrealistic elements because he believed that strict realism is incapable of bringing out the rich multiplicity of what is real. The fog of Chongqing becomes a nightmarish symbol of the Guomindang secret police's "white terror" campaign against Communist activists. ("Fog" was a slang term for this campaign.)

Tang wrote "Time and Banner" for the first volume of *New Chinese Poetry* (June 1948). The volume's featured theme was "the flag," and Tang's poem is a companion piece to Mu Dan's poem "The Flag." Published in Shanghai when the city was still under Guomindang control, Tang's piece celebrates in veiled language the soon-to-be-founded "people's government." To elude Guomindang censors, Tang never describes the flag he is celebrating; the repetition of "the people," a term dear to Mao, hints that it is the people's government flag – the Communist banner.

Publishing underground, the Nine Leaves poets ignored the literary prescriptions of Chiang Kai-shek, but they were also free to ignore Mao's literary dicta. After the Communist takeover, their disregard of Communist Party guidelines for literature caused them to be banned from publishing. When in 1956 Tang Qi did resume publishing during the censorship thaw of Mao's Hundred Flowers Campaign, he was sentenced for what he wrote to a labour camp in the far northeast of China. After Deng Xiaoping returned to power Tang would publish a remarkable collection of poems that describe his camp experiences, one of the few accounts of life in Mao's gulag. "The First Light of Dawn" comes from that collection.

Fog

1

Fog white as ash
Roves through the night
With strides huge and clumsy as a polar bear's.

Lower, damper, filthier than a cloud,
It stalks and prowls, squats
On its enormous weightless buttocks,

Then slowly, slowly
Rises
And stalks off to lower places.

2

It has forgotten everything it passes:
Tranquil mountains, trees, intersecting roads,
Grass shacks packed tight as the teeth of combs.
Only fog can pull a curtain across the sky,
Covering people's eyes
As it slowly leaves things shapeless and obscure
In the vile breath of its nostrils.

At once the city is ashen, truncated,
A poor man's den, cramped and flattened.
The street, shrouded in the damp vapour of dusk,
Sprawls like a paralytic before the myopic eyes of passers-by.
The fog envelops everything.
Shapes arise, towering and vague;
On the wharfs, leaden grey piles of cargo wait
For grey rats to pilfer.

Far apart, the ferry boats whistle.
Night, hypnotic, comes ahead of time.
The great Customs House clock drowses
But the street lamps think of things remote –
Sprawling vagrants, too free, detained
In wall-less jails of thick white.
Gradually, roof after roof disappears
In fog more encompassing than ever,
Known only to itself.

3

Those imprisoned in dark rooms,
Reporters, thinkers, students,
Scratch their heads and sigh,
Hands clutching their unpublishable news.

It peeps through a lamplit window
At a virgin's insomniac yawn
That expresses her incandescent solitude, as her wide eyes
Gaze out on a nightmare world.

It stands alert, on guard
Like a white throng of secret police,
Shielding the most remote, secluded tall building
Where intriguers, strategists, and dealers in arms
Make peace their white smokescreen

While they lay out a map with human bones
To mark every square foot of their territory,
Employing the latest means
To gather flesh and blood into a symbol of death,
While they grin hideously, pretending ignorance.

4

Fog! Expanding, concealing,
Drawing an interminable downpour after it –
People don't need to explore it further.
Underneath the grey of peace is the black
Quagmire of battle.

1946, in the fog of Chongqing[1]

from *Time and Banner*

6

Look up! The winds of war!
The shocking tempo of the storms increases daily.
Their blast has wakened the bleak winter trees that stretch out their arms;
It has roused seeds buried in the mud. And people roused by the storm of revolt
Will hurl themselves into the battle.
At this prospect
We will laugh with joy. Those who never laughed will part their lips in laughter.
It is the enormous wind – millennia of brutal tyranny

1 The Guomindang's wartime capital.

Shattered in one decisive moment.
The whole land transformed, bleeding, shining with a mighty fire
To light up a glorious life and death.

7

The struggle will outdo imagining,
And in the vast process the future will unfold in a Time, ruthless
But beneficent, fulfilling its promise
By bringing forth a banner of the people.

8

Little by little, day by day, this banner will endure the storms of battle to
 show the people
The earth renewed, the beauty of the flowers, the joyful cry of the birds.
Humanity dawns anew.
Through conquest by labour, through awakening in war
We will seize Time itself. Though people will still suffer,
Jubilant winds will blow
In festive days to come.

The past remains here,
But not completely past; the present swells inside it,
As does the future – all with a single, unwavering direction.
An enormous historical pattern is fulfilled
In this radiant banner of the people, flaunting its brilliance like the sun,
Brightening all time before and after,
Then, now, and yet to come.

1948

The First Light of Dawn

The first light of dawn! Soon our train will reach its destination.
A deathly stillness in the prison-car muffles every sound
Save the frightened click-clack, click-clack of the wheels.
Glimpsed through the window in the dark of night,
Black snowflakes swirl above the wilderness.[2]

Over the dim, bleak prairie
A muddy line has been trodden in the white snow,
A long chain of footprints,
Silent, dreary, cold.

Countless hearts,
Framed in case after case,
But though their suffering is deep
There is neither sigh nor moan.
Their fate
Is forced labour in primeval forests,
With saw and axe to sever the growth rings of their lives,
With ploughshares to uproot the bright spring of their youth.
O the ceaseless plowing of the soil!

The turquoise light of early dawn
And the pure white snow
Shall bear them witness:
They neither sigh nor moan
As they advance – a long human chain
Into the bleak and snowy prairie
Where no smoke tells of human presence.

1957–58

2 "During nighttime snowfalls in the bitter winters of the Northeast, the north wind swirls the snow into 'cannon smoke,' mixing the black of night and the white of the snow until the two are indistinguishable. As a train rushes through the night with enormous flakes of snow falling outside the window, the white flakes and the black of night take on the appearance of a mingled swirl of black and white points, until suddenly the black dots knit into the shape of snowflakes." (Author's note.)

Hang Yuehe
(1917–95)

Hang Yuehe was the pen name of artist and book designer Cao Xinzhi. Born in Jiangsu province, Cao studied at a ceramic arts institute, then trained as a teacher at Jiangsu Normal College. When the Japanese occupied Jiangsu in 1937, Cao fled inland to study at the Communist-run National Revolutionary University in Shanxi province, then at Mao's Lu Xun Academy of Literature and Art in Yan'an. In 1940 he was sent by the Communist leaders to Chongqing, the Guomindang's wartime capital, where he worked as one of the Communist delegation serving with Chiang Kai-shek's government during the wartime alliance between Chiang and Mao, the United Front.

After the defeat of the Japanese Hang lived in Shanghai, where he joined Zang Kejia in founding the underground poetry journal *Poetry Creation*. With Chen Jingrong and Wang Xindi he also founded a second underground journal, *New Chinese Poetry*. The two publications featured the poetry of the nine writers who later came to be known as the Nine Leaves Poets. When the Guomindang authorities banned the magazines in November 1948, Cao fled to Hong Kong. After the Communist takeover he moved to Beijing to work in publishing. In 1957 he was branded as a rightist and sent (like fellow Nine Leaves poet Tang Qi) to a labour camp in remote northern China. After the Cultural Revolution he was permitted to return to Beijing, where he took a position at the China Arts Publishing Company and resumed writing. In 1981 he served as editor of the *Nine Leaves Anthology*, the collection that established the identity of the Nine Leaves Poets as a distinct group.

Hang's "Last Performance" develops with surrealistic imagery a commonplace theme in traditional Chinese poetry: the critique of the unjust ruler. The leftist narrator, living underground, is compelled to witness Chiang Kai-shek's theatrical celebration of himself as leader of China at the very moment when the Communist armies are about to drive him out of the country. The poem is written in stanzas composed of lines of regular length, each containing the same numbers of characters, but without rhyme.

The year is 1948. The poem's mock-festive occasion is the Guomindang National Assembly's election of Chiang as the first President of China under a new constitution, promulgated the year before. Chiang's installation as president of a democratic government representative of the Chinese people is the "performance" mocked in the final lines of the poem. The serio-comic effect of Chiang's pomp is all the more ironic in that his audience is "captive" – constrained to watch his inauguration under the eye of his secret police. Cao's allusions sketch the history of the relationship between Chiang's Guomindang and Mao's Communists from 1927 to 1948. "Ten years of mutual hatred – of blood mixed with tears" (line 7) refers to the warfare between the Guomindang and the Communists from 1927 to 1937. Line 8 refers to Chiang's agreement in 1937 to an alliance with the Communists to fight the Japanese invaders in a "life-and-death struggle for our country." This alliance, the United Front, officially lasted until 1947, two years after the Japanese surrender. In fact all genuine cooperation between the two forces ceased in 1941, after Guomindang forces allegedly attacked the Communist New Fourth Army. Hang blames the breakup of the United Front on Chiang's betrayal of "your promises" (line 9), likely with reference to this attack. Open civil war between the two sides resumed in 1947. By the date the poem was written, the Communists controlled nearly half of China, so that Chiang can only "half fulfill [his] longed-for wish" (line 11) to rule the nation. Hang's poem anticipates Chiang's ultimate defeat, a year after the poem was written, in 1949.

Last Performance

You'd like us to set off firecrackers to show our delight
And unfurl banners in celebration.
You want us to raise our hands and clap and cheer you,
As, all smiles, you perform your masterpiece.

Though memory and reason are twins,
We have studied the art of forgetting:
We swallowed ten years of mutual hatred – of blood mixed with tears –
To coax you into joining the life-and-death struggle for our country.

But since you've betrayed both humanity and your promises,
The old scars have once more opened in our hearts.

Now you can only half fulfill your longed-for wish
With your motley company in this monotonous farce.

You mount the stage with your entourage. What a magnificent program!
Firecrackers! Flags! Hurrahs! But you must realize
That all these don't quiet the storm that rages around you.
You laugh convulsively, laugh till you shake, but you must understand

That we are a captive audience, tied up and dragged here
So that our bloodshot eyes can admire
Your final performance, with hundreds of millions
Of shouts and clapping hands – as you await the curtain call.

1948

Yuan Kejia
(1921–2008)

Born in Nanjing, Yuan graduated in 1946 from Southwest United University in foreign languages. He then moved to Shanghai where he became the youngest of the poets who would be known as the Nine Leaves. After the Communist takeover he moved to Beijing, where he briefly taught at Beijing University.

Yuan wrote many essays in the late forties advocating the modernization of poetry. His work is an example of the hybrid nature of the Nine Leaves Poets, a synthesis of select elements of symbolism and formalism, cast in formal stanzas. Three of his poems in this collection are in a loose sonnet form: fourteen lines of uneven length with strict rhyme. Like that of other Nine Leaves poets, Yuan's work reflects the political tumult of the late forties. "Shanghai" mirrors the social chaos of the last years of Chiang Kai-shek's regime: rampant inflation, starving refugees crowding a Shanghai dominated by foreign capitalists. "Nanjing," Yuan's comic psychoanalysis of Chiang on the brink of his downfall, evinces the author's disdain for the Guomindang regime which had moved its capital to Nanjing after the defeat of the Japanese.

But though he ridiculed Chiang, not least for his reliance on the Americans, Yuan was no leftist but a progressive who embraced the intellectual traditions of both China and the West. He took the position that poetry should not be shackled to politics, that the authorities should afford the writer a degree of latitude to reflect on major political issues. "Thinking about Our Times" expresses his dismay at the radicals' hatred of scholarship in the apocalyptic period of the late forties, just before the Communist takeover. Once Mao took power, Yuan's notion of the poet as unfettered commentator on public events became a dead letter. He and the other Nine Leaves poets never wrote slogan-poetry according to the Party's formula, so after the Communists took power they were frozen out of publication. In the new political climate they turned to translation and literary research. Yuan's translations included a collection of the poems of Robert

Burns. After Deng Xiaoping's return to power, Yuan published the first Chinese anthology of Western modernist poetry in translation. Against establishment critics, he defended the new "obscure" poetry which began to appear in the 1980s.

Nanjing[3]

Thirty years of one unbroken dream, then you wake, surrounded by hostile eyes;
You scurry about frantically, forgetting that the enemy is yourself.
Before the spring tide comes, red dragonflies fill the sky:
Blame here, blame there, blame everyone – the third stage of an inferiority complex!

Still imagining that you grasp a high-voltage wire,
Your whimsical hates and likes still enough to rule the world;
Flatterers everywhere conspire to deceive you,
And whoever refuses to deceive, you think is reactionary, a traitor!

Bureaucrats clog the streets, hold meetings, collect their pay.
Hands clutching phones, their agitation bids them silence others.
They issue declarations to all points of the compass, all in rebellion: The Four Great Empties.

Beholding you, bunglers feel sick at heart.
Psychiatrists call you "schizoid,"
And Washington gropes in the bottomless pit, its money bag.

1948

3 At the time of the poem, the Communists were sweeping down from the north upon Nanjing, the Guomindang capital. "You" is Chiang Kai-shek.

Shanghai

How many prophets have foretold the demise of this city,
Proclaimed that it is sinking several inches every year?[4]
New buildings keep stretching skyward like the Devil's talons,
Robbing the earth of sun and rain,

Casting the Devil's shadow. Greed rises through the air.
Telephones ring battle-alarms against commercial rivals.
Prices of goods in display-windows balloon. Nerves tighten.
Eyes of scavenging famine-refugees scour the ground.

Injustice everywhere! Yet some go on, smooth and graceful,
From office to saloon – their undeviating track:
Ten hours of money-grubbing, ten of orgy.

The gentleman patting his belly strolls into the office,
Greeted by a typist's red-mouthed yawn.
He picks up the paper, covering his face, awaiting a rumor from
Nanjing.[5]

1948

Pregnant Woman

A lacerating pain wakes you in the depths of night.
Exhaustion flows from your eyes out the window toward the stars.
O wayfarer on a long journey, you have reached another crossroad
In the rugged, luxuriant forest that stretches around you.

You are greeted like unconfirmed news.
A strange feeling they cannot put a name to throbs in people's hearts;
Your husband's joy is full of anxious advice,
And old wives make you the occasion of their wit.

4 Shanghai is built on a marsh. The section near the river lies below water-level, protected by a dyke.
5 The Guomindang capital. See note 3, page 370.

As children we entrusted the past to adults;
As adults we commit our future hopes to children.
O Source of Creation, with your head bowed at this solemn moment,

And bodily filth heaped around you,
Does the round of repeated births plunge you into this grave solitude –
To bear the doubt of every creator: what can one add to the universe?

1948

Thinking about Our Times

Still bent over your desk, still writing,
When your publisher's advance won't even pay for paper,[6]
When no one cares any more what you have to say,
But only asks what party's flag you're waving as you shout,
When unorthodox talent is damned as mortal sin,
And the spittle of party-pals is gathered like shining pearls?

Why still keep your head buried in old books
When intellectuals raise their voices cursing knowledge,
When students stare at a textbook as if it were poison,
And at teachers like doomed bookworms,
Shunning both the classics and foreign books like nerve gas,
Cramming their gullets with esoteric foolery like nutriment from heaven?

A disgrace surrounds us, something unparalleled in our history.
Centres of culture launch inquisitions against ideas.
Someone must arise amid this depravity
And abolish the superstition that ignorance is all-powerful against ignorance;
Someone must dispel the black hell that is closing round us
And raise the glimmer of a star as we await a dawn after this calamity.

1948

6 A reference to the rampant inflation during the last stages of the Guomindang regime.

Chen Jingrong
(1917–89)

One of the foremost women poets of twentieth-century China, Chen was born in Leshan, Sichuan Province. She was especially encouraged to study by her mother, whose ambition to become a teacher had been thwarted by her traditionalist family. The daughter stole books from her grandfather's library and read them in secret. In this way she gradually read the Chinese classics. The struggle of a woman to control her own life was to be a major theme in her verse.

At the age of thirteen she first met Cao Baohua, a new poet who was her English teacher in middle school. At fifteen she tried to run away with him, and was locked up at home for six months. At seventeen she joined Cao in Beijing. Here she met He Qifang, who encouraged her interest in the New Poetry. In 1944 she moved, alone, to Chongqing where she eked out a hand-to-mouth existence as a substitute teacher. Here she met the prominent novelist Ba Jin, who would edit her poetry. In 1946 she moved to Shanghai, where at first she found shelter sleeping in the apartments of friends. To support herself she produced a six-volume translation of the stories of Hans Christian Andersen as well as a translation of Victor Hugo's *Hunchback of Notre Dame*. Her first volume of verse appeared in Shanghai in 1948. Here she began to translate Rilke and became acquainted with Tang Qi, Tang Shi, and Hang Yuehe, with whom she edited *New Chinese Poetry*, publishing the verse of many of the Nine Leaves Poets.

Chen's poetry first appeared in the literary supplements of Beijing newspapers in the mid-thirties, when she had begun writing with the encouragement of He Qifang. Her early verse reflects her mentor's symbolism and his neo-romantic self-expression. In her Shanghai poems of the late forties her use of symbol verges on surrealism, as in "Weavers of Nets" and "The Radio Strangles Spring," where a kaleidoscopic series of twisted images renders the media's distortion of real life. The grotesque city scenes in the Shanghai poems give expression to the disillusionment that enveloped Chinese society in the period of rampant inflation and prolonged civil war that followed the defeat of the Japanese.

Chen's choice of free verse as her mode of expression befits her commitment to liberation, above all the liberation of woman, as in the narrator's refusal of the marriage proposal in "A Knight's Love." "In "Left Behind" she treats every human tie as ephemeral. "The Unknown Me" explores her role as poet as a reaction to the alienation she that feels is inevitable in human relationships. The theme of female independence reappears in her work of the 1980s in such poems as "What the Painted Eyebrow Sings." The late poem "The Walls of the Ancient City of Gaochang" alludes to the subjection of women in traditional Chinese society.

Of all the Nine Leaves poets, Chen proved to be the one most committed to the Communist cause. "The Pearl and the Seeker after Pearls" can be interpreted as the private monologue of an underground activist (like Chen in Shanghai in 1948) waiting for the approaching Communist army to arrive so that she can come above ground and work openly with them. After the Communist takeover in 1949 she trained as a party cadre and worked as a prosecutor in the national Supreme Court in Beijing to convict opponents of Mao's regime. Her service to the Communist state did nothing, however, to facilitate the publication of her work. Chen's 1946 poem "Idle Chat" was to be condemned by Communist establishment critics for its personalism (a violation of Mao's prescription for socialist art). Like other Nine Leaves poets, she abandoned poetry for translation during the Mao era. In the fifties she published translations of Soviet fiction and, with Zou Difan, translations of the Indian Muslim poet Iqbal. In 1956 she joined the editorial staff of *Translation* magazine, renamed *World Literature* in 1959. In 1965 she transferred to the staff of *People's Literature*, the foremost literary journal in China. Chen was sent down to the countryside for "political reeducation" during the Cultural Revolution in 1967. "Moth" alludes to the tribulations suffered by many during this period. She began publishing her poetry again in the early eighties, when censorship was eased under Deng Xiaoping. Her last collection appeared in 1983.

Zhou Liangpei complains that Chen's poetry omits the personal and political occasions of her introspection. Chen consciously strives to overcome such solipsism in the masterpiece of her Shanghai period, "Spring Comes to One Sick of Logic," with its vivid details of the post-war metropolis. When Chen resumed writing in the 1980s her verse became more concrete, structured on images from real life like the caged bird in "What the Painted Eyebrow Sings." The expressive symbolism of poems like "The Walls of the Ancient City of Gaochang" distinguishes Chen's work of the 1980s as perhaps the most significant of any new poet who survived Mao's death.

Yellow

Yellow sands, yellow sands –
A jaundiced memory
Recovered from the dust.
The shadow on the wall is sighing.

Welling up in the imagination
Is a vast sea like a mirror.
In its translucent waves,
I glimpse my solitary footsteps.

1936

To Xingzi[7]

I'll come to you with August,
And in the stillness we will listen
To September twilight rain.

Chrysanthemums will bloom,
Chrysanthemums will wither.
Go, travel to the banks of time
And build a dam.

Go there and weep
For youth, for love.
Go to the far-off ocean and seek ... what?
Will you cast it away? Gather it up?
In the invisible wind, in the sunless dark,
Chrysanthemums will bloom,
Chrysanthemums will wither.

1942

7 Xingzi means "apricot." Here it is the name of the person addressed in the poem.

A Knight's Love: A Dialogue

"What arrow do you shoot
To fell the soaring bird?
Tell me, knight at arms!"

"The candid crimson of my heart
Painted with a lie that's redder still."

"And what potion do you use,
O knight at arms,
To heal those bloodied wings
That they may spread again."

"I use a fitting reprimand,
And at the right moment, force."

"And can she still soar joyfully,
O knight at arms, and can she still
Sing in April sunlight?"

"Neither soar nor sing,
But hover within my garden walls."

"Return then to your garden
And let me soar at ease, gazing down alone
At clouds that sail across the earth."

1944

Pulsation

A wave's rise and fall,
The patter of rain,
The throb of a distant bell,

The hot yet gentle
Beating of a heart –
Whose the will, whose the hand
That instills rhythm
In each movement,
Every sound?

As I breathe in and out
The cosmos breathes,
As a blade of grass, an ant
Breathes in, breathes out.

Pulsating breath,
Pulsating sobs,
Pulsating song –
Whose will, whose hand
Endows every action
With rhythm?

The universe stands everlasting,
Life is eternal
And so is rhythm.

At my window
Every evening, you quiver,
Everlasting starlight.

1945

Left Behind

The music of the flowing current
Unsteadies me like drink.
Walking on the white stones in the river,
I remember Eve –
The strange, fresh exhilaration
At her first taste of forbidden fruit.

Sometimes on a gloomy evening
The sadness of other days and twilights
Glides swiftly back
Through the shadowy depths of memory,
Then disappears.

Have I merely buried yesterday?
I cast today behind me
And the moment that has just slipped by,
And shall cast away
Each fleeting instant
That becomes the past.

So I stand
On the prow of a speeding ship
Carried off by the current,
Watching each of my brief selves,
Each "I" of each past encounter,
Left standing mute
On the cliffs towering eternally behind me.

1945

A Painting of Running Water

On a blank white wall I hang
A painting of running water.

Whose is that white dress
That floats on the evening grass
And vanishes down the shadowed path?

The flame of a dying candle
Illuminates a half-open book.

Notes lie bleeding on the keyboard –
A phrase in an unknown language
Condenses into fog.

Lightly the wind passes,
Abandoning the melancholy trees.

1945

The Web of Images

Rivers and streams
Crisscross the broad Earth;
Intersecting roads
Stretch to the horizon.

No blade of grass
Boasts of solitude;
No single syllable
Constitutes a sentence.

Arms and arms
Intertwine in the night;
Together, pairs of eyes
Gaze toward tomorrow.

1946

Idle Chat

Idle chat is the season's reverberation,
Bringing spring back to a winter's night.
When cold shadows sway beneath my feet
The sky and its stars call me
To think of April.

The stars too are swaying.
They have shaken down memories,
Jerked hopes awake:
The hooves of horses are tramping
Past my soul's door.

But I can't just jump
To fling it wide;
I fear a furious rainstorm
Will rush in.

No, I'll wait for
A soft low knock,
For the sound
Of an intimate voice.

1946

Isolation

Frequently I stop short
As a stray breeze blows past.
Often I lose my way
At the chance peal of a bell.
A cloudless sky
Induces me to muse
On the unfathomable blue-green
Of pines and grass.

About to be launched, a ship stands poised.
An arrow is ready to soar;
The taut bowstring contains its feathered flight.

Terrified by fire alarms,
Vague human forms rush through the tormented night.

Amid the sudden unfamiliarity of daily things
We are isolated from the cosmos.

1946

Crossing Paths

In joy I encounter pain forgotten.
Suffering we meet again, weeping.
The bygone years recede,
The tightened bowstring
Snaps!

A flood of feeling sweeps away considerations
That search acres of sunlight for shadows.
Before my drowsy eyes the damp March night
Sinks into a dream;
Flowers dance, stars sing,
In the wink of an eye time dies young.

1946

Writing in Chinese

Each character is a piece of sculpture,
Currents of thought flowing through static shape,
Rivulets from every direction
Harmoniously blending into a sea.

City ponds cover the graves of ancient dynasties,
But characters repeat their history with passion:
Centuries of battles, piles of corpses –
All that remains now, a few desolate verses.

Your shadowy images roam the air,
Your poses now distinct, now blurred.
When I am feverish with anger, I seek your coolness.
In the dark of night I seize you as if seizing light.

Through your fixed mouths, I speak my formless language
To launch my thoughts from ocean depths.
From every mountaintop you call me.
I hoist my sail, I catch your winds and skim the waves.

1947

The Radio Strangles Spring

People out for a stroll, enjoying spring,
Reach at leisure for a willow branch,
Pluck peach blossoms
To bring home to the frenetic metropolis.
The sky looks bluer than ever,
Suddenly reminding them of life's agonies.

The wireless strangles spring:
"Shangri La"[8] yelps like a bitch in heat,
And then the commercials –
Banks, department stores, shops – abacus beads
Click back and forth too fast to see, but all the profits
Cannot fill the war's greedy maw.

A night of debauchery, tumult all around,
But the din cannot drown the street's biting chill.

8 A song then popular in Shanghai.

Late at night the Huangpu sighs,
Suzhou Creek groans.[9]
  In their dreams some men still calculate –
  Oil, salt, wood, rice – anxious that the morning paper
  Will just bring news of more disasters.[10]

1947

Weavers of Nets

The rooftops are in a trance:
Dusk sky.
On the radio
Someone pulls a long face and wails –
Rock it! Rock it!
An enormous raven
Bears on its wings
The weeping eyes of victim sons and daughters.

Someone stealthily
Takes up a sharp, sharp pen
And pokes a hole through human life.
The many holes line up
And become a net
Across the sky,
Vast, hazy.

Hey there, want a smoke?

1947

9 The Huangpu River and Suzhou Creek are Shanghai's two principle waterways.
10 A reference to Communist advances in the north.

The Sculptor

Beneath your fingers a murmuring river flows,
Infusing lifeless clay with being.
Light, shadow, voice, colour
Solidify,
As your chisel breaks mute stone, freeing its age-old dream.

Let each image have its place:
A beauty's warmth, the tiger's fierce strength,
The victim's brow, furrowed in mute accusation,
The prophet's wisdom brimming over,
Spilling waves in all directions.

Sometimes, at one of your gestures, everything
Suddenly falls silent.
Under your chisel
Space contracts, time hesitates,
But you retain, forever changeless, your primal openness.

1947

Spring Comes to One Sick of Logic

1

Water flowing too fast
Seems not to flow,
Too fast a spinning wheel
Seems not to spin,
A face smiling too intensely
Appears to weep,
Too strong a light dazzles the eye
And, just like darkness, leaves you
Blind.

Perfection equals flaw,
Satiety, emptiness;
The greatest is the least,
Zero, infinity.

Ancient, and twice ancient, this world
Seems eternally fresh:
Rummage through your Grandma's cupboards and wardrobes,
And you can open the latest fashionable boutique.

2

Of so many forms, poses, symbols, voices
We've long gone weary. Hey,
You're never old, blue sky.
On a warm spring morning
Bombers circle in the sunlight.

Nature is one enormous hospital,
Spring the doctor, sunlight the panacea
Resurrecting withered trees and grass
To waken weary, ailing spirits.

Ours are a thousand indolences, ten thousand fatigues
That the days pile carelessly on our shoulders.
Now that spring is here we long
To stretch our weary backs and yawn.

Even though endless green fills our imaginations –
Water, ah, water! –
We still cherish
An eternal thirst.

3

In the midst of life –
Eating, drinking, working, sleeping,
Laughing or weeping for some reason or other –
Everything seems to be going just as expected
When a dove wails beneath the clear blue sky,
Crying disaster borne on a showery wind –
Wretched, wretched, most wretched of all is hope,
Thirsting to death in despair.

Raise a rampart of will,
Then pace back and forth,
Both forgiving
And despising yourself.

4

In my dream a sudden gale
Stealthily brings the bark of a dog.
When the wind subsides, somebody's massive
Door thuds shut
As if it were mine, and so I'm shut
Off from sleep,
And listen, alone, to the frantic
Roar of a distant train.

Ah, Siberia's
Frigid blast is long gone.

So is this the true
Spring? Yes! Can't you see?
The sunlight turns softer,
The willows dangle their branches,
The whole earth sprouts green,

Intoxicating even the wind.
We are waiting for the sound of thunder
To shock insects from their doze.
A peal of true spring thunder,
And not merely the sky's
Rheumy cough.

5

Children's Day:[11] a few lucky ones,
Dressed splendidly for the festivities,
Salute, recite from memory, accept prizes,
Even as so many others toil
Eight, ten, twelve hours
In sweat shops that devour their health:

Festivity and hoax are brothers.
Spring, we know that you possess
An abundance of brief flowers –
A memorial service for the dead;
The funeral horn resounds,
But we the living spare no time
To shed a sudden tear.

In this modern metropolis
We are insignificant, crushed together on packed streets,
Squeezed for clothes, for food, a flat, a seat on a bus.
You have to shove your way to the front;
If you don't squeeze ahead, there's no place for you.

The birds, the animals, the insects and the fish of springtime
Can't attract our gaze. Even
Life's joys and griefs, family partings and reunions have become humdrum,

11 A Chinese holiday celebrated on 1 June.

Shoved aside,
Leaving a blank.

Last night's dream of horror leaves no morning sorrow,
In its nightmare, mountains and rivers stand in isolation, their bridges
gone.
Qingming is indifferent now to spring rain.[12]

There is always more business, one more word to say,
Something ends, something else begins,
And the moment you suddenly stop,
Like it or not, you're dead.

Shanghai, April, 1947

The Unknown Me

Often I see myself
As an unfamiliar being
Thinking unfamiliar thoughts,
Speaking unfamiliar words.
As I stand alone on the street
Buffeted by a sudden gust of wind,
I see myself a stranger
Facing an alien world.

Many familiar things –
The clothes I wear,
The house I live in,
My favourite books,
The music I love –
Are not really mine.
Even the five senses of my body,
My voice,
My gait as I walk down the street,

12 Qingming: literally "clear and bright," the period in the solar calendar – generally around the 5th of April – when the Chinese pay respects to the dead. The holiday is traditionally associated with spring rain.

Are just casual accidents,
Part of the usual.
Now I occupy space and time,
Now I vanish.
How can I boast of giving all that's in me,
Even if in life's theater
I play every part?

I am not my own woman.
When I write a short poem
Or a long, long letter,
I am only trying to stitch
A single beam of sunlight out of my dreams
Into your reflections.

1947

Spring Song of Youth

To my young brothers and sisters

Do you know why flowers bloom,
Fish swim, deer bound?
Do you know why lips tremble,
Hearts leap?

Even young grasses are fragrant,
Even raindrops warm,
Even night shines.

Spring in your heart,
In your hair, in your step,
Silently quickens.

Earthworms say the earth is soft,
The sparrow hawk watches white clouds drifting.
Small birds, bees and butterflies

Bustle about in the sunlight,
While crickets love nothing
But the little wheel of the high moon.

Spring hovers in every wind,
Hovers and sings.

When you sigh, when you weep,
Spring turns to pond-water to match your tears.
When you smile, when you sing at the top of your voice,
Spring changes again
To the rose-coloured sun just after dawn.

1947

The Pearl and the Seeker after Pearls

Within the oyster shell the pearl is waiting.
It knows the greatest joy is
Giving, not painfully concealing in its depths
The many sunshine days,
The many moonlit nights,
And milk-white waves roused now and then by storms.
It has gathered them inside itself as it ripens,
And has made them all its own, walled up within its shell,
Buried, hearing steps on every side,
Hasty or loitering,
Hordes of footsteps
Passing. It lives still sealing its light
Within, refusing to shine at an untimely hour.
There is something it must wait for.
It knows from where
And with what heartfelt passion the seeker of pearls
Will come.
Then the shell will open, the pearl appear,
Yielding to a world completely new.

1948

On Reading a Midsummer Biography

Who ever had to bear such irritation?
To be compelled to endure
Such stupid coyness over and over,
To listen to these never-ending lamentations,
These cheap and sentimental sighs!

Well I suppose it's true
That even crocodiles shed tears
When embroiled in enervating struggles.

In heaven or on earth, where can one escape it?
O, how one aches with longing
For a drink of clear, cold water,
But everything around this spring
Is a quagmire to trip my feet.

1980

The Walls of the Ancient City of Gaochang[13]

In Response to a Letter from My Daughter

White snow glitters on the summits of the Heaven Mountains.
Blossoms of cloud drift under a blue canopy of sky.

Autumn forests of willow and elm bind with sashes of jade
The flaming skirts of Fire Peak.

Everywhere across the vast Gobi Desert,
Distant oases flash sparkling emerald eyes.

Standing at sunset beneath the walls of Gaochang
One senses vague echoes of camel-bells from westward caravans.

13 Gaochang: an ancient city in Northwest China's Xinjiang Province, the homeland of the Uighurs, a Turkic people.

Child, in my dreams each night fantastic mists
Take on the forms of the majestic landscapes from your letter –

The heavenly horse gallops across the sky, leaping peaks,
Its silver hooves scattering petals of crystal frost,

But where in all this land is the birthplace of Fragrant Concubine,[14]
Her homesickness clinging like a grapevine to its arbor?

1981

The Long Cry of the Peacock

For a crowd of visitors at the zoo
The peacock unfolds the fan of his tail,
Igniting stars of green and gold.
Mothers say it's trying to outdo the beauty of their children.
But a scientist among us remarks
This is no competitive display,
But a living creature's instinct –
A sort of self-defense.

Like all flying creatures
The peacock comes from dense woods deep in the mountains.
He's used to the sound of running springs, leaping waterfalls,
And the sight of the sun, moon, stars, clouds.

Now, suffering
Half-teasing praise,
The peacock suddenly conceives
A pang of compassion for this tangled world,

14 The author's footnote explains that Xiang Fei (Fragrant Concubine) was a Moslem Uighur girl from the region of Northwest China where the poem is set. She was the favourite of the aged Qianlong Emperor (reigned 1736–96), who built within his Beijing palace an elaborate imitation of her native countryside, including a mosque and grape arbours like those of her homeland. None of this cured Xiang Fei's homesickness, and she died young.

Folds up the fan of its tail
And utters a long cry to the wind.

1982

Moth

Between sleep and waking, I was half-aware
That a spot on the ceiling
Had moved.

I rushed for a flyswatter
And climbed onto my desk to eliminate the speck.
I struck! A moth
Flew off in panic, and flung itself at the window;

A tiny moth
With a white pattern on its brown wings –
What harm could it do – a moth?

In the end I did not kill it,
Mindful that in this boundless universe
There still lurk a thousand calamities.

1982

A Porcelain Bas Relief of Bodidharma[15] Walking across the Sea

O ancient sage
Who meditated in the mountains
So deeply and so long,
What waves are these that bring you
To this corner of the Forbidden City Museum?

15 Bodhidharma was a sixth-century Indian monk who traveled to China, where he is credited with founding the Chan sect of Buddhism (known in Japan as the Zen sect).

You who deeply love all sentient beings,
But disdained imperial diadem and throne,
Stand here in an attitude of respect
As if to honour the laughing, chattering crowd,
Come to view antiquities.

The time since the age of the South and North Dynasties[16]
Is just a few days to your mountains,
But a millennium in this world of ours.
Beneath your broad robe and long sleeves
You join your hands and cup them in benediction,
Silently pouring forth
Long-intended good fortune on the visitors.

Behind your broad, high forehead
Stretches the deep, deep ocean.
Its vast expanse surging night and day
Is stilled beneath your feet.
A few persisting blossoms of spray
Join together to sustain your august figure,
Harbouring ever-increasing wisdom.
You raise a foot, about to take a step.
On voyage to what future are you bound?

1982

After an Illness

If the day comes
When my fingers suddenly tremble
And my lutestring snaps,

When that day comes,
The images in my heart
May still be only sketches,
And my song left unfinished.

16 420–618 CE.

O how many times have I approached
That primordial abyss,
Heard that faint call
From beyond time and space?

Life's loving hands
Have grasped me once again,
And returned me to this arduous, joyful journey.

All that was so familiar on my way
Seems rather strange after a short absence:
These clouds, these trees, this window,
These passers-by suddenly appearing and disappearing.

Again I hear the distant bell
That tolls the rhythm of life.
Again I glimpse a flock of pigeons
Flashing silver-white wings across the blue sky.

When that day comes
Will all my burdens be lifted?
Will nothing remain of all I hold dear
But watery moonlight, the feeble glimmer of a star,
The fresh scent of a forest clearing
And mother-of-pearl clouds at dawn?

May the ancient constellation of joy
Shine on your dreams forever,
O my friends, familiar and unknown,
O my children and my kin!

1984

What the Painted Eyebrow Sings[17]

Bird with yellow-brown plumage
Hopping back and forth in your exquisite cage,
What are you thinking
Beneath those white eyebrows, your jet-black eyes
Ever vigilant, ever shifting?

From nearby trees
Come intermittent calls
As if in friendly competition –
Or rather in stubborn defiance.
In reply you beat your wings
And join the immemorial chorus.

Perhaps you have long known
That your fellows too shift back and forth,
Each in a cage, elegant or plain,
And that all these restless cries
Express one longing:
O, to fly! To fly!

1986

17 The painted eyebrow is a thrush-like bird with white eye-rings resembling women's eye-makeup in ancient China. It is among the species of pet birds that old men bring in the morning to public parks, where they hang the cages on the branches of trees and the birds sing together. The date and the fact that the author is a woman suggest both political and feminist themes.

The Sound of Footsteps

– Haigeng, on the shore of Lake Dianchi[18]

From this height I gaze
On Dianchi, this vast sea.
Beyond Dragon Gate that beautiful maiden[19]
Has lain in silence so many centuries!
Whose footsteps does she await?
Sleep, sleep –
In the solemn stillness of your fragrant dream
Mountain camellias bloom.
The sea-waves are your turquoise breath
As in deep blue-green you await
Me –
Your fellow native of the Southwest
Who roamed the North many years,
A wandering poet.

1987

18 Lake Dianchi: a large lake surrounded by mountains, located south of Kunming, Yunnan Province, southwest China. Haigeng ("Sea-embankment") is the name of a park on the east shore of the lake, facing Dragon Gate (see the following note).
19 Dragon Gate is a lofty mountain pass on the west shore of Lake Dianchi. The sleeping maiden is a rock formation which legend says is a beautiful girl who fell asleep in that spot long ago.

Zheng Min
(1920–)

Zheng Min is a native of Minhou county, Fujian province. Her parents gave her to be brought up by her uncle and his wife, who were childless. Her adoptive father was a mining engineer who had studied for a long period in France, so she was exposed to Western culture from an early age. Her family moved to Liuhegou, Henan province, a strife-torn area where they occasionally had to hide in mineshafts from clashes between rival warlords' armies. She did not adapt to the local school, so they took her to Beijing for her primary education. Later they moved to Nanjing, where Zheng Min entered Nanjing Women's Middle School. Here she encountered Western fiction like *Jane Eyre*. When the Japanese swept south toward Nanjing her family fled to Chongqing.

In 1939 Zheng Min entered Southwest United University in Kunming, where she studied philosophy. Her professors included many of the foremost names in modern Chinese literature; she studied classical poetry with Wen Yiduo, the history of Chinese fiction with Shen Congwen, and Goethe and Rilke with Feng Zhi. She encountered the poetry of Eliot and Auden, and began writing down in a little notebook poems that spontaneously came to her. In 1948 she went to America, where she studied English at Brown University. To support herself she worked at various jobs, washing dishes in the college cafeteria and stringing pearls in a jewelry factory.

In 1949 she published her *Collected Poems: 1942–1947*. In 1952 she received her MA in English. Prevented from returning to China during the Korean War, she and her husband resided in New York City until 1955, when the American authorities finally permitted them to return home. In 1960 Zheng Min began teaching English and American literature at Beijing Normal University.

Her study of Goethe and Rilke as a student of Feng Zhi was a definitive influence on Zheng Min's work. Many of her poems address subjects found in Rilke: animals, paintings, flowers, birds. Often she writes in the sonnet form, one that both Rilke and Feng Zhi favoured. But her more usual form is irregular free verse like that of Dai Wangshu, varied from line to line in order to render mood. Even in her sonnets her rhyme scheme tends to be irregular and the length of her lines uneven.

Like Rilke, Zheng Min portrays works of art that transcend time and space to enlighten and transform the beholder. Her poetry seeks to achieve a mood of solitude and calm like the sonnets of Rilke and Feng Zhi. Such themes and such an atmosphere set her works apart from other Chinese poets of her era, who portrayed dramatic scenes to stir readers to take sides in the political struggle or to dedicate themselves to fighting the Japanese. It was Zheng Min's conviction that poetry should steer clear of any political or social agenda. Indeed, it was her conscious intention to achieve a philosophic detachment. In her 2012 interview with Debra Bruno, she explained the integral relationship between philosophy and her poetry: "I started to study philosophy to have a better understanding of literature, because I don't think you can really understand literature without a background of philosophy ... Philosophy without literature is too hard. Literature without philosophy has no depth. So you have to combine both." Her poem "The Student" deals with the search for a higher Socratic wisdom in the midst of the social upheavals of the late forties. At the age of ninety-two she recalled that such Socratic self-knowledge helped her survive the Cultural Revolution. "Always know yourself ... It's like watching a play. You have two selves. One self is standing on this earth, another self is looking down from the air."

The influence of Western modernist poetry is evident in Zheng Min's use of images. Her poems depict symbolic scenes, but unlike those of French symbolists, her scenes convey philosophical content. Her reference to Socrates is revealing. Like Socrates in the dialogues of Plato, her poems seek some higher spiritual reality beyond the vicissitudes of daily life. In "Horse" the horse becomes the image of the suffering sage. In "Tree" the tree becomes an image of a meditative tranquility that transcends the conflicts of earthly existence. Feminine consciousness is a theme in poems like "Golden Rice for Threshing," where the peasant woman stands as the new image of humanity. Zheng Min's critique of the role of woman in classical Chinese society is the subject of "Portrait of an Imperial Maid of Honour by Wu Guxiang," where an elegant hairpin represents the material splendour for which the imperial maid has exchanged her personal integrity.

Zheng Min published nothing during the Mao era. During the Four Clean Movement (1963–66) she was sent to the countryside, where she was put to manual labour. Asked by Debra Bruno if she considered writing in secret during the Cultural Revolution, she replied, "You didn't have time to think of all that. Your whole mind was so full of all kinds of slogans ... You had to revise yourself." She began to write again in 1979 at the start of Deng Xiaoping's reforms. "I'm surprised myself when I look back. How could I have left [writing], just forgot all about it? And then picked it up?" *Zheng Min's Poems: 1979–1999*, appeared in 2000. In her later works she develops the theme of the unconscious as the source of all language. Her sonnet cycle *Death and the Poet*, published in 1991, treats the themes of love and mortality.

The German romantic philosophers who influenced her teacher Feng Zhi held that a concrete thing embodies a spiritual reality. Her "Wild Beasts" is not ultimately about animals but about primitive urges in human beings; the poem's last six lines are addressed to people who live like brutes. The idea of a resonance between the natural world and the human psyche, as taught in the German romantic philosophers and expressed in the poems of Feng Zhi, bears a resemblance to the Confucian doctrine of the *qi*. The objective of the traditional Chinese artist is to render the *qi* of the subject, its vital energy. Similarly, Zheng Min's "realism" expresses the energy that quickens her subject. "A Glance" conveys the vital spirit of the girl in her silent pose. This concept of *qi* is central to the use of symbolism in Chinese classical poetry, where natural images stand for what takes place in the human psyche. Because *qi* is present everywhere, both in nature and in the human, there is a resonance between the external world of nature and the inner world of the poet, so that symbols from nature can express the human spirit. Zheng Min's rendering of a natural symbol can sometimes assume a mystical sense, as in "Tree," where the tree becomes a symbol of eternal peace. The similarity of her natural symbolism to that of classical poetry gives her verse a more traditional flavour than that of her contemporaries. With this in mind, it is not surprising that in the nineties Zheng Min called for poets to return to classical poetry as a source of inspiration and criticized the translation style of Westernized verse, including the modernist work of the younger "obscure" poets.

At this writing, Zheng Min is the last surviving writer of those who appear in this collection. MacDougall and Louie mention her as one of the rare modern Chinese writers who attempt to portray a panoramic vision of Chinese culture. She has urged young Chinese to study recent history in order to understand the suffering her contemporaries endured.

Golden Rice for Threshing

Golden yellow sheaves of rice stand
In the field just harvested.
I remember the exhausted mother,
Her beautiful, wrinkled face in the twilight.
The full moon of harvest-time
Rests at the topmost branch of a tree.
In the twilight, the distant mountains
Mark the boundaries of the heart.

No statue is more silent.
As you trudge this autumn field that stretches into the distance
Your shoulders bend under a massive weariness
And you lower your head in thought.

Silent, silent. History is the little stream
Flowing at your feet.
You stand there,
About to become the image of humanity.

1942–47; published 1949

Forest

This too is a symbol:
Of silent thought in the midst of the universe,
Not lofty like a mountain, nor like the sea
Bright and clear. The forest stands in a corner of the earth
Wrapping within its somber hue
An abundant gift from heaven:
Beneath tangles of dry, twisted branches, leaves upon leaves,
An invisible recess.

Squirrels are lost in the sun's reflection, leaves flutter down,
Light and shadows float, tender shoots bare themselves,
But the forest never speaks.
Despite the soaring of the eagle on the horizon,
The passing of a wayfarer on the footpath,
Or the occasional storm at sea,
It is like some great personage, dignified, silent.

1942–47; published 1949

Meeting at Night

I don't raise my hand to knock:
It would sound too brusque.
A small boat returns,
Its oars at rest,
Waiting for the evening wind off the sea.
If you are seated beneath your lamp,
Hear quiet breathing outside,
And feel that someone is approaching softly,
Throw down your cigarette,
Open the door in silence,
And there you will find me, waiting on the threshold.

1942–47; published 1949

Village in Early Spring

Closely I observe this village
Huddled at the foot of a city,
Presenting itself to the universe
With dark-roofed huts
And countless flapping rags,
As if its inhabitants
Spoke, painted, shouted out their lives
As does their work-coarsened skin.

Their grateful tongues savour like ripe fruit
The sweetness of life returned,
The tree's endurance
Persevering through winters, perplexing springs
And stormy summers.
A sympathetic heart penetrates
This village smiling in the sun,
Beholding again the dark, damp nights in the long downpours
When shaking grass roofs and swaying walls
Shield crowds of crouching people,
While at their backs poverty
Lurks like a vicious dog in the forest.
But now see how proudly the village opens its heart
Like a well in the blazing heat of summer,
Drawing the water of sympathy for passing strangers:
A spectacle to evoke compassion
For these people who, for no reason, are thought stupid
For their bare muddy feet and weary shoulders,
Their sallow faces and lonely, disregarded hearts.
Now the women wash clothes, the children play,
Dogs run, and thin chimney smoke leaps into the sky.
The stream gradually thaws like their long-imprisoned delight
As every evening they see the treetops
Add a few more banners of green hope.

1942–47; published 1949

Dipping My Feet in the Water

From deep within her bosom, the forest offers a path
That leads – ah, to where ancient trees
Ring a pool, and the pool reflects a face
Brimming over with a smile, like a motionless blossom
Offering life to the thousand moving creatures.

Look there – green pours from the tender leaves,
Then melts into delicate verdant sunlight. As you dip your feet

You merge with the forest's cool, secluded silence. In the dimness –
Ah, young lady – you wait happily for the other half of yourself.

Here it is! A squirrel jumps over the fallen leaves.
He's whistling, and a pair of birds whisper together.
Finally the forest mist is blown away by drowsiness.

You dream that you become a squirrel, an enormous tree,
Tiny grasses, a deep pool.
Your pale feet sleep in the water.

1942–47; published 1949

Two Lotus Flowers: On a Painting by Zhang Daqian

One blossom's never-withering goblet,
Filled to the brim with the joy of blooming,
Rises mountain-like into an eternity
For which there are no words.

Its young leaves, reluctant to uncurl,
Conceal within their pure heart
The hope to rise through the mist over the pond
To gaze at a world in drab, old-fashioned garments –

But what is the theme
Of *this* troubling gesture – this sagging stem,
Dropping its blossom toward its underwater roots?

This is no story of the wind's buffeting,
The lashing of the rain, but a gift from the creator's hand:
The solemn burden of abundant life.

1942–47; published 1949

Wild Beasts: A Painting

Around them the desolate city of the jungle
Nurtures its denizens as usual.
Only the breathing wind can penetrate its gloom
Where no glimmer parts the night.
These beasts endure a life cold and fearful.
It fills their tough veins, swirls
Through their salty blood until their sullen eyes
Mirror the loneliness of the vast wilderness.

Your petty impulses shame you.
Your fine language is nothing but talk. Your knowledge brings
Only prejudice. Better let the harsh wind blow unchecked
And the pitiless cold lash you
Until the fresh intensity of life
Blows its way into your awkward shapes.

1942–47; published 1949

Apparition on a Winter Afternoon: A Painting

The painter has dozed off
And let the great road lie here colourless –
Perhaps lost in meditation,
Musing upon a pair of tender, naked feet
And a checkered parasol,
The road's face has turned all white.

In tears the white willow complains,
"When will the beauty reappear?
The wind sings my praises no more."
A crow reposes on a stone wall.
The sky hangs too low.

Loneliness drips from the branches.
I pass the lovely girl, drowsing,
Waiting for a fragrant breeze.
Someone lightly touches my elbow,
Gently tugs at my sleeve –
A pair of timid hands.
A tiny voice seems to say,
"Can't you see me?"
Whereupon I stay my steps and turn back:
Not a soul on the road.

A branch of white rose, slender and fragile,
Reaches out through a low hedge,
Still trembling by itself.

1942–47; published 1949

The Student

One step forward,
Then I stumble back.
I join the ranks,
Then slip aside.
I stare at posters on the wall to the left,
And the crowd surrounding them.
I stare at posters on the wall to the right,
And the crowd surrounding them –
Opposing battle lines that fire
Crisscrossing volleys over my head.
O Socrates of the street,
Where are you? I have heard
You can lead the young toward truth
As a shepherd guides his flock,
Like a compassionate passerby
Returning a lost child to its mother.
Why have you abandoned this country,
More perplexing than any other,

And now more troubling than any other?
Here right and wrong are like day and night at the north pole.
Truth is a puppet that plays two roles,
One wrestling with the other.
One cries, "Only mine is truth!"
The other cries, "Only when your 'mine' is changed to mine
Can it be truth!"
Truth is lovely bait
Enticing small fry that gape, enthralled.
There's no such thing as a baited hook
To their wide, myopic eyes.
Socrates, if you cannot appear
In this twentieth-century labyrinth of streets,
Why then can't truth become a child,
Laughing when it's happy, wailing when it's sad,
Showing me exactly truth herself?

1942–47; published 1949

A Glance

Rembrandt: Young Girl at an Open Half-door

Exquisite, those shoulders vanishing into shadows
Framing the bosom, rich as an orchard laden with fruit;
Like a sudden dream appearing, that radiant face
Harmonizes with the hand, so slender, resting on the half-door.

From the calendar-tree, time's river bears away another fallen leaf.
Her enigmatic eyes betray a giddy quiet.
Even the leisurely, changeless pace of her narrow life is too rushed.
In the half-light of a fortuitous dusk, she watches endlessly the ever-changing world.

1942–47; published 1949

Drought

The hot wind has wrinkled the vegetables in the field.
Everywhere it whispers, "Die, die."
A peasant walks by, shouldering
A gorgeous new waterwheel,
But it is an infant god powerless to be born.
All the canals and ditches bare
Their dry, mud-cracked beds,
Like sailors' bones revealed by dried-up seas.
Leafless trees thrust desiccated branches.
A calf stands in vain at the edge of the dried pond,
Gazing uncertainly at the people. The small brook
Runs through the sheltering canopy of entwined green branches,
Runs through the cave beneath its little low bridge, like
An old person lost in recalling happy days long past.
It utters no sound of merry leaping
And passes like an uncouth visitor who brings no gift.
The fields are silent as death.
On the desolate land the people
Now have no word for one another.
Every voice, every hope
Is turned toward heaven. And there, nothing but
A ceaseless hot wind rushing over the treetops
With the sound of fleeing feet.
In people's hearts is
The agony and terror of a mother
Who hears the mute wail of the whole earth.

1942–47; published 1949

Tree

I have never heard any voice
Like the voice of a tree
With all its tones –
Grieving

Or exultant.
On a dark winter's night
You ought to walk by as if
Passing a people denied their freedom –
Can't you hear the voice locked in its blood?
When spring comes
In every one of its brawny arms
A thousand wailing babies lie concealed.
Never have I felt a tranquility so deep
As in the posture of a tree.
No matter what thought I wake from,
My eyes encounter it
Looming above me.
Stars revolve between its arms,
The brook flows slowly off beneath its gaze,
And in its bosom small birds flit.
Thus it prays eternally, meditating
As if it grew on a peaceful earth.

1942–47; published 1949

Horse

Once on a heath full of wind and rank grass
This primitive, heroic figure stood quietly,
Vibrant with the latent power of speed,
Disdaining the distance to the firmament.

Once resolute as an arrow, mane unfurled,
It reared, then rushed ahead
Like water from a broken dike.
But for this rough world, such a shape is too dazzling an ideal.

The endless road unrolls beneath its feet.
By day it treads the creaking planks of bridges
Over mountain chasms, and grazes in the wilderness.
At night it is tricked into the confines of a city street.

Maybe it realizes that the fellow at its back, whip in hand,
Endures in his own life lashes even more ruthless.
And so it arches the taut muscles of its neck, doesn't groan
Under a load too heavy, and silently trudges on.

Day by day it loses its old heroic beauty,
The natural ease of its posture worn away.
Perhaps one day it will collapse beside the road
And cast off its burden together with its pitiful companion.

No trace of its gallant form remains.
The hero of past years has become a saint,
Having completed its journey
Over earth's tortuous roads.

1942–47; published 1949

Portrait of an Imperial Maid of Honour by Wu Guxiang

The painter has given you clouds of hair,
Layer upon layer, piled upon your head,
A tight silk gown, roomy sleeves,
Like a water scallion
Yellow-green, soft and supple.
Your eyes, gently traced by the artist,
Smother your suffocating soul.
All you can do is stare at the jade hairpin in your hand.
The pathetic life behind this lovely pose
Has forgotten even how to sigh.

Silk and damask have long bound tight
The naked cries and longings of childhood.
Even on so radiant a spring day, the sunlight
Cannot pierce this elegant frigidity
In which people have wrapped your flesh.
That pale white belt constricts your veins,
O cold, cold lady!
If you could tear apart these satins

And plunge back to bathe in the sea of life
And find again the lost pulse of your blood,
The loves and hates of your flesh would bring you emblems of life
Far truer than the jade hairpin in your hand.

c. 1984

Silkworms

Life is condensed in these miraculous black specks
That transform overnight into a swarm of tiny strands.
They swim in a sea of green leaves,
Growing into tender flesh – slender forms
Perfectly round, with crimson mouths.

With a ceaseless rustling
You greet the first sign of that precious translucence.
And lift up your heads, ecstatic,
Pondering, dreaming,
Foreseeing tomorrow's construction
Of your white palace.

You spend your lives to build a future,
Your resurrection,
Using a long, long thread of shining silk,
Winding and winding it again around your flesh,
A passing stage in your life,
Awaiting in seclusion your metamorphosis.

However it may be,
Your diaphanous abodes
Are not sleeping chambers,
Nor mausoleums.
Life pulsates inside.
In boiling water you exchange a death
For silver threads that reach through time and space.

c. 1984

The Wings of Swans

Swans swim on the lake in the park.
Flying overhead, herons come and go,
Their wings unclipped.
Swans live in elegance between
Captivity and freedom.
Who can say
If they are fortunate?

1988

Glossary

ANTI-RIGHTIST CAMPAIGN (1957–58): during this government campaign the Communist regime denounced hundreds of thousands of persons, mostly intellectuals, as pro-capitalist counter-revolutionaries. The majority were people who had taken the opportunity to criticize government policy and officials during the brief Hundred Flowers Campaign (see below), which Mao abruptly terminated in June, 1957. Those denounced were banished to the countryside or imprisoned. The Chinese government still maintains a ban on critical discussion of the Anti-Rightist Campaign.

APRIL 12TH INCIDENT (also known as the Shanghai Massacre): On 12 April 1927, Chiang Kai-shek's right wing forces within the Guomindang began a systematic purge of the party's Communist members. (See "Guomindang" below.) In Shanghai, where a Communist faction of the Guomindang was in control, Chiang's forces captured their strongholds and executed their men with the help of gangsters.

CHIANG KAI-SHEK (1887–1975; we use the conventional romanization of the name, as pronounced in a southern dialect; in *pinyin* the name is Jiang Jieshi): Chiang was head of the Guomindang and recognized ruler of China from 1927 to 1949. He was a close associate of the party's co-founder, Sun Yat-sen. He assumed leadership of the Guomindang after Sun's death, and commanded its 1927 Northern Expedition (see below), moving northward from Guangzhou to wrest control of south and central China from local warlords. That same year he purged the Guomindang of its Communist faction, made a deal with northern warlords, and was recognized as titular ruler of all China. For the next nine years he carried out military campaigns against recalcitrant warlords and Communist guerrillas.

Beginning in 1937, Chiang led China's national army against the expanding Japanese occupation. After the defeat of the Japanese, he engaged in civil war against the Communists. When the Communists emerged victorious in 1949, Chiang and his remaining forces withdrew to the island of Taiwan, which he ruled as president until his death in 1975.

CHINESE CIVIL WAR (1946–49): fought between the government forces of Chiang Kai-shek's Guomindang party and the Communists under Mao Zedong. The war ended in a Communist takeover of mainland China. In 1946 the Communists, who held much of northwest China, sent forces to the countryside of northeast China, which their Russian allies had seized from the Japanese. The Communists' land reform policy won them widespread popularity among the peasants. Rampant inflation in Guomindang areas sapped public support for Chiang Kai-shek's regime. Communists captured the cities of the northeast, then north central China, then central and south China. Guomindang forces withdrew to the island of Taiwan.

COMMUNIST PARTY OF CHINA: the CPC was founded in 1921 as a Marxist party devoted to promoting revolution among the lower classes. In the early and mid-twenties Soviet advisors, sent by Moscow, urged CPC members to join the Guomindang. (See "Guomindang," below.) In 1927 Guomindang leader Chiang Kai-shek purged Communists from the Guomindang's ranks, killing many. Surviving Communists took to guerrilla warfare, taking control of several rural areas in south central China. In the largest of these zones, Mao Zedong (see below) undertook a land reform program, reallocating land to poor peasants.

In 1933 Chiang Kai-shek launched the fifth and most powerful of his anti-Communist offensives. Communist leaders planned set battles (as opposed to Mao's guerrilla warfare). The result was a military disaster for the Communists. Their remaining forces were compelled to withdraw on the Long March. (See below.) Along the way, in January 1935, the party reinstated Mao to a role in the military command. A remnant of Communist forces established a small base in Yan'an in northwest China.

From 1937 to 1945 the Communists and the Guomindang joined in an uneasy alliance against the Japanese invaders, who surrendered in 1945. Mao's forces defeated Chiang Kai-shek's army in the Chinese Civil War of 1946–49. The Communist regime nationalized industry and organized peasants into collective farms. The government controlled the media. After Mao's death the CPC steered a more liberal economic policy under Deng

Xiaoping, gradually allowing room for private enterprise and more self-expression in the arts, while retaining one-party rule.

CREATION SOCIETY: an association founded in Japan in 1921 by a group that included Guo Moruo. Later the same year its members moved to Shanghai. The society's agenda involved the development of new vernacular literature characterized by expressionism, romanticism, and a striving after poetic beauty. Its members shared a belief in the writer as inspired genius. After the government's massacre of demonstrators in Beijing on 30 May 1925, the society espoused revolution.

CRESCENT MOON JOURNAL: founded in 1928, this journal published the poetry of members of the Crescent Moon Society. Edited by Hu Shi, the journal gradually shifted to political subjects with a relatively conservative stance, in opposition to the Communists.

CRESCENT MOON SOCIETY: the society evolved from a private literary circle in Beijing founded in 1923 by Xu Zhimo and Hu Shi. Xu and Hu moved to Shanghai in 1927, where the club was formally inaugurated, with Xu, Hu, Wen Yiduo, and Shen Congwen among its founding members. It advocated the development of New Poetry within strict patterns of rhythm and rhyme. Its members endorsed "freedom of ideals" and open, unrestricted debate of ideas. They opposed what they considered the obscene poetry of Guo Moruo's Creation Society. Lu Xun and other leftist intellectuals attacked the Crescent Moon Society for its opposition to revolutionary political change. The society disbanded after the death of Xu Zhimo in 1931.

CULTURAL REVOLUTION: the Great Proletarian Cultural Revolution (1966–76) was a political movement orchestrated by Mao Zedong to regain absolute authority after the disasters of the Great Leap Forward (1958–61; see below) diminished his day-to-day control of the government. Responding to Mao's appeal, young people formed Red Guard units and seized supposed counter-revolutionaries who were subjected to public humiliation, tortured, and often killed. The victims included many intellectuals as well as party officials. Those apprehended were sent to menial labour in the countryside. Production plummeted and the economy was paralyzed. The movement fulfilled Mao's objective, forcing his rivals Liu Shaoqi and Deng Xiaoping, along with many others, from political office. Mao Zedong Thought became the official ideology, and adulation of its author became government policy. After warfare broke out between Red Guard factions, Mao ordered the young people sent to the countryside to "learn revolution from the peasants."

The number of those who died is impossible to calculate. Few records were kept. Estimates range from half a million to 20 million. Hu Yaobang, former head of the Communist Party, has been quoted as saying that one million died, but many scholars believe the figure was higher.

"DRIED BEAN CURD" METER: this metric system, influenced by European prosody, was developed and popularized in vernacular poetry by Xu Zhimo and Wen Yuduo. Poems were written in stanzas consisting of a set number of lines, usually four. Each line contained an equal number of "feet." Each foot consisted of one stressed and one or two unstressed syllables. The poetic form was sometimes jokingly referred to as the "dried bean curd style" because the stanzas on the page resembled rectangular blocks of tofu.

GREAT LEAP FORWARD (1958–61): a nationwide economic campaign to turn China into a modern state by drastically increasing production in both agriculture and industry. Mao sought to compensate for China's technical deficiencies by harnessing her enormous manpower. Households were organized to smelt iron ore in miniature blast furnaces. Some nine hundred million peasants were ordered to move onto newly established collective farms. The government dictated new techniques in planting based on the now-discredited methods of Soviet agronomist Trofim Lysenko. Crop failures led to widespread famine and death by starvation, mostly in the countryside. As a result of this disaster, the government temporarily scaled back Mao's collectivization of agriculture, and he temporarily had to relinquish control of economic policy.

There is considerable divergence in the estimates of the number of those who perished. Calculations are based on statistical extrapolation from incomplete records. Ó Gráda's estimate of eighteen million represents the low end.[1] Banister reckons the mortality at thirty million.[2] Yang and

1 Cormac Ó Gráda, *Great Leap into Famine*, University College Dublin Centre for Economic Research Working Paper Series (Dublin: University College Press, 2011), 9.
2 Judith Banister, *China's Changing Population* (Palo Alto: Stanford University Press, 1987), 118–20.

Dikötter's estimates are generally considered more authoritative. Yang sets the death toll at thirty-six million.[3] Dikötter's total of forty-five million includes some two or three million killed for political reasons.[4]

GUOMINDANG (in Wade-Giles romanization, "Kuomintang"): literally "National People's Party," sometimes referred to in English as the Chinese Nationalist Party. Under the leadership of Sun Yat-sen (see below) it was founded after the fall of the Qing emperor in 1912 as a democratic socialist party. The party dates its administration (called in English "The Republican government") from this date. After losing control and being outlawed in Beijing, the party moved to Guangzhou, where it established a rival center of power in 1920. Refused recognition by Western powers, Sun sought assistance from Moscow. In 1923, Lenin sent advisors who reorganized the party along Soviet Communist lines and encouraged Chinese Communists to become members of the Guomindang.

After the death of Sun in 1925, control of the Guomindang passed to Chiang Kai-shek. (See above.) In 1927 Chiang led his troops on the Northern Expedition (see below), defeating the southern warlords. He then purged the Guomindang of its Communist members. After a deal with the northern warlords, Chiang was recognized as ruler of China. The Guomindang regime lasted until it was overthrown by Mao's Communist forces in 1949, when its survivors, including Chiang, fled to the island of Taiwan, where they continued to hold power.

HAKKA: a distinct subdivision of the Chinese nationality who speak their own dialect of Chinese. The term "Hakka" literally means "guest family" or "guest people." Originally from Guangdong province, the Hakka migrated to other provinces of south and central China where they formed a distinct subgroup, often looked down upon by the indigenous population. Many Hakka joined the Communist movement, including Deng Xiaoping.

HUNDRED FLOWERS CAMPAIGN: initiated in January 1957, this official government campaign encouraged open expression of a wide spectrum of opinions, together with criticism of party officials. Its slogan was, "Let a hundred flowers bloom, let a hundred schools of thought contend."

3 Yang Jisheng *Tombstone: the Great Chinese Famine, 1958–1962* (New York: Farrar, Straus, Giroux, 2008).

4 Frank Dikötter, *Mao's Great Famine: the History of China's Most Devastating Catastrophe, 1958–1962* (New York: Walker, 2010), 333.

Ostensibly the campaign's purpose was to encourage people to criticize corrupt lower-level party officials.

The campaign unleashed a flood of criticism of party policy in every field of life. In May 1957, when criticisms of Chairman Mao himself began to resound, the party clamped down. Authorities denounced as counter-revolutionaries many thousands of those who had spoken out. This crack-down was the start of the Anti-Rightist Campaign (see above). Some historians believe that the Hundred Flowers Campaign was a ploy of Mao and the Communist Party to flush out covert opponents.

IMPERIAL EXAMINATION: in Imperial China, this system of state-run exams was designed to select the most qualified candidates for positions in the government administration. Successful candidates constituted a class of scholar-bureaucrats without regard to class or family background. The subject matter of the exams focused on the ancient Chinese classics. Preparation for the examinations could be costly, since tutors were usually involved. Consequently, the largest number of successful candidates tended to come from the wealthy land-owning class, although any man was eligible to try the exams. The examinations were abolished in 1905.

JAPANESE OCCUPATION OF CHINA (1931–45; in China this conflict is referred to as the War of Resistance against Japan): the conflict began in 1931 when Japan occupied northeast China. In 1937 the Japanese invaded Beijing, then swept southward through China's major coastal cities and the lower Yangzi River basin. While Japan eventually was to seize most of north and coastal China, including most of China's great urban centres and industrial capacity, their area of control was largely limited to railroads and cities, "points and lines," leaving most of the countryside unoccupied. After 1941 China's ongoing war with Japan merged into the Second World War, accounting for the greater proportion of casualties in the Pacific Theater.

Japanese troops committed numerous atrocities, the most famous of which is the 1937–38 Rape of Nanjing. Chinese historians refer to the policy of the Japanese in parts of North China from May 1942 onward as the "Three Alls": "Kill All, Burn All, Loot All." Japanese historian Mitsuyoshi Himeta estimates that this policy claimed the lives of some 2.7 million Chinese civilians. The Chinese regard Japanese war crimes, which included the use of poison gas and bubonic plague germ-warfare, as Hitler's atrocities are regarded in the West.

JULY GROUP: founded in 1937 around critic and poet Hu Feng, these leftist poets' objective was to write simple, direct poems to rouse the Chinese public to resist the Japanese. Members included, at various times, Tian Jian, Ai Qing, A Long, and Zang Kejia, among others.

LEAGUE OF LEFT WING WRITERS: a group founded in 1930 under the auspices of the Communist Party. Its original three-man governing council included Lu Xun. Members engaged in ongoing polemic against the aestheticism and political conservatism of the Crescent Moon Society. Against growing Guomindang censorship they advocated freedom of the press. Influenced by Soviet writing, their theories about the political role of literature to inspire the masses anticipated Mao's "Talks on Literature and Art at the Yan'an Forum." (See below.) The Communist Party dissolved the League in 1936 after it was convulsed by debate over Mao's formation of a temporary alliance with Chiang Kai-shek against the Japanese.

LITERARY RESEARCH SOCIETY: established in Beijing in 1921, this society numbered among its founders Zheng Zhenduo, Wang Tongzhao, Ye Shaojun, and Bing Xin. Its membership would eventually include Zhu Ziqing, Xu Yunuo, and Liu Yanling. Their objective was to liberate Chinese literature from classical tradition by the study of Western models. Their periodical, *Poetry Monthly*, published the new verse. In 1922 they produced the first multi-author anthology of New Poetry, entitled *A Snowy Morning*. The society encouraged literature that reflected the life of the people, under the slogan "literature for life's sake" in opposition to the "literature for art's sake" of Guo Moruo and his Creation Society. Against Guo's romanticism, they advocated humanism. At first they espoused social realism, although they soon ventured into new styles. The Society's formal activity ceased around 1925.

LONG MARCH: an extended retreat undertaken by Communist forces from south central China to northwest China, lasting from October 1934 to October 1935. It began when the Communists broke through a Guomindang encirclement of their base in Jiangxi province. They trekked west, then north, then northeast to a small, remote Communist base in Shaanxi province, under attack along the way from Guomindang troops, warlords, and local non-Chinese minorities. The distance covered on the Long March has been reckoned at six thousand miles. Of the original one hundred thousand who began the trek only about eight thousand reached Yan'an. Since the establishment of the People's Republic of China, the Long March has been portrayed as the defining event of the Communist Revolution.

MAO ZEDONG (1893–1976): founding member of the Chinese Communist Party, a leader on the Long March, Party Chairman, and virtual ruler of China from 1949 until 1962 and from 1966 until his death in 1976. Mao was the son of a prosperous peasant in Shaoshan, Hunan province. He attended the first meeting of the Chinese Communist Party in Shanghai in 1921. In the course of his party work, Mao developed the doctrine of armed revolution based on the support of the peasant class. In 1927 Mao's forces gained control of parts of rural Jiangxi province, where he set up a Soviet-style government, confiscating and redistributing land. Over the years 1931–33 the Chinese Communist Party replaced Mao as leader of the Jiangxi forces. After the Communists were compelled to flee the Guomindang during the Long March (1934–35), Mao regained his leadership, and in Yan'an in northwest China he achieved paramount control of the Communist Party and its army. After a 1936 truce with the Guomindang, he directed guerrilla warfare against the Japanese from 1937 to 1945. His "Talks at the Yan'an Forum" (1942) established the cultural policy of the Communist regime. After defeating Guomindang government forces in the Civil War (1946–49) he set up the Communist government. After the failure of the Great Leap Forward (1958–61), party leaders Liu Shaoqi and Deng Xiaoping scaled back agricultural collectivization and temporarily took control of the economy. Mao considered their action a betrayal of Communist ideology. He purged them during the Cultural Revolution (1966–76), which promoted the ideology of Mao Zedong Thought and adulation of its author to a paramount role in Chinese life. In 1973 Mao reinstated Deng, who was eventually to become China's leader.

Mao's policies during the Great Leap Forward and the Cultural Revolution brought about the deaths of an estimated forty to seventy million people. He is honoured in his native land as the architect of the People's Republic of China.

MAY FOURTH MOVEMENT: a movement advocating the radical transformation of Chinese political, social, and literary culture, which brought together currents of thought already present on the periphery of Chinese society for several decades. The movement is named for the day in 1919 when Beijing students led demonstrations to protest the Chinese government's acquiescence to the Versailles treaty, which had granted German-controlled Shandong province to Japan. (China had joined the Allies with the understanding that Shandong would be returned to China, but the Allies had made a secret agreement with the Japanese.) The protests rapidly evolved into a movement for democracy, attacking Confucianism and classical literature, and advocating new vernacular writing.

NANCHANG UPRISING: after the April 12th Incident (see above) Communist forces tried to take control of Nanchang, the capital of Jiangxi province in south central China. They were defeated by right-wing Guomindang forces loyal to Chiang Kai-shek.

NEW CHINESE POETRY (*Zhongguo Xinshi*): an underground Shanghai poetry magazine which appeared for a few issues in 1948. Its co-editors included Hang Yuehe, Chen Jingrong, Tang Qi, and Tang Shi. The magazine was soon suppressed by the Guomindang authorities. It published work by the group of writers later dubbed the Nine Leaves Poets.

NEW CURRICULUM (also referred to as the modern curriculum): an alternative education model introduced in the late nineteenth century. It deemphasized classical Chinese and the traditional canon of Chinese literature and philosophy in favor of Western subjects including European languages, modern science, and Western philosophy, and introduced democratic political ideas.

NINE LEAVES ANTHOLOGY (1981): a poetry anthology edited by Hang Yuehe and Tang Shi which combined the work of nine poets whose verse had appeared in two underground poetry journals in Shanghai in 1947–48. After its appearance these poets became known as the Nine Leaves Poets. The works of all but Xin Di are included in this anthology.

NORTHERN EXPEDITION: the 1927 campaign of the Guomindang forces under Chiang Kai-shek. Chiang led his forces northward from their enclave in southern Guangdong province to wrest control of south and central China from local warlords as far as the Yangzi River. When the Communist wing of the Guomindang declared a provisional government in Wuhan, Chiang's right-leaning faction crushed them, then purged Communists from the Guomindang, executing many. (See "April 12th Incident," above.) Chiang then made a deal with the northern warlords and was recognized as titular ruler of all China.

POETRY CREATION (*Shi Chuangzao*): an underground Shanghai poetry magazine which appeared for a few issues in 1947 and 1948. It was soon suppressed by the Guomindang authorities. The magazine published work by writers later numbered among the Nine Leaves Poets. It also included work by leftist poet Zang Kejia, who assisted its production manager, Hang Yuehe.

POETRY MONTHLY: a magazine established in 1922 by Zhu Ziqing, Liu Yanling, and Ye Shaojun, dedicated to publishing the poetry of writers associated with the Literary Research Society. (See above).

SOUTHWEST UNITED UNIVERSITY: located in Kunming, Southwest United University was organized by prominent faculty of major universities in Japanese-held territory, especially Beijing's Qinghua and Beijing Universities and Tianjin's Nankai University. Among its professors were poets Wen Yiduo, Shen Congwen, and Feng Zhi. Younger poets who enjoyed their tutelage included Mu Dan, Du Yunxie, Yuan Kejia, and Zheng Min.

SUN YAT-SEN (1866–1925; we use the conventional romanization of the name, as pronounced in a southern dialect; in *pinyin* the name is Sun Yixian): the titular leader of the revolution that overthrew the Qing emperor in 1912. A physician, Sun was co-founder of the Guomindang party and served as the first president of the Republic of China, but soon lost power and spent the rest of his life in a fruitless struggle with warlords who had taken piecemeal control of China. He did not live to see his party reassert its control over China under Chiang Kai-shek.

TAGORE, RABINDRANATH (1861–1941): Nobel-prize-winning Indian poet. His visit to China in 1924 gave added impetus to the New Poetry movement. His collection of brief poems, *Stray Birds* (English translation by the author, 1916), initiated a fashion for similar poems in vernacular Chinese.

TALKS ON LITERATURE AND THE ARTS AT THE YAN'AN FORUM (1942): two addresses delivered by Mao Zedong on the role of the arts in society, later published in 1943, which became official party policy for over forty years. Authors, Mao said, were to overcome their sense of superiority about their personal emotions and learn from the masses – i.e. workers, peasants, and soldiers. He urged writers to employ genres of popular literature such as folk tales and folk songs. Creativity was subordinate to politics. Proletarian literature was to serve the needs of the Communist Party in its leadership of the masses.

"THIRTEEN-TRACKS" RHYME SYSTEM: a system of rhyme used in the composition of Chinese opera *libretti*. It classifies all possible Mandarin Chinese syllables into thirteen rhyme-groups: mostly groups of exact rhyme, but some of near-rhyme, and a few of artificial rhyme. New Poets adopted versions of the "Thirteen-Tracks" system in place of the artificial rhyme system of classical Chinese poetry.

TRANSLATION STYLE POETRY: poetry written to appear as if it were a translation into Chinese of a poem in a European language. In the early stages of the New Poetry movement, when interest in importing Western culture was at its height, Zhou Zuoren advocated the writing of vernacular poetry with syntax, diction, and imagery that made it appear to be a translation from a Western language.

UNITED FRONT (sometimes referred to as the Second United Front): an alliance formed in 1936 between Chiang Kai-shek and Mao Zedong to oppose the Japanese occupation. Officially the arrangement placed Communist troops under Guomindang command, but in fact there was relatively little coordination of the two military forces. The Front lasted until 1941, when Chiang's forces fought the Communist New Fourth Army. This ended all cooperation, and the two forces fought the Japanese independently until the end of the war in 1945.

YAN'AN: a small, undeveloped city in Shaanxi province, northwest China, Yan'an was the destination of Mao's troops on the Long March of 1934–35. (See above.) It became the central Communist stronghold until the late forties, and served as Mao's guerrilla base against the Japanese. In the late thirties and forties, Yan'an came to represent leftists' hopes for transforming China. Many Communists trekked to Yan'an to join Mao's forces, evading Guomindang checkpoints along the way, often traveling hundreds of miles on foot.

Bibliography

GENERAL

Haft, Lloyd, ed. *A Selective Guide to Chinese Literature, 1900–1949: The Poem*. Leiden: Brill, 1989.

– *The Chinese Sonnet. Meanings of a Form*. CNWS Publications No. 69. Leiden: Centre of Non-Western Studies, 2000.

Lin, Julia C. *Modern Chinese Poetry: An Introduction*. Seattle: University of Washington Press, 1972.

Yeh, Michelle. *Modern Chinese Poetry: Theory and Practice since 1917*. New Haven: Yale University Press, 1991.

MULTI-AUTHOR ANTHOLOGIES

Anthology of Contemporary Chinese Literature: Taiwan, 1949–1974. Edited by Chi Pang-yuan et al., 2 vols., volume 1, *Poems and Essays*. Taipei: National Institute for Compilation and Translation, 1975.

Anthology of Modern Chinese Poetry. Translated and edited by Michelle Yeh. New Haven, CT: Yale University Press, 1992.

China China: Contemporary Poetry from Taiwan, Republic of China. Edited by Germain Droogenbroodt and Peter Stinson. Ninove, Belgium: Point Books, 1986.

Columbia Anthology of Modern Chinese Literature. Edited by Joseph Lau and Howard Goldblatt. New York: Columbia University Press, 1995.

Contemporary Chinese Poetry. Edited by Robert Payne. London: George Routledge and Sons, 1947.

Earth-Shaking Songs: Epic of Chinese Revolution. Translated by Xu Yuanchong. Hong Kong: Commercial Press, 1981.

The Fontana Collection of Modern Chinese Writing. Edited by Christine Liao. Melbourne: Fontana/Collins in association with the Chinese Literature Publishing House of Beijing, 1983.

Frontier Taiwan: An Anthology of Modern Chinese Poetry. Edited by Michelle Yeh and Goran Malmqvist. New York: Columbia University Press, 2001.

The Isle Full of Noises: Modern Chinese Poetry from Taiwan. Translated and edited by Dominic Cheung. New York: Columbia University Press, 1987.

Lyrics from Shelters: Modern Chinese Poetry, 1930–1950. Translated by Wai-lim Yip. New York: Garland, 1992.

Modern Chinese Poetry. Translated by Harold Acton and Chen Shih-hsiang. London: Duckworth, 1936.

Modern Literature from China. Edited by Walter J. Meserve and Ruth L. Meserve. New York: New York University Press, 1974.

Modern Verse from Taiwan. Translated and edited by Angela C.Y. Jung Palandri with Boert Bertholf. Berkeley: University of California Press, 1972.

New Chinese Poetry. Edited by Kwang-chung Yu. Taipei: Heritage Press, 1960.

New Voices: Stories and Poems by Young Chinese Writers. Translated and edited by Nancy Ing. Taipei: Heritage Press, 1961.

One Hundred Modern Chinese Poems. Translated and edited by Bingjun Pang, John Minford, and Sean Golden. Hong Kong: Commercial Press, 1987.

The Orchid Boat: Women Poets of China. Translated and edited by Kenneth Rexroth and Ling Chung. New York: McGraw-Hill, 1972.

The People Speak Out: Translations of Poems and Songs of the People of China. Edited by Rewi Alley. Peking: no pub., 1954.

Poetry Hong Kong: An English Translation of a Selection of Chinese Poetry. Translated and edited by J.S.M. Leung. Hong Kong: no pub, 1991.

Sailing to Formosa: A Poetic Companion to Taiwan. Bilingual Anthology. Edited by Michelle Yeh, N.G.D. Malmqvist, and Xu Huizhi. Seattle: University of Washington Press, 2005.

Twentieth Century Chinese Poetry: An Anthology. Edited and translated by Kai-yu Hsu. Garden City, NY: Doubleday, 1963.

Twentieth-Century Chinese Women's Poetry: An Anthology. Translated and edited by Julia C. Lin. Armonk, New York: M.E. Sharpe, 2009.

Zhongguo Xinshiku. Edited by Zhou Liangpei. 10 vols. Wuhan: Changjiang Wenyi Chubanshe, 1993.

INDIVIDUAL AUTHOR ANTHOLOGIES

Ai Qing, *Selected Poems of Ai Qing*. Bloomington: Indiana University Press, 1982.

Bei Dao, *The August Sleepwalker.* Translated by Bonnie S. McDougall. London: Anvil Press, 1988.

Chen Jingrong, *The Poetry of Chen Jingrong: A Modern Chinese Woman Poet*. Translated by Shiu-Pang E. Almberg. Stockholm: Skrifter Utgivna Av Foreningen For Orientaliska Studier, 1988.

Dai Wangshu, in Gregory Lee, *Dai Wangshu: The Life and Poetry of a Chinese Modernist*. Hong Kong: Chinese University Press, 1989.

He Qifang. *Paths in Dreams: Selected Prose and Poetry of Ho Ch'i-fang [He Qifang]*. Translated and edited by Bonnie McDougall. St Lucia, Queensland: University of Queensland Press. 1976.

Li Po [Li Bai], *The Works of Li Po*. Translated by Shigeyoshi Obata. New York: Paragon, 1965.

Lu Xun, *Complete Poems: A Translation with Introduction and Annotation*. Translated by David Y. Ch'en. Tempe: Center for Asian Studies, Arizona State University, 1988.

– *Poems of Lu Hsun*. Translated by Hsin-chyu Huang. Hong Kong: Joint Publishing, 1979.

– *Selected Poems*. Translated by W.J.F. Jenner. Beijing: Foreign Languages Press, 1982.

Wen Yiduo. *Red Candle: Selected Poems by Wen I-to [Wen Yiduo]*. Translated by Tao Tao Saunders. London: Cape, 1972.

– *Wen Yiduo: Selected Poetry and Prose*. Beijing: Panda Books, 1990.

PIONEERS

Hockx, Michel. "Art for Whose Sake? The Poetry of Xu Yunuo and the Esthetic Principles of Ye Shengtao." In Lloyd Haft, ed., *Words from the West: Western Texts in Chinese Literary Context: Essays to Honor Erik Zurcher on his Sixty-Fifth Birthday*, 5–25. Leiden: Centre of Non-Western Studies, 1993.

– *Snowy Morning: Eight Chinese Poets on the Road to Modernity*. Leiden: Centre of Non-Western Studies, 1994.

– *Questions of Style: Literary Societies and Literary Journals in Modern China, 1911–1937*. Leiden: Brill, 2003.

Kubin, Wolfgang. "Lu Xun's Dreams on the Eve of May Fourth and Thereafter." In Marian Galik, ed., *Interliterary and Intraliterary Aspects of the May Fourth Movement 1919 in China,* 59–65. Bratislava: Veda, 1990.

Tang, Xiaobing, with Michel Hockx. "The Creation Society (1921–1930)." In Kirk A. Denton and Michel Hockx, eds., *Literary Societies in Republican China*, 103–36. Lanham, MD: Lexington Books, 2008.

Weinberger, Eliot. "A Few Don'ts for Chinese Poets." In *Works on Paper,* 70–6. New York: New Directions, 1986.

FORMALISTS

Cheung, Dominic. *Feng Chih [Feng Zhi]*. Boston: Twayne, 1979.

Crespi, John. "Form and Reform: New Poetry and the Crescent Moon Society." In Joshua Mostow, ed. and Kirk A. Denton, China section, ed. *Columbia Companion to Modern East Asian Literatures*, 364–70. New York: Columbia University Press, 2003.

Haft, Lloyd. "Some Rhythmic Structures in Feng Zhi's Sonnets." *Modern Chinese Literature* 9, 2 (1996): 297–326.

Hockx, Michel. "The Chinese Literary Association (*Wenxue yanjiu hui*)." In Kirk A. Denton and Michel Hockx, eds., *Literary Societies in Republican China*, 79–102. Lanham, MD: Lexington Books, 2008.

– "Wu Xinghua, the Poetics of New Poetry, and the Taiwanese Poetry Scene of the 1950s." In Christina Neder et al. eds., *China in Seinen Biographischen Dimension: Gedenkscrift für Helmut Martin*, 313–30. Wiesbaden: Harrossowitz Verlag, 2001.

Hsu, Kai-yu. *Wen I-to [Wen Yiduo]*. Boston: Twayne, 1980.

Hsu, Tsemou [Xu Zhimo]. "Art and Life," *Chuangzao jikan* (*Creation Quarterly*) 2, no. 1 (July 1923), *zalu* section, 1.

Hutt, Jonathan. "La Maison d'Or: The Sumptuous World of Shao Xunmei." *East Asian History* 21 (June 2001): 111–42.

McClellan, T.M. "Wen Yiduo's 'Sishui' Metre: Themes, Variations and a Classic Variation." *Chinese Literature: Essays, Articles, Reviews* 21 (1999): 151–67. [available online on Project Muse]

van Crevel, Maghiel. "Who Needs Form? Wen Yiduo's Poetics and Post-Mao Poetry." In Peter Hoffmann, ed., *Poet, Scholar, Patriot: In Honour of Wen Yiduo's 100th Anniversary,* 81–110. Bochum / Freiburg: Projekt-Verlag, 2004.

SYMBOLISTS

Fokkema, Douwe and Elrud Ibsch, *Modernist Conjectures: A Mainstream in European Literature, 1910–1940*. London: C. Hurst, 1987.

Haft, Lloyd. *Pien Chih-lin [Bian Zhilin]: A Study in Modern Chinese Poetry*. Dordrecht: Foris Publications, 1983.

Lee, Gregory. *Dai Wangshu: The Life and Poetry of a Chinese Modernist*. Hong Kong: The Chinese University Press, 1989. [a study with extensive translations]

McDougall, Bonnie S. "European Influences in the Poetry of Ho Ch'i-fang *[He Qifang]*." *Journal of the Oriental Society of Australia* 5, 1/2 (1967): 133–51.

"PEASANTS AND SOLDIERS" POETRY

Crespi, John. *Voices in Revolution: Poetry and the Auditory Imagination in Modern China*. Honolulu: University of Hawai'i Press, 2009.

Denton, Kirk A. "Literature and Politics: Mao Zedong's 'Talks at the Yan'an Forum on Art and Literature.'" In Joshua Mostow, ed. and Kirk A. Denton, China section, ed., *Columbia Companion to Modern East Asian Literatures*, 463–9. New York: Columbia University Press, 2003.

Eoyang, Eugene. "Editor's Introduction." In Ai Qing, *Selected Poems of Ai Qing*, i–x. Bloomington: Indiana University Press, 1982.

Feng, Jin. "Ding Ling in Yan'an: A New Woman within the Part Structure?" In Feng, *The New Woman in Early Twentieth-Century Chinese Fiction*, 189–96. West Lafayette, IN: Purdue University Press, 2001.

Feuerwerker, Yi-tsi Mei. "The Uses of Literature: Ding Ling in Yan'an." In W. Kubin and R. Wagner, eds., *Essays in Contemporary Chinese Literature and Literary Criticism*. Bochum: Brockmeyer, 1981.

Ho, Ch'i-fang [He Qifang]. "The Anti-Party, Anti-Marxist Literary and Social Thought of Feng Hsueh-feng." In Hualing Nieh, ed. and co-trans., *Literature of the Hundred Flowers Volume II: Poetry and Fiction*, 310. New York: Columbia University Press, 1981. [He Qifang's political attack on Feng Xuefeng]

Hsia, T.A. "Lu Hsun [Lu Xun] and the Dissolution of the League of Leftist Writers." In Hsia, *The Gate of Darkness: Studies on the Leftist Literary Movement*, 101–63. Seattle: University of Washington Press, 1968.

– "Twenty Years after the Yenan Forum." In Hsia, *The Gate of Darkness: Studies on the Leftist Literary Movement*, 234–60. Seattle: University of Washington Press, 1968.

Laughlin, Charles A. "The All-China Resistance Association of Writers and Artists." In Kirk A. Denton and Michel Hockx, eds., *Literary Societies in Republican China*, 379–412. Lanham, MD: Lexington Books, 2008.

Mao Zedong. *Mao Zedong's "Talks at the Yan'an Conference on Literature and Art": A Translation of the 1943 Text with Commentary* by Bonnie S. McDougall. Michigan Monographs in Chinese Studies, Ann Arbor: University of Michigan Centre for Chinese Studies, 1980.

NINE LEAVES POETS

Haft, Lloyd. *The Chinese Sonnet. Meanings of a Form.* CNWS Publications No. 69. Leiden: Centre of Non-Western Studies, 2000.

Ling, Chung. "Her Dexterous Sensibility: On Zheng Min's Poetry," *Modern Chinese Literature*, 3, 1/2 (Spring/Fall 1987), 47–55.

For a list of suggested further readings visit www.modernchineseverse.com.